THE UNREAL LIFE

OF

OSCAR ZARISKI

Oscar Zariski, 1960 (courtesy of Yole Zariski)

"Geometry is the real life."

Oscar Zariski (signature)

—Oscar Zariski

THE UNREAL LIFE

 OF

OSCAR ZARISKI

Carol Parikh

ACADEMIC PRESS, INC.

Harcourt Brace Jovanovich, Publishers

Boston   San Diego   New York

London   Sydney   Tokyo   Toronto

Copyright © 1991 by Academic Press, Inc.
All rights reserved.
No part of this publication may be reproduced or transmitted in any form or by any means, electronic or mechanical, including photocopy, recording, or any information storage and retrieval system, without permission in writing from the publisher.

ACADEMIC PRESS, INC.
1250 Sixth Avenue, San Diego, CA 92101

United Kingdom Edition published by
ACADEMIC PRESS LIMITED
24–28 Oval Road, London NW1 7DX

Library of Congress Cataloging-in-Publication Data

Parikh, Carol Ann.
    The unreal life of Oscar Zariski / Carol Ann Parikh.
        p.   cm.
    Includes bibliographical references and index.
    ISBN 0-12-545030-3 (alk. paper)
    1. Zariski, Oscar, 1899–1986.   2. Mathematicians—United States—
Biography.   3. Geometry, Algebraic.   I. Title.
QA29.Z37P37   1990
510′.92—dc20
[B]   90-43919
                                                                                   CIP

Designed by Camille S. Pecoul.

Printed in the United States of America

90 91 92 93   9 8 7 6 5 4 3 2 1

For my father,
Frank T. Geris

and in memory of my friend
Erika Mumford

❧ CONTENTS ❧

◼ PREFACE ◼

Oscar Zariski transformed the foundations of algebraic geometry. The powerful tools he forged from the ideas of modern algebra allowed him to penetrate classical problems with a clarity and depth that brought a new rigor to the way algebraic geometers carry out proofs. The strength of his work was matched by his forcefulness as a teacher, and the students he trained at Johns Hopkins and later at Harvard have made essential contributions to many areas of mathematics.

A man who called geometry "the real life," Zariski lived intensely in the world of mathematics, and it was here that his temperament had its most free expression. Curious, optimistic, arrogant, stubborn, demanding, he was in some ways the embodiment of intellectual romance — the boy genius marked out for greatness by his teachers, the idealist torn between his love for Russia and his devotion to mathematics, the student who surpassed his masters, a precursor of the great influx of European talent that would transform academic and artistic life in America.

Neither a prodigy like Gauss nor the victim of an early death like

Galois, he saw himself as having chosen mathematics. Aware from an early age of his mathematical talent, he only later discovered how much his character had contributed to the development of his gifts. As his boyhood interest in algebra ripened into love, his pragmatism drew him to geometry; the tenacity with which he attacked fundamental problems was already evident in the intensity of his early studies at the University of Kiev. "A faithful man," as he termed himself, he remained totally committed to algebraic geometry for more than sixty years.

His commitment led him safely through the turbulence of the twentieth century. Having left Kobrin to attend the gymnasium in Chernigov as a child in 1910, he went on leaving places for the sake of mathematics until he settled at Harvard in 1947. He was an undergraduate in Kiev during the 1917 revolution, a graduate student in Rome during Mussolini's rise to power, an assistant professor in Baltimore during the Depression, and a visiting professor at the University of São Paulo in 1945 when he learned that his family in Kobrin had been murdered by the Nazis. In his eighty-five years he contributed to the radical transformation not only of algebraic geometry, but also of what it meant to be a Jew, a communist, and a university professor.

While his "real life" is recorded in almost a hundred books and papers, this story of his "unreal life" is based upon his memories and the recollections of his family, colleagues, and students. Whenever it was possible I supplemented oral accounts with letters and journals. I have used outside sources only to provide a historical context and to resolve the inevitable inconsistencies of a remembered past.

Carol Parikh

▨ ACKNOWLEDGMENTS ▨

This book grew out of the loving efforts of Oscar Zariski's family and students to create a record of his life. Because the Zariski Archives in Widener Library are sealed until 2001, my account is based almost entirely on my interviews with those who knew him and on his own memories as they were preserved in a series of tape-recorded interviews made a few years before his death.

I would like, first of all, to thank Yole Zariski, Zariski's wife of more than sixty years, and his daughter, Vera DeCola, for having so generously shared their recollections with me, and for joining two of Zariski's students, Heisuke Hironaka and David Mumford, in asking me to write this biography. I would also like to acknowledge my indebtedness to Ann Kostant who, with the help of Heisuke Hironaka, Wakaiko Hironaka, and David Mumford, conducted the series of interviews with Oscar Zariski between 1979 and 1981 that form an important part of this book.

David Mumford's help with all aspects of this project, especially the sections on algebraic geometry, was invaluable, as were the corrections and suggestions of Michael Artin and André Weil.

George Mackey's knowledge of the history of the Department of Mathematics at Harvard and Ray Zariski's understanding of the intricacies of the Russian Revolution added other important dimensions to my account. I would also like to thank all the friends and colleagues of Zariski who spoke to me at length and who almost all gave their permission to be quoted in this book, and to express my indebtedness to Erna Alfors, Karin Tate, Elizabeth Walsh, and Vera Widder for their lively descriptions of the Harvard community in the forties, fifties, and sixties.

Zariski's remarkable success as a teacher was evident in the enthusiasm with which his students and protégés contributed material for this book. I am grateful to Daniel Gorenstein and Maxwell Rosenlicht for their memories of Zariski's first years at Harvard; to Shreeram Abhyankar and Jun-ichi Igusa, who provided letters and stories about the middle fifties; to Heisuke Hironaka for his autobiographical writings; and to Peter Falb and Robin Hartshorne, who seem to have forgotten nothing. The accounts and letters provided by Zariski's last students, Steven L. Kleiman and Joseph Lipman, and by his French protégé, Bernard Teissier, were indispensable to my description of the final years of his research career.

Although the book is living history, there were a great many facts to be checked and rechecked, and I was always readily assisted by the archivists at Columbia, Harvard, Johns Hopkins, and MIT. I would also like to thank Everett Pitcher at the American Mathematical Society, and to express my gratitude for the editorial comments of Judith B. Herman and Eliza Wyatt, for the many practical suggestions of Barbara Solomon, and for the support and helpfulness of Klaus Peters, Susan Gay, and Camille Pecoul at Academic Press.

I would, finally, like to acknowledge my debt to my husband, Rohit Parikh, whose experience as a research mathematician and former student in the Harvard Mathematics Department contributed an important dimension to this book, and to thank my children, Vikram and Uma, for occasionally lending me their perspectives.

early dedication to communism and his later, more sober, reflections on the success of capitalism. He was torn between an allegiance to an intellectual world that ignored the politics of race and his emotional need to find safety for those members of his family who escaped the Holocaust. Intellectually, he was torn between a love of the free-spirited, creative Italian vision of geometry and his appreciation of the need for strict logical rigor which he found in the Bauhaus-like school of the abstract German algebraists.

Unfortunately, like all working mathematicians, I have led my life with the realization that most of what I care about so passionately is nearly impossible to explain to the educated layman. "What do you mean," they say, "when you say this theorem is *beautiful* or that theorem is *deep*?" One cannot appreciate what drove Zariski and why his colleagues were so excited by his contributions without having some idea of the intellectual world in which he moved. Is it possible within the confines of this foreword to convey some idea of this world and why it is so vital for the dedicated group of mathematicians who pursue it? I won't try to explain all the terms needed to state Zariski's deepest theorems, but I think something of what draws people to his subject can actually be explained in two fairly easy illustrations.

Before I embark, I have to make one thing clear about the way mathematicians think about their world. Everyone knows that physicists are concerned with the laws of the universe and have the audacity sometimes to think they have discovered the choices God made when He created the universe in thus and such a pattern. Mathematicians are even more audacious. What they feel they discover are the laws that God Himself could not avoid having to follow. Now some would say all such laws must be obvious, that you can find nothing truly new beyond what you assumed in the beginning. But this isn't what mathematicians find. They find that by following the thread of logic, just as you would follow a river to its source, at every bend you find things that are totally unexpected. Because these things follow by logic, they have to be true in any world God creates, and yet there is no way in which they are evident on first sight. Or at least so it seems until some mathematician finds a way of rephrasing or recasting the facts; then, by some sleight of hand, they appear immediately evident. That's one of the things mathematicians mean by a beautiful proof. Yet other theorems continue to fascinate mathematicians because they have never been fully reduced to something intuitively obvious. Such theorems live on in a state of tension between seeming new and surprising and seeming clear and evident.

To be a mathematician is to be an out-and-out Platonist. The more you study mathematical constructions, the more you come to believe in their objective and prior existence. Mathematicians view themselves as explorers of a unique sort, explorers who seek to discover not just one accidental world into which they happen to be born, but the universal and unalterable truths of all worlds.

My first illustration will attempt to show in the simplest possible way how algebra and geometry come together in the field Oscar Zariski made his own, algebraic geometry. We want to go back to what was perhaps the first and arguably still one of the deepest mathematical truths — Pythagoras's theorem. We start with a right triangle A, B, C (see Figure 1), with a right angle at B, the side AC being the longest, the so-called hypotenuse. Pythagoras's theorem states that the square of the length AC equals the sum of the square of the length AB and the square of the length BC.

We're not going to prove this theorem; rather, we'll use it to build a fundamental link between algebra and geometry. To do this, we first need to use an idea of Descartes: we can name points in the plane by means of pairs of numbers, called their x and y coordinates. That is to say, to each point, we can assign two numbers, and conversely to any two numbers, we assign a single point (see Figure 2). This idea, although commonplace to anyone who has taken high school math, was an amazing step for Descartes; it was a step that

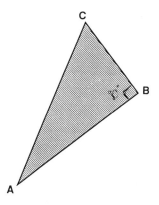

Figure 1. A right triangle

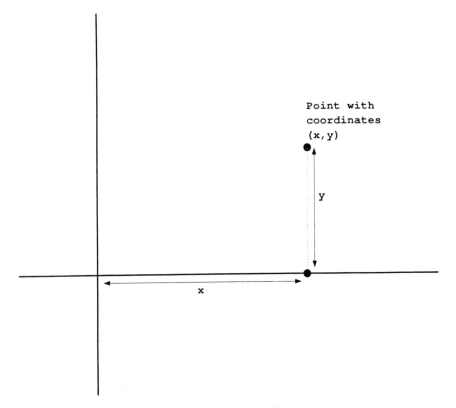

Figure 2. Cartesian coordinates

the Greeks never took. In fact, the Greeks had terrible techniques for doing simple arithmetic, and they would never have thought of the reduction of geometry to arithmetic by means of coordinates as any sort of simplification (which was perhaps why they didn't think of it).

Now take Pythagoras's triangle and put point A at the origin of Descartes' coordinates and make side AB horizontal. This makes side BC vertical. Also let x be the length of AB and let y be the length of BC. Then we see that the pair of numbers x,y is simply Descartes' coordinates for the point C (see Figure 3). Finally, consider the circle whose center is the origin and whose radius is one. If C lies on that circle, then the length of AC is one, and Pythagoras's theorem tells us that the sum of the square of x and the square of y is one:

$$x^2 + y^2 = 1.$$

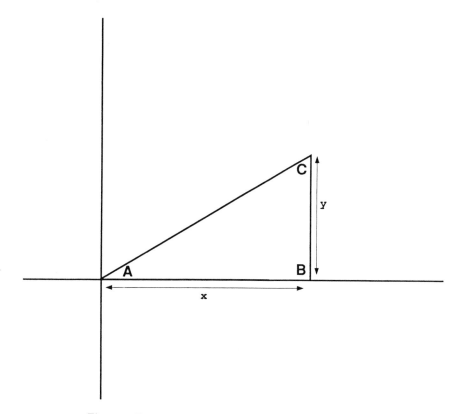

Figure 3. Pythagoras' Theorem in Cartesian coordinates

On the other hand, if C doesn't lie on that circle, then $x^2 + y^2$ is the square of some other number, less than one or greater than one, so $x^2 + y^2$ does not equal one. In other words, we have shown that the set of solutions of the equation

$$x^2 + y^2 = 1$$

is the same as the set of coordinates (x,y) of the points on our circle! We have an equation, and a simple one at that, for the most basic object of geometry. We have reduced the circle, one of the great building blocks of geometry, to a polynomial $x^2 + y^2$.

This idea, of taking equations of any kind and plotting their set of solutions using Cartesian coordinates, is the secret to the link between algebra and geometry, and the origin of algebraic geometry. What happens with other equations? We can take any equation made up by adding, subtracting, and multiplying x and y and ordinary numbers and out of it get a curve, which is called an algebraic curve. The curve is the set of points whose coordinates x,y solve the equation. In Figure 4, we have drawn three such curves to give you an idea what can happen. Clearly the algebra can produce a whole lot of geometry.

What sort of rules apply to this dictionary between equations and curves? We need some terminology. The equations are built by adding and multiplying the coordinates x,y by various numbers and by each other, and we call x and y the "variables" in the equation

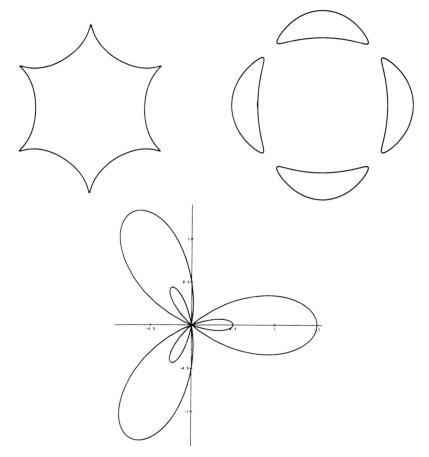

Figure 4. Some algebraic curves

because they can be given any value. Some rules are easy: for instance, if the equation is linear (it doesn't multiply variables by each other, but only adds them up after multiplying them by known numbers), then the curve is a straight line. If the equation is quadratic, meaning that each side is a sum of pieces in which at most two variables are multiplied (i.e., x^2, xy, or y^2), then we get a circle or a stretched circle, called an ellipse, or a few other simple types (see Figure 5). Newton was the first to make a systematic study and to classify the curves obtained from cubic equations.

Now, here's our second illustration of the way mathematics

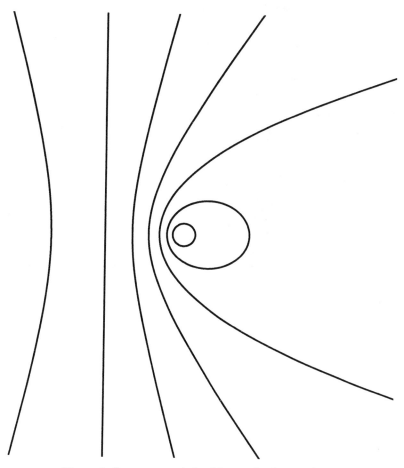

Figure 5. Some curves defined by quadratic equations

works. We ask a simple question: If we start with two algebraic curves, is there a rule for predicting how many points they have in common, that is, how large is their intersection? Well, two lines always meet in exactly one point — unless they are parallel, a special case that we shall leave aside for the moment. A line and a circle can meet in two points, or in one point if they are tangent, or in no points if the line doesn't go near the circle at all (see Figure 6). Looks like a mess!

But here we can adopt another strategy that mathematicians love and that often leads to great surprises: If you find a mess in the world you start in, why not change the world? Invent a new and better world, a castle in the sky, in which you can make your theorem come true; looking back at the dreary reality with which you started, maybe you can understand your more complex reality as a departure from this simpler picture. If you plunge ahead like this, now really pretending to be God, one of two things happen. You may find that the reality you want contains the seeds of its own self-destruction: it leads to a contradiction. Or you may find it holding up, and if you are lucky, you eventually prove that it is consistent. In either case, you have understood the original situation more *deeply*.

For the case of the parallel lines, this leap of faith, this audacious idea of altering the rules of the game, was one of the great inventions of the Renaissance, when it was declared that *parallel lines meet at infinity!* Painters realized that, in order to draft accurately rectangular buildings, they should draw the horizon on their canvasses, even where it was obscured behind nearer objects. Then the parallel lines would be drawn correctly if, when extended, they met on the

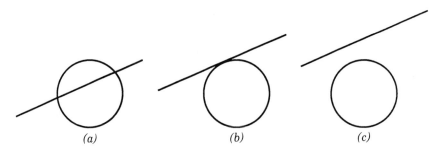

Figure 6. (a) A line and a circle that meet twice; (b) A line and a circle that meet once and are tangent; (c) A line and a circle that never meet

horizon. Mathematicians realized that these points on the horizon depicted places that didn't literally exist in the real world because they would have to be infinitely far away. But why not say they do exist somewhere? Increase the stock of points in the plane by adding new ones, which we then call ideal or infinite points. Don't treat them as second-class citizens either, because on the canvas, they appear just like real points and the canvas can be treated as a kind of map showing points at and near infinity all at once. The new points are where the train tracks meet, where the lines of Leonardo's drawing intersect (see Figure 7). We come up with a richer geometry, in which there is more elbow room. In fact, if you go out on a line in one direction, you actually reach infinity, pass it, and then reenter the finite world from infinity but now at the other end of the line. This way of thinking is called "projective geometry."

Now how about the circle and the line? Ignore for a while the case where the circle is tangent to the line, as it is a special case. The two basic cases are where they meet twice and where they don't meet at all. We don't want to lose any points, so we are forced to add points again until a line totally outside a circle still "meets" it somewhere. Here is where some old ideas that originated in the Middle Ages

Figure 7. Leonardo da Vinci: Perspective study

come to our help: the square root of -1, called i, and the complex numbers built up from it, e.g., $2 + 3i$ or $-4.5 - 5i$. It had been known for a long time that solving polynomial equations seemed to work better if you allowed complex numbers in, either as the solutions themselves or, even if you only wanted the usual real roots, as intermediate steps in calculating the solutions. Such numbers had had an air of mystery and black magic about them at first, but, gradually it was realized that there was nothing inconsistent about them; if you suspended your disbelief and admitted them for the sake of the game, you didn't reach any contradiction. A beautiful way of describing them by points in the plane, due to C. F. Gauss, the founder of the modern era of mathematics, made it totally clear that they were a perfectly consistent rigorous construction.

So where are the missing points, for example, where the line $x = 1.25$ and the circle $x^2 + y^2 = 1$ meet? One of them is the point $x = 1.25$, $y = 0.75i$, and the other is $x = 1.25$, $y = -0.75i$. (Just square 1.25 getting 1.5625, and square $.75i$ getting $-.5625$, which add up to 1.0.) With a little algebra, it's easy to see that this always works, so long as we let the coordinates x,y of the points in the plane be complex numbers. But what has this technique done to our geometry? In fact, it has made it much richer. Although we continue to treat it like a two-dimensional world, to specify a point requires two coordinates, and each of them, being complex, needs to have a real and an imaginary part (thus $2 + 3i$ has real part 2 and imaginary part 3). This means that we need in all four numbers of the ordinary sort to specify a point, so our geometry has now become four-dimensional. Moreover, we still have to add the line of points at infinity, including complex points at infinity. For instance, a circle, which in the ordinary sense doesn't go out to infinity at all, now can do so, provided the direction in which it goes has imaginary slope (the points at infinity on circles used to be called I and J and were nicknamed Isaac and Jacob by students in the college days of my colleague Lars Ahlfors). The whole affair is called the *complex projective plane* and is the place in which to "draw" algebraic curves and to do algebraic geometry.

To complete our story, what have we gained by these mental gymnastics? In fact, we have gained a tremendous amount, but to tell the story is to tell a large part of algebraic geometry. For this foreword, I'll only tell about Bezout's theorem — actually a theorem of Poncelet, I believe, but mathematicians are notorious for crediting things rather arbitrarily. Remember that any polynomial equation in x and y defines its curve of solutions. The degree of the equation is simply the largest number of times the variables are ever multiplied together (so 2 is the degree of $x^2 + y^2 = 1$, and 5 is the degree of $x^3 \cdot y^2 = -1$). Bezout's theorem states that two such curves, of degrees n and m, meet almost always in $n \cdot m$ points, and always in $n \cdot m$ points if special points of intersection, like a point where a line is tangent to a circle, are counted more than once in a careful way. (Finding techniques for counting these special points was, by the way, one of the principle technical accomplishments of Zariski's archrival Weil, *cf. Ch. 12*.) In other words, we have found a strong general link between the algebra of the polynomials on the one hand and the geometry of the curves on the other. Such links, many quite amazing on first sight, are the main concerns of algebraic geometry.

I want to touch on one more thing in this quick tour of the mathematician's world. The lay picture of the mathematician (as seen in *New Yorker* cartoons) shows a bespectacled, white-coated, rather unworldly man looking at a blackboard of bizarre equations. This man is probably dry and precise, following rules without fail; his failing to do so is cause for humor (see Figure 8). As discussed below, much of Zariski's life was devoted to seeking the right way to make precise a huge amount of writing and thinking produced by other mathematicians who were anything but precise. In fact, one of them was an out-and-out romantic and another a dictatorial dramatic man with a flair for wild driving. Let the truth be known: mathematicians are as subject to human error and emotion, as subject to the fashions of intellectual trends and as often personifications of their national characteristics, as thinkers in any other field. They do strive, or claim, to be better and more detached, but their history reveals marvelous episodes in which they have driven right off the road in pursuit of their particular vision of truth.

This book deals with one of the most colorful episodes of this type. The Italian school of algebraic geometry was created in the late 19th century by a half dozen geniuses who were hugely gifted and who thought deeply and nearly always correctly about their field. They extended its ideas over a huge new area, especially what is called the theory of algebraic surfaces (we were discussing algebraic curves;

"I THINK YOU SHOULD BE MORE EXPLICIT HERE IN STEP TWO."

Figure 8. © *1975 by Sidney Harris —* *American Scientist magazine*

surfaces come from equations in three variables, $x, y,$ and z, instead of two). But they found the geometric ideas much more seductive than the formal details of proofs, especially when these proofs had to cover all the nasty special cases that so often crop up in geometry. So, in the twenties and thirties, they began to go astray. It was Zariski and, at about the same time, Weil who set about to tame their intuition, to find the principles and techniques that could truly express the geometry while embodying the rigor without which mathematics eventually must degenerate to fantasy.

The 20th century has been, until recently, an era of "modern mathematics" in a sense quite parallel to "modern art" or "modern architecture" or "modern music." That is to say, it turned to an analysis of abstraction, it glorified purity and tried to simplify its results until the roots of each idea were manifest. These trends started in the work of Hilbert in Germany, were greatly extended in France by a secret mathematical club known as "Bourbaki," and found fertile soil in Texas, in the topological school of R. L. Moore. Eventually, they conquered essentially the entire world of mathematics, even trying to breach the walls of high school in the disastrous episode of the "new math." Now the trend has reversed: postmodern mathematics is quite different and has reintroduced the love of the baroque; it embraces the tool of the computer and seeks out rather than shunning the complexities of applications. The theory of chaos is the best-known example of this trend, but it extends from the vast number–theoretic speculations on modular forms to the paradoxically flat yet knotted "non-standard" four-dimensional spaces. Zariski's life is the story of a mathematician of this century, who lived with and loved and gave his soul to these struggles. He began his career with naive beliefs inherited from the nineteenth century; the middle part of his career was wholly devoted to "modern mathematics"; and in the last part, he began to look again at the richness and complexities of his material. But this is the story Carol Parikh has told so ably in the book that follows.

David Mumford

1 ◧ THAT DARLING OLD LADY

KOBRIN AND CHERNIGOV

1899 – 1918

Oscar Zariski was born on April 24, 1899, in Kobrin, a small city in White Russia in what was then known as the Pale of Settlement. Jewish by birth, Russian by culture, carrying a Polish passport and educated in Italy, he eventually settled in the United States. "I have never felt more comfortable with one nationality than with another," he used to say, and indeed, students of algebraic geometry were drawn to him from all over the world.[1]

The sixth child and third son of Bezalel and Hannah Zaritsky, Oscar, or "Ascher," as he was named after his maternal grandfather, spent his first eleven years in a traditional, almost exclusively Jewish society.[2] Like many of the predominantly Jewish towns in Eastern Europe, Kobrin had become part of the Russian Empire with the partition of Poland in the eighteenth century and would be returned

---

[1] Zariski's own words throughout the book, unless otherwise noted, have been taken from interviews made by Ann Kostant, Hei Hironaka, Wakako Hironaka, and David Mumford between 1979 and 1981. All other interviews have been made by the author.

[2] He chose the Westernization "Oscar Zariski" as a graduate student in Rome.

to Poland again, briefly, between the two world wars.[3] As Zariski once explained to a Soviet official, "Russia left me before I left her."

The Kobrin in which Oscar grew up, with its two-story houses and the broad cobblestone road that led out to the railway depot, had served for generations as the commercial center of the flat, often swampy countryside. From his front windows he could watch peasants gathering with their horse carts in the main square on market day to trade their produce for money and their gossip for news of the wider world. From the garden behind his house he could catch sight of rabbis gliding in and out of the neighborhood *shul.*

His father, had he lived to occupy this house, would have preferred the quiet garden view, but his mother thrived on the commercial bustle of the marketplace. The lively daughter of the owner of a prosperous pub, Hannah Tannenbaum had enjoyed serving customers before her marriage to Bezalel Zaritsky, a young Talmudic scholar. They were supported by her family, in keeping with convention, until the sudden closing of the pub in 1882. Her father retired, and her four brothers, after finding a husband for her slightly retarded younger sister, sailed for New York.[4]

Left to take care of her scholarly husband and her growing family without their help, Hannah mustered what capital she could and opened a small store on the ground floor of her old wooden house. During these difficult years she was usually pregnant, and when she wasn't minding the store she was nursing a baby or mourning its death or taking care of her husband, who had become an invalid as a result of an ill-fated attempt to avoid the draft. Anticipating the treatment he would find as a Jew in the czar's army, Bezalel had drunk a potion designed to cause a severe but temporary illness and had never quite recovered. He died in 1901 when Oscar was two, leaving Hannah with a new baby, six young children, and one picture of himself looking dignified and thoughtful.

---

[3] "The Jewish Pale of Settlement," which extended from Lithuania through Eastern Poland, the Ukraine, and Bessarabia, was made up of areas that had been annexed or conquered by the Russian Empire. Etymologically, "pale" is derived from the Latin "palus," a stake used for making fences — and, by extension, boundaries.

[4] The sudden and inexplicable pub closing was perhaps connected with the May Laws of 1882, which forbade "the registration of deeds of sale and mortgages in the names of Jews . . . as well as the attestation, in the name of Jews, of leases on real estate situated outside of cities and towns." See George Vernadsky, ed., *A Source Book for Russian History from Early Times to 1917,* New Haven: Yale University Press, 1985, III, 682.

Hannah Zaritsky (courtesy of Yole Zariski)

Zariski always remembered his mother's strength and independence, and enjoyed telling his own children stories about their lively grandmother. According to one story, Hannah took to visiting Bezalel's grave once a week to seek his advice on business matters and entertain him with family news and town gossip, even though an orthodox Jewish conscience would have forbidden such behavior.[5] Aware of the narrow confines of Kobrin, she did her best to prepare

---

[5] I am indebted to Zariski's daughter, Vera DeCola, for her vivid recollections of her father's stories of his early childhood.

her children for the world beyond the Pale.[6] Although this was a
time when many Russian Jews, struggling to preserve their identity,
considered it sinful to learn Russian and she herself spoke only
Yiddish, she encouraged her children to attend secular schools.

She was not, however, blind to the limits of pragmatism. One
night shortly after her husband's death she had a dream in which
one of her brothers urged her to take her family and all their belong-
ings out of the house because there would be a terrible fire. The
vividness of the dream compelled her to tell it to the children the
next morning, but as the day wore on she began to consider how
foolish she would feel if she wasted so much effort on what was, after
all, only a dream. That night the fire struck, destroying the old
wooden house on Pusky Street and all its contents. Oscar heard the
story many times as he was growing up: perhaps his mother liked to
tell it as a cautionary tale, to show what happens when you fail to
trust your dreams.

A wealthy uncle rescued the struggling family by buying Hannah
the beautiful stone house on the main square that Zariski would
remember so fondly. She rented out half of the second floor to a
family and the other half to a movie theater (which admitted the
Zaritskys free of charge) and moved her seven children and her shop
into the ground floor. Oscar shared one of the three large bedrooms
with his oldest sister, Zippa, and his small bed with the family cat. A
live-in maid was hired to manage the household so that Hannah
could devote herself to her rapidly expanding business.

Oscar was sent to study at _heder,_ a religious school for young
children, as soon as he turned six. He was forced to memorize pas-
sages in Aramaic, and then more complicated things, like the legal
codes of marriage and divorce, in Hebrew from the Talmud:

> Seven of us boys would sit around a long table in a small room in the
> rabbi's house, and if he didn't like you he would rap your hands with a
> stick. You go there in the mornings and you stay there all day and you
> come back in the evening and it's dark in the winter and you carry
> with you a lamp, a kerosene lamp, to light the way.

---

[6] Discrimination against Jews in the Russian Empire seems to have been more legal than
racial. Baptized Jews, university graduates, and certain other specific categories (including
prostitutes) were routinely granted permission to live permanently outside the Pale.

The Zaritskys rapidly became one of the richest families in Kobrin, and by the time Oscar was seven Hannah was able to afford a tutor for him in the two subjects that would lead him out of Kobrin — Russian and arithmetic. Two years later she enrolled him in a secular elementary school, where he became an avid reader in Russian, especially of the adventure novels of Jules Verne.

His oldest brother, Moses, seems to have been the first member of the family on either side to demonstrate a talent for mathematics. A man with little formal training but with immense enthusiasm, he took advantage of Oscar's growing interest in arithmetic to teach him algebra. Oscar must have learned very quickly, because soon they were working on problems together, competing fiercely with each other for solutions. Although Moses often quarreled with Hannah and was known in the family for his irascible temper, he never resented it when Oscar beat him, which was more than half the time, and never pushed but always encouraged him to do what was most difficult.

"I spent hours and hours doing math problems without a teacher forcing me," Zariski remembered almost eighty years later. "Whole books of algebra problems — I did them one after another. I was only seven or eight, but I always wanted mathematics." Moses told his little brother that someday he would be a mathematician.

Although Zariski was by all accounts an exceptionally quick and eager math student, the full extent of his gifts became apparent relatively late in life. He was almost twenty-five before he published his first paper, and almost fifty when he did his great work on holomorphic functions. The romantic convention that mathematicians, like poets, burn early and rapidly consume themselves was also belied by his work on equisingularity, which was completed when he was almost eighty.

His memories of his early childhood also give very little hint of the passionate tenacity he would later bring to mathematics. Moses taught him chess, a game at which he would excel and which would bring him pleasure all his life. His other brother, Shepsel, taught him to ice skate on the Mukhavets, a small tributary of the Bug River. In the summers he liked to bicycle out to the countryside or play chase games through the town streets with the other boys. Often he would wander down to the sprawling bathhouse to swim, or explore the riverbanks in a small boat. Hannah grew vegetables and fruit in the garden behind their house, but although she encouraged him to eat the apples and cherries as they ripened, he sometimes took more pleasure in stealing them from the trees of the Polish family next door.

In 1909 Hannah married a gentle man who, with his youngest son from a previous marriage, became part of her Kobrin household. The following year Moses moved with his wife and first child to Vladimir-Volynskiy, where a government-supported college preparatory school (called "gymnasium" after its European cousins) had recently been opened. When an imperial decree doubled the quota for the admission of Jews to gymnasiums, Moses urged Oscar to take the entrance exam.[7] In spite of his trepidation, Oscar agreed and soon found himself one of four Jewish students in an entering class of forty.

Although Vladimir-Volynskiy was more than a hundred miles from Kobrin, Oscar felt only excitement at the prospect of leaving the big house on the square, and Hannah, although he was her youngest son and favorite child, encouraged him, just as she had encouraged all the others. Moses had gone to a yeshiva only because Jews were not allowed to attend institutions of higher learning outside the Pale at that time, but Oscar's other brother and all four sisters were sent by Hannah to gymnasiums and would go on to study in professional schools. Shepsel would become an engineer. Oscar's three older sisters would become dentists, and his younger sister, Zila, would be educated at the University of Rome.

During the first of his eight years at the gymnasium, Oscar lived with Moses and his family. After Moses, who was always restlessly changing jobs, left Vladimir-Volynskiy, he moved into a boarding house that had been assigned to Jews. With six other boys he lived in

---

[7] From September 1908 to August 1909, quotas for the admission of Jews "to state-supported institutions of secondary education" had been increased by imperial decree — from 3% to 5% for "educational institutions in the capitals," and from 5% to 10% for "educational institutions outside the Pale of Jewish Settlement" (*A Source Book for Russian History*, III, 818).

two rooms, closely supervised by the gymnasium authorities. The housemaster kept a diary in which he described the conduct of each boy, and teachers appeared unexpectedly in the evenings to see if the students were doing their assignments.

He had classes every day in Russian literature and grammar, Russian and general history, the natural sciences, French, German, Latin, art, gym, geometry, arithmetic and, later, algebra (which, of course, he already knew and liked). Students were allowed outside only from three to five o'clock each day, a recess he took advantage of to ice skate in the winter and to swim, boat, and bicycle when the days grew warm. Three times a year, at Christmas, Easter, and during summer vacations, he took the five-hour train ride north to Kobrin. He was always happy to see his family, although while he was at the gymnasium he was so involved with his studies, particularly mathematics, that he hardly had time for homesickness.

His mathematics teachers recognized his talent immediately. Before the start of each class one teacher would open his book to some difficult problems in geometry. "Don't listen to what's going on in class," he would whisper. "You do that."

Ignoring the rules, another teacher would come to the boarding house and spirit him away to the river to talk about mathematics. It was this teacher who said to him one evening, "Good God, what a pity that you are Jewish! You will have great difficulty. You will never become a professor of mathematics. Why don't you convert? Then you will be free to go to university. What does it matter?"

And yet it did, even though since moving into the boarding house he had become an atheist and most of his friends, including his best friend, were Russians. He had also begun to smoke, even on Saturdays, and to eat nonkosher food, which Hannah, with her usual pragmatism, ignored. "She was a very intelligent woman," Zariski once explained, "so she tried to make believe she didn't know."

But this adventurous breaking-away from a provincial background, which looked so much like a rejection of Jewishness to the mathematics teacher, seemed to Oscar and to many others of his generation simply the natural consequence of an awakening to the wider world. "I felt no hostility toward the Jewish past or Jewish laws," he later said. "I thought, 'They exist, but not for me.'"

He made his bar mitzvah in a way that again suggests an adroit balancing of past and present, and a practicality that rivaled Hannah's. Having asked permission of the gymnasium authorities to absent himself for an hour, he went alone to a small synagogue and told them that he needed a *minyan*. When ten people had been gathered he said the necessary prayer, gave them money for vodka, and returned to class.

His ability to preserve what he found valuable and to reject the rest without sentimentality would prove indispensable to his revolutionary work in mathematics.

World War I broke out in August 1914 while Oscar and Moses were home on vacation. Terrified, Kobrin followed the eastward march of German troops and watched the ragged remnants of the czar's army straggle through the cobblestone streets. "I was too young to be in the army," Zariski remembered, "but I read the newspapers and rejoiced every time the czarist army was beaten."

When Hannah heard that the Germans had reached Warsaw, only a hundred miles away, she decided that her three sons should leave Kobrin immediately. Oscar's gymnasium had already been evacuated from Vladimir-Volynskiy to Chernigov, and one sister, Rebecca, was settled in the Ukraine, so it was decided that Oscar and Shepsel would go with Moses to Chernigov. Hannah herself, although she was particularly afraid of Germans, chose to stay in Kobrin with her store and her second husband.

Feeling fortunate to have found space on a platform between two cars of a freight train, Oscar and his brothers traveled east for several days, deep into the Ukraine. The unfamiliar countryside with its frightened knots of peasants at the crossings excited the imagination of the fifteen year old boy. Too excited to sleep, he spent the nights with his eyes on the vast expanse of stars.

During his remaining four and a half years of gymnasium education, from 1914 to 1918, Oscar lived comfortably in Chernigov with Moses and his family. Cut off by the Germans from his mother in Kobrin and free of the constraints of boarding-house life, he was able to devote himself entirely to his studies. His favorite subjects were still mathematics, particularly algebra and number theory, and Russian history and literature. As his taste matured, he immersed himself in the great Russian novelists, Dostoevsky and Tolstoy, and joined a literary club where students took turns reading their own critical essays to one another. He found that he was just as good in literary composition as in mathematics. Every year he won a certificate of honor as one of the two or three best students in his class.

Having become a salesman, Moses took advantage of his frequent trips to Moscow and Petrograd to buy books for Oscar. He gave him Salmon's algebra and a little geometry book after one trip, and a book on differential equations and Goursat's integral calculus after another. Once he brought him a whole collection of philosophy books because Oscar had explained that he was trying to decide whether to study mathematics or philosophy.

Edited by a German historian of philosophy, the seven volumes included Descartes, Spinoza, Schilling, and Hegel, who was of particular interest to Oscar because of his growing enthusiasm for the ideas of Karl Marx. As he reflected later, "Naturally a man at that time would sympathize with the movement in which you nationalize industry and everything belongs to the working man, to the state."

In 1918, the year after the Reds took control of Chernigov, Oscar graduated from the gymnasium and taking advantage of a lull in the war, returned to Kobrin. The Bolsheviks had not yet reached the German-occupied territories of western Russia, and he was pleased to discover that Hannah had not only overcome her fear of Germans but had also managed to use their patronage to make her store into the largest in Kobrin.

One day shortly after his return Oscar woke to find the house in a turmoil because their cow, a sweet-natured creature whose milk he regarded as ambrosial, had not returned home with the other cows. Neighbors who had lost cows told Hannah to forget about it since it was the habit of German officers to take cows as they needed them. Not a woman to ignore so bold a theft, however, she set off briskly for the front lines and by evening had found and chastised the offending officers. They must have been pleased by her spirit because they not only returned the cow, but treated her to a splendid meal by way of reparation.

The German commander of the town was a frequent guest in the big house in the square, and he and Oscar often played a friendly game of chess. Breaking the silence one evening, the commander

looked across the board at Oscar and asked him what he was going to
do for a living. When Oscar replied that he was planning to become a
mathematician, the officer laughed. "Look," he said, "I am not
asking you what you are going to read, but what is your aim in life."

Knowing that the German was not an intellectual, Oscar didn't
take his attitude toward mathematics seriously, but the question of
his aim in life remained with him and a few days later he made the
following entry in his diary:

> Incidentally, what is my aim? It goes without saying that mathemat-
> ics will not be in the back seat. I feel exceptionally sure of that darling
> old lady, and I also feel exceptionally certain that she will not betray
> me, because I feel inside me the presence of a mathematical talent.
>
> I have two notebooks consisting entirely of my own original mathe-
> matical work: research in number theory. Some of my results, as I
> found out later on, were known; some apparently are new. The happi-
> ness one finds in letting one's self be carried by the current of one's
> thoughts! That current takes you inevitably to new results.
>
> You begin with some question (in the present case it was the
> theorem of Euler), and step by step you witness the wonderful func-
> tioning of your own intellect. You stumble on new problems, which in
> their further development lead you to new results. Association of
> ideas plays here a superlative role. . . . Well, to put it briefly: in
> mathematics I feel absolutely sure of myself.

2 ▨

BIRDS WHIRLING

LIKE NUMBERS

KIEV 1918–1920

In the fall of 1918 Zariski enrolled at the University of Kiev, in the philosophy department because there was no room in the faculty of mathematics. He took only mathematics courses, however, and his main interest during the following two years remained in algebra and number theory. In order to save money he commuted thirty miles to the embattled streets of Kiev from his brother's house in Chernigov, which was already basking in the peaceful aftermath of the Bolshevik success. Most of the time he worked at home alone. Moses had been temporarily cut off from Chernigov while on a business trip to Vladivostok, where fighting between Reds and Whites was particularly fierce, and disruptions in transportation made even local traveling difficult; once Zariski's shoes were stolen by soldiers and he made the long journey to Kiev in his bare feet.

The seat of a newly formed Soviet executive committee, Chernigov had rapidly become the propaganda center of a large and prosperous district. One of its most important projects was the publishing of a weekly newspaper with which Zariski, as a convinced

Marxist and skillful writer, soon became involved. He did not, however, join the Communist Party, but became instead a member of the *Po'alei Zion* (Workers of Zion), a heterogeneous socialist Jewish party that included both workers and students. Unlike later Zionist groups, the aim of the *Po'alei Zion* was not the establishment of a homeland, but of equal rights for Jews wherever they chose to live — an ideal shared by many Jewish political organizations before the Holocaust.

Writing for the paper seemed at first to reconcile his political and intellectual interests, and in just a few months he became their main editorial writer. He held this position for more than a year, during which it became increasingly clear that his work for the revolutionary cause was interfering with his commitment to mathematics. That "darling old lady" demanded silence and solitude, a withdrawal from the world that was the very opposite of the intense involvement with the details of everyday life exacted of a writer for the revolution.

Perhaps he also grew wary of this involvement because of his precocious and rather romantic intuition about the attractiveness of force. Three weeks after his nineteenth birthday, he wrote the following passage in his diary:

> I'm afraid to read Nietzsche who is a believer in, even proselytizer of, force; afraid of the effect it will have on me, the socialist. I am a very young man and it's very well known what Nietzsche does to young men. The philosophy or theory of Nietzsche is a philosophy of youth, of youthful cruelty, a philosophy full of admiration of force, of the (persuasive) force of physical beauty (and psychological vigor) — after all, only the young are cruel and at the same time are full of the will to live.

More difficult to avoid than Nietzsche, however, was the violence that raged in the streets of Kiev. While the 1917 revolution had already put control of the most important cities into the hands of the Bolsheviks, the next three years saw the rest of the country rent by civil war. The recently signed Treaty of Brest-Litovsk had not resulted in the German support for the Bolsheviks that Lenin had hoped for, but rather in Polish independence and the loss of a good part of industrial Russia.

Ukrainian nationalists in Kiev, fearing the Red Army's search for grain almost as much as the White Army's support of landlords, struggled with peasant partisans and Poles. A Red takeover of the city on January 27, 1918, was quickly followed by a German victory, but by the end of the year Ukrainian leftist nationalists had managed to form a "people's republic." A few weeks later this, too, fell to the Reds, who were soon vanquished by the Whites but were able to regain control of the city by the end of 1919. After a Polish takeover, which lasted barely a month, the Reds again declared victory on June 12, 1920.

One morning on his way to class Zariski found himself surrounded by hundreds of students carrying the red flags of the Bolsheviks, and moments later truckloads of Ukrainian soldiers came wheeling around the corner. They jumped down, formed two lines, and began to fire into the unarmed crowd. At least fifty students were killed, and Zariski was wounded in the leg by a bullet that ricocheted up from the sidewalk. For more than eight weeks, the longest time he'd ever spent in Kiev, he shared a hospital room with two other wounded students, one of whom died. His own leg healed without infection, even though the doctors hadn't been able to remove the shrapnel (which traveled with him to Italy and from there to the United States, where it worked its way out in Berkeley, California, in 1949).

In spite of the unceasing violence, it was with reluctance that he accepted the fact that there was no mathematical future for him in Kiev. The university itself had come under siege and professors were having trouble just keeping classes open. As sympathetic as he was to the socialist cause, he began to think of leaving Russia for Western Europe. When the victorious Communists abolished examinations, he went secretly to the houses of his professors to take tests, the results of which he planned to bring to his new university, wherever it might be.

In the summer of 1920, in the wake of the Red Army as it battled the Poles westward from Kiev, Zariski traveled to Kobrin to see his mother after almost two years of being away. That October the Russians and the Poles declared an armistice, and a few months later the Treaty of Riga was signed, returning much of that region to Poland. Residents of Kobrin were given the choice of retaining their Russian citizenship by moving eastward or of remaining where they were and becoming Polish citizens.

To Hannah, "citizenship" meant very little compared to her attachment to the town where her family had lived for generations and to the store that she'd maintained for almost forty years. To Zariski's stepbrother, an ardent Communist, "citizenship" meant everything: he left Kobrin immediately to offer his considerable talent as an engineer to Trotsky and the Red Army. For Zariski, however, the choice was particularly difficult. Torn between his commitment to the socialist cause and his love for mathematics, he spent three agonizing months trying to decide whether to return to Kiev with the Bolsheviks or to stay in Kobrin and apply for Polish citizenship so that he could get a passport quickly.

He eventually found it impossible to relinquish his dream of studying mathematics in Western Europe: as he had predicted more than a year before, his "darling old lady" steadfastly refused to sit "in the back seat." Hannah, as always, supported his decision, and with her help he found a lawyer who was willing to speed the process along by bribing officials.

Increasingly impatient to be gone, he considered several destinations. France and Switzerland seemed attractive but not affordable, and Germany was still reeling from its defeat. At last he decided upon Italy, where university tuition was waived for foreigners and living cheaply would be possible. There were other, less practical reasons, too, as he would remember many years later: "I had the same romantic idea of Italy that most Russians had—the land of song, the land of poets, the land of Galileo Galilei. I might also have had some ideas of good-looking girls."

After several months of feeling like a foreigner in his hometown, a Russian ill at ease in Poland, he obtained his passport and his Italian visa, and carefully tucked the letters of exam results from his professors in Kiev into the pockets of his heavy overcoat: "Boarding that train meant the end of a whole way of life," he said later, "but I loved it. I knew that I was destined to do mathematics. I was so fascinated that when I looked at the sky I saw the birds whirling like numbers."

He crossed the border into Italy in the late winter of 1921, having decided to enroll at the University of Pisa. On the platform at Udine, where he had stopped to change trains, he was recognized as Russian, and before he could even step into the waiting room he found himself surrounded by a crowd of railway workers who were eager to find out about the revolution. Their curiosity made him lively, and never considering that he might be in any danger, he answered them as enthusiastically as he could in his halting Italian.

Had there been a Fascist among the workers, the warmth of his welcome might have been quite otherwise, as he himself would later recall. The Black Shirts, a band of disillusioned soldiers and officers from World War I who had been organized and equipped by Mussolini, were roaming the countryside, attacking anyone who might have leftist sympathies. As a recent arrival from the country of the triumphant revolution, Zariski was, of course, particularly vulnerable. The Fascist government was not yet in power, but Mussolini's triumphant "March on Rome" was only a year and a half away.

Crossing into Italy, Zariski had traded one politically unstable country for another, one set of violent imperatives for another, but he had carried with him like a magic cloak his devotion to mathematics. Although he would be attacked by Fascists in Rome, he would remember this attack, like the one in Kiev, with less intensity than the theorems he was studying at the time. Standing in that crowded waiting room in Udine, surrounded by strangers and besieged by questions in a language he only barely understood, what he felt was not fear but excitement at having reached the land of Galileo Galilei.

He arrived in Florence at midnight and was unwilling to wake the Polish friends who'd invited him to stop on his way to Pisa; he was too curious to sleep anyway. Hungry but not cold — after the Russian winter, Florence felt very mild — he spent the night in the streets. Like a man without a destiny, he followed the narrow lanes, surprised by the dark shape of a cathedral, delighted by the moonlight of a square. Unlike Rousseau, he found that the reality surpassed his dreams.

Enrolling at the University of Pisa for the spring term, he found room and board with an Italian family that seemed, like the workers at Udine, particularly hospitable to foreigners. Unfortunately, however, the son of the house turned out to be a Fascist who spent mealtimes trying to provoke Zariski into fights so he could demonstrate "how much stronger Italian Fascists are than Russian Communists." But it was only after he'd begun attending classes that he realized the full extent of his mistake in having chosen Pisa. The mathematics department was not as good as the one he'd left behind in Kiev; his courses were taught on a disappointingly low level, and the professors he'd looked forward to working with, especially Bianchi, whose book he'd admired in Russia, were no longer at the university.

He was also disappointed in the city itself, which he found very provincial; there were no theaters where he might occasionally spend an evening, and he was unhappy to discover that unmarried girls were not allowed out alone. He was only twenty-one, and Pisa's significance as a historical center of scientific studies, the home of Galileo and the leaning tower, was not enough to keep him there for very long.

That summer he moved to Rome, a relatively small city in 1921, with fewer than 700,000 inhabitants. The streets were noisy, not with cars but with strikes and demonstrations occasioned by high inflation and widespread unemployment. Roving bands of Fascists kept a sharp eye out for communists and anarchists.

Many years later he would say that had he gone to study in another country, or even to another university in Italy, he wouldn't have become an algebraic geometer but would have been content to remain an algebraist, since he was "not geometrically inclined by nature. . . . But it's so much nicer when you have geometry combined with algebra," he would smile, as if amused by this hint of arbitrariness in his mathematical destiny.

3 THREE GREAT

MATHEMATICIANS

ROME 1921 – 1926

In the fall of 1921 the University of Rome was the most important center of algebraic geometry in the world. What is now known as "the Italian School" had been started by Luigi Cremona soon after the unification of the Kingdom of Italy, a generation before Zariski's arrival in Rome. It was only after 1900, however, as a result of the combined efforts of three great Italian mathematicians — Guido Castelnuovo, Federigo Enriques, and Francesco Severi — that the Italians had carried algebraic geometry off in a startling new direction.

Speaking of "geometric intuition," they pushed their way into the gray area between "proof" and "rigorous proof," on what would turn out to be an exciting but perilous journey. They used "whatever tools were at hand, whether algebro-geometric, transcendental or topological, coupled with a geometrical imagination that gave the subject a beauty to match that of the Italian scene."[8]

---

[8] David Rees, "Efforts to restore geometric paradise," *The Times Higher Education Supplement* 10 Oct. 1980:12.

Zariski with fellow students, Rieti (left) and Corbellini, 1923 (courtesy of Yole Zariski)

More than fifty years later Zariski would write, "I had the great fortune of finding there on the faculty three great mathematicians, whose very names now symbolize classical algebraic geometry: G. Castelnuovo, F. Enriques, and F. Severi. Since even within the classical framework of algebraic geometry the algebraic background was clearly in evidence, it was inevitable that I should be attracted to that field."[9]

The first of the "three great mathematicians" to recognize Zariski's talent was Guido Castelnuovo. Stern and forbidding, he brought to his task as Zariski's teacher and, later, thesis advisor the formal classicism of his own early education. Although he was a central figure in the development of the Italian School, his commitment to reason and discipline made less than rigorous proofs distasteful to him, and he watched with dismay as his colleagues became increasingly dependent on "intuition." Full of natural dignity, he was always a little distant without quite wanting to be, so that it was impossible for Zariski to imagine him otherwise, even with his own family.

Standing in front of the class with his long black beard and quiet hands, Castelnuovo often reminded Zariski of the Moses of Michelangelo, although Zariski would also remember "the sweet smile that suddenly transformed his face." His lectures, which were on analytic geometry during Zariski's first term at the university, were tightly structured, reflecting the formality of his manner. Zariski enjoyed them so thoroughly that it was almost a month before he realized that he was wasting his time.

One day after class he found the courage to introduce himself and was relieved when Castelnuovo, as cordially as his forbidding manner would allow, said, "Come with me. I am going home." As they made their way through the narrow streets, Zariski explained that he knew all of analytic geometry and more calculus than had been taught in his college because his study had been based on the French textbooks on integral calculus (which were more like the analysis courses given in the first year of graduate school). He told Castelnuovo how he'd been forced to enroll as a student of philosophy at Kiev because the mathematics department had been full, and how

---

[9] *Collected Papers,* 4 vols. (Cambridge: MIT Press, 1972) I, xii.

he'd studied only mathematics. He described the books that he'd read, including Salmon's algebra and Goursat's calculus, and how he'd studied alone at home and taken examinations secretly after they had been abolished by the Communists.

Castelnuovo, who'd been quiet during all this time, suddenly began to ask mathematical questions, simple ones at first, and then more and more advanced and searching ones. By the time they stood in front of his house he seemed to have reached a decision. "Well, Zariski, you go tomorrow to the registrar's office and tell them that I sent you there, and that I suggested that you should change your application, which has already been accepted, in the following way: instead of asking admission to the first year, you ask to be admitted to the third year. Then you come to my course."

As Zariski himself liked to put it, on that short walk he gained two years. He also gained a thesis advisor who would encourage his independence. Once Zariski complained that he needed to know more about the functions of complex variables in order to understand the abelian functions that Castelnuovo was covering in his third-year course on algebraic geometry and algebraic functions. "Go to the library," Castelnuovo said. "There are books and you can read them."

Federigo Enriques, another of "the three great mathematicians" and a brother-in-law of Castelnuovo, was also quick to recognize the talent of the young Russian. "Castelnuovo was my official teacher — I mean, he gave me the topic for the dissertation — but Enriques became especially close to me, took me under his protective wing. Of all the mathematicians at the University of Rome, he was the most affectionate and outgoing, at least towards me," Zariski would later recall.

Warm and lively, a descendant of Spanish Jews, having befriended Zariski during this first difficult year in Rome, he maintained their friendship until his death, in spite of the war and his aversion to letter writing. Unlike Castelnuovo, who in six years of close association saw Zariski only by appointment and never anywhere but in his study, Enriques often invited Zariski for drinks or Sunday dinner with his wife and daughter. There was in fact some

Federigo Enriques (courtesy of Springer-Verlag Archives)

speculation that Enriques hoped to have a mathematician for a son-in-law.

After dinner he would invite Zariski to walk with him in the Villa Borghese and they would talk for hours "about everything," but especially about modern mathematics and ancient Greek philosophy, the two subjects in which Enriques was most interested. A dapper man with a well-trimmed beard, Enriques enjoyed serious conversation, pretty girls, and good wine, and had an unusual tolerance for eccentricity. One evening Zariski arrived two hours late for dinner because he'd been thinking and walking very slowly. Although this would have been a serious matter to most Italian professors, Enriques simply asked if he was hungry.

Enriques' easy attitude toward life seemed to extend to mathematics, for Zariski described his third-year course in algebraic geometry as "just geometry, just playing around with curves and figures, very informal, no proofs. If somebody quizzed Enriques, he would plead, 'Ah, come on.' If something was missing in his proof, he would say, 'Well, this is only *"dubbio critico"* — or, in a phrase still credited to him, 'Theorems are aristocratic, but proofs are plebeian.'"[10]

André Weil recounts a well-known anecdote in which Enriques is walking along the street speaking to a student about mathematics. The younger man finally stops and says, "Well, professor, I don't see that." Enriques looks at him with great contempt and says, "What do you mean, you don't see it? *I* see it just as clearly as I see that little dog over there!"

Many years later Zariski would find the beginning of the end of the Italian school in this cavalier attitude but at the time, as Zariski's wife put it, "Enriques' lack of rigor was also his charm."

He was not, however, incapable of meticulousness. One day as he and Zariski were preparing their first joint paper for publication, he suggested the Italianization of Zariski's name:

> First of all, look at it. "Ascher Zaritsky." Your name in Russian is very hard for Italians. Why don't you shorten it? Omit the "t" and the "y" and make "Zariski." Because to reproduce the sound "Zaritsky" phonetically in Latin letters, you'd have to use "tz ky." That's why, in Italian, "Zariski" is better.
>
> And then "Ascher." Well, it's a Biblical name, but Italians don't have a letter "sha" like the Jews have "shi." Italians have to write "Ascer," and "sc" in Italian is either "sh" or "sk," depending on the letter which lies after it. So why don't you change the "e" after the "c" into an "a" and the "A" into an "O" and become "Oscar"? That would be a reasonable thing.[11]

Zariski seems always to have found his name amusing. He would explain that "Ascher" meant "blessed are you who live in your mansion which is God's house," and that it was the name of his mother's father who owned the local pub. About "Zaritsky" he also liked to joke. "When I learned Russian history as a child, I found

---

[10] Kunihiko Kodaira remembers Zariski quoting Enriques in a less eloquent form: "'We aristocrats do not need proofs. Proofs are for you commoners.'" In the same article Kodaira speaks of his own admiration for the intuition of the Italian geometers, "which enabled them to derive correct results by obscure reasoning" ("Algebraic Geometry of the Italian School, A Japanese Mathematician's Reminiscence," *Creativity and Inspiration*, December 1987).

[11] Yole Zariski suggested that Zariski could and should have spelled it "Ascer."

that during the time of Peter the Great, or a little before him, a very well-known Russian Cossack leader had been called 'Zaritsky.' So I said, 'God knows what happened! You know, maybe I have Russian blood in me! Even my Jewish name is purely Russian!'"[12]

The new Russian student also attracted the attention of Francesco Severi, the youngest of the three founders of the Italian school and the only non-Jew. A tall heavy man from Tuscany, he lectured in a way that was particularly disquieting to Zariski. Lacking both the playfulness of Enriques' *"dubbio critico"* and the meticulous formality of Castelnuovo, Severi's dictatorial style seemed designed to make it impossible for his students to distinguish between guesses and assertions, hunches and hypotheses.

Severi was at the center of a famous controversy over the rigor of an Italian geometric "proof" that concerned the theorem of the existence of continuous families of curves $\{C\}$ on an arbitrary algebraic surface made up of a q-dimensional family of linear systems, where the number q, called the irregularity of the surface, was computed by elementary geometric means.

This theorem was discovered by the Italians — by Enriques, in fact — but no complete proof was found until the transcendental methods of Poincaré were used. The picture was later clarified by comparing the classical situation with characteristic p geometry: the theorem was found to be false in characteristic p, and a complete geometric analysis was eventually given using Grothendieck's extensions of Zariski's theorems on holomorphic functions.[13]

However, the question of whether Enriques or Severi had a purely geometric proof was the subject of considerable controversy over several decades. Years later, Severi looked back on what he called "a wearisome episode," but far from apologizing, he used it as the basis of a spirited defense of the Italian style of doing mathematics:

---

[12] His sense of the absurdity of racial divisions never left him. In the last decade of his life, a protégé remembered "a discussion about Arthur Koestler's book on the thirteenth tribe and Oscar's laughing at his own nose, which was not Semitic according to Koestler" (Bernard Teissier, letter to the author, 20 January 1990).

[13] See David Mumford, *Lectures on Curves on an Algebraic Surface* (Princeton: Princeton University Press, 1964).

In December 1904, Enriques gave a proof of the theorem that if the series $\{C\}$ is complete then the characteristic series is always complete even if $\{C\}$ is not linear. From that followed the characterizations of irregular surfaces, where $q = p_g - p_a > 0$, as those on which there exist complete irreducible systems made up of ∞^q linear systems. This proof was accepted as beyond reproach by all the geometers, and in 1905 I presented the proof myself in another form, based on the same line as that of Enriques.

But unfortunately this reasoning was not successful [*n'arrivait pas au but*]. And people have taken this wearisome episode as an accusation of lack of rigor in Italian algebraic geometry!

I note first of all that rigor is not a method of discovery; it has its place, after the discovery, in the critical analysis; and it should not be surprising if one has not made this analysis immediately in the period of the fever of creation, all the more so as our use of the theorem (the existence of a complete system of ∞^q linear systems) was entirely legitimate and *never* led to mistakes, because the applications were directed and informed by intuition about the facts that we were discovering.

One can, on the contrary, assert that it was a *felix culpa,* because otherwise the discovery of a mass of important properties would have been held back several years.

I remember in Pisa something which happened with one of my colleagues from Turin, about 1900, when Lindemann published a false proof of Fermat's last theorem. My friend, always lively and considered very learned, assured me that Lindemann's proof was completely correct because he had been able to reduce it to symbols of mathematical logic. Fifteen years later, Lindemann himself published a second note to say that his proof was false. My friend had therefore made a mistake of logic, that is to say, he was deceived even while using one of the most formidable instruments of rigor.

Another colleague, an eminent foreign geometer,[14] wrote me recently that he believed in Enriques' proof up to the time when it was recognized not to work and that from that time on, while still thinking like an Italian geometer, he distrusted all the results until he had been able to put them in algebraic terms. Personally, I believe that our methods, when they are well analyzed, give a confidence as perfect as purely algebraic methods (perhaps I have given examples of this even in this paper).

In any case, I reply to my colleague with a question: Was the gap in

---

[14] David Mumford suggests that this was Zariski.

the proof discovered by the algebraists, or rather by us, with our methods?[15]

Outside of mathematics Severi was also a forceful and disquieting presence. "I love you, Zariski, but you don't love me," he once said, a surprising statement from a man as vain as he often seemed to be. His wild driving was legendary; oblivious to the pleading of his passengers, he would careen through the hills above Rome. Even old age seems not to have slowed him down behind the wheel; Zariski remembered with terror being driven through Rome by Severi, when Severi was already eighty-one.

When Mussolini asked university professors to give an oath of allegiance to the government in 1933, most agreed. But just a few years later, when he abolished the ancient Accademia dei Lincei[16] and formed the Accademia d'Italia, which began to expel Jewish members soon after its creation, many non-Jewish professors protested by resigning from the new academy. Among the few who didn't resign was Severi.

A socialist after WWI and a *"democristiano"* after WWII, his loyalty to the Fascists seems to have arisen from self-interest rather than from any particular political or racial opinion. While Castelnuovo was hiding somewhere in Rome and Enriques was trying to make his way to France, Severi was being honored by Mussolini. Many of the mathematicians who had resigned in protest were given makeshift positions by the Accademia Vaticana, but Severi was appointed president of the Accademia d'Italia.

In spite of their deep mathematical and political differences, however, Severi was never less than cordial to Zariski and Zariski never less than loyal to his old professor. In 1953, when Zariski found serious problems in a paper of Severi's he had been asked to read for *Math Reviews,* he chose to write his objections directly to Severi "in an attempt not to be too nasty with him in a public review." [17] And even after Severi's death Zariski tried to dissuade one of his students from publishing an attack on his work.[18]

---

[15] "La geometrie algebrique italienne," *Colloque de Geometrie Algebrique* (Liege: Georges Thone, 1950) 40–41. Translated by David Mumford.

[16] The Accademia had been named for the keen eyesight of the lynx in 1603.

[17] Oscar Zariski, letter to Shreeram Abhyankar, 23 July 1953.

[18] David Mumford, personal interview, June 1987.

Zariski would always feel grateful for "the geometric paradise" he
found in Rome and for "the very humane reception" he received that
first year, both from his professors and from the university administration. The free tuition they offered him as a foreign student turned
out to be of crucial importance: a few months after he had reached
Rome he had been cut off from his mother's support by the war
between Russia and Poland. Since he knew no one in Rome well
enough to borrow from, he found himself for half a year "without a

Oscar Zariski, 1924 (courtesy of Yole Zariski)

penny," as he said, remembering how hard it had been to face morning exams without even a cup of coffee.

When he told his landlady what had happened, she was very sympathetic, unlike her husband, who growled, "Don't believe the scoundrel." She agreed to wait for the rent and sometimes brought him food, stealing up to his room so that her husband wouldn't find out. Fortunately, the owner of a small *trattoria* that catered to students also believed his story and gave him credit during these long hungry months, and an organization of foreign Jews granted him, on loan, a small monthly stipend. He quickly discovered for himself, however, that the best way to economize was simply not to eat.

But compared to his pleasure at discovering algebraic geometry the difficulties of his first year in Rome seemed trivial to him. Why would he be more daunted by poverty than he had been by bullets? In his eager courtship of that "darling old lady" it simply never occurred to him to give up and go home.

He was also helped through that year by the general warmth of Italians. Pretty girls on trains offered to teach him Italian and strangers often smiled. "I wasn't used to being treated equally by people who weren't Jews," he once explained. "Back in Russia I had friends, but in the streets it was different. The Russians, especially after the revolution, were very talkative, very outgoing, but there was still not the same friendly open atmosphere that I found in Italy at that time."

He flourished in that "friendly open atmosphere." He not only found a direction for his talent in classical algebraic geometry, he also discovered love.

4 ▨   READING PUSHKIN

AND DANTE

One warm spring day near the end of his first year in Rome, Zariski was stopped on the steps of the university library by a friend and fellow countryman, an "eternal student" named Derechin. In high spirits, Derechin introduced him to the pretty girl beside him, a literature student at the university named Yole Cagli.

"He looked like he was starving," Yole would remember, and of course to a rather alarming extent he was. But he must have spent a good part of his summer holidays in Kobrin just eating, because when Yole met him accidentally in the street that fall she almost didn't recognize him. "He looked very different. He'd been really fattened up by home cooking." She helped him with directions to a shoe store, and on the way suggested that now he should begin to improve his Italian.

"I still have no money for a private tutor," he said, and she suggested that perhaps he could exchange lessons with someone. "But with whom?" he asked, and they walked for a while in silence. "Well, I could do it," she finally offered. "For mathematics?" he smiled. "No," she said, "no mathematics."

Having agreed to exchange Italian for Russian, they began to meet regularly, and soon they were exchanging confidences as well as languages. Yole was unofficially engaged to Zariski's friend Derechin, while Zariski was interested in an Italian Catholic girl from the South who was studying mathematics. She was willing to convert to please Hannah, but when he went to meet her family her sister took him aside for a serious talk that led him to consider more seriously what life would be like for two people from such very different backgrounds. Afterwards he asked Yole for advice; she agreed that he should think the matter over carefully, and he soon began to go out with other girls.

Yole remembered that he learned Italian "very very fast," picking it up in the streets and from the newspapers, and after a few months he no longer needed Yole's help. Fortunately, however, they still had a reason for meeting regularly, because Yole, who was also very adept at learning languages (having studied Latin for twelve years and Greek for eight), had a more formal approach and wanted to learn Russian grammar.

Money from his mother began to arrive that fall, and little by little he paid his debts. The owner of the *trattoria* was particularly surprised. "Good boy!" he exclaimed. "You are really a very honest man!" The money also made it possible for him to socialize with other students and he began to go regularly to the Caffe Greco, where other mathematics and physics students (among them Enrico Fermi) gathered to gossip and play chess.

The pleasure that Zariski had taken as a child in his games of chess with Moses had, if anything, intensified over the years. He played countless games at the Caffe Greco with Beniamino Segre, a mathematics student and a nephew of the algebraic geometer, Corrado Segre, and occasionally he went to a chess club to test his skill against the best players in Italy. Once, to his great delight, he managed to beat a Master.

He was perhaps most amused by a game he once played with the elegant analyst from Gottingen, Edmund Landau. Landau had come to give a talk at the university and Tullio Levi-Civita held a party in his honor. A wealthy and well-traveled Jew, remembered by Zariski as "never quiet, all afire," Levi-Civita had married a tall beautiful Italian Catholic woman who enjoyed entertaining as much as he did, and his frequent parties introduced Zariski to many important mathematicians working abroad. During the course of one

evening Landau found out that Zariski liked chess and invited him
to play. "But how can we play with all these people around?" Zariski
asked. "Easily," Landau said. "Blank. You know, without a board."
Zariski was pleased when he managed to last for twenty moves.

The relative isolation of the Italian algebraic geometers was not,
however, a serious drawback for Zariski at this point, because although he was vaguely aware of a lack of rigor in many intuitive
proofs, he basically felt quite happy with the kind of "synthetic" (an
adjective dear to his Italian teachers) geometric proofs that constituted the very life stream of classical algebraic geometry, Italian
style.

He was also increasingly happy in the company of Yole Cagli. In
the fall of 1923 he took his doctoral exams and a few months later he
began work on his thesis. Yole, having finished her doctorate in
literature the preceding summer, found a job teaching in a high
school. Their language lessons had progressed to the point where
they were reading Pushkin as well as Boccaccio and Dante together.

They had, in fact, become very good friends. Although Yole had
broken her engagement to Zariski's friend Derechin, she frequently
asked Zariski for news of him. Because he always seemed happy to
give it, she was particularly shocked when one day he shouted, "Stop
worrying about him!" He went on to confess that he'd been in love
with her for a very long time. Completely taken aback, she managed
to tell him that she was going to Florence for a few days. "And when I
come back we will see. . . ."

On the day that she returned to Rome Zariski went to see her and
she confessed that as soon as she'd recovered from her surprise she'd
realized that she, too, had been in love with him for a long time. They
saw each other the next day and the next. As often as they could they
took a train to the Castelli Romani in the hills above the city and
walked until evening.

Some days Zariski wouldn't speak at all and Yole would understand that he was thinking about a problem in his thesis. "Oscar was
a man of many moods," she would explain years later, "and his
moods were always very much affected by his work. He could only
feel happy when his work was going well."

They both enjoyed the theater, particularly the plays of Piran-
dello and Bontempelli (who was the husband of Yole's aunt); some
evenings they managed to find a chaperone but usually they made do
with movie matinees because Yole was not allowed out alone with

a young man after dark. They were too happy with their days to mind about the evenings, although the strictness of customs governing the conduct of unmarried girls in Italy was still strange to Zariski after what he called the "complete freedom" of Russian women during and after the revolution.

Many of Yole's friends regarded even her daytime freedom as "criminal indulgence" on the part of her parents, well-educated intellectuals from prosperous Jewish families in Ancona, the small city on the Adriatic Sea where Yole had been born in 1901. "Often my parents wouldn't ask whom I had seen that day because they were so busy," Yole remembered. "They had five children and they worked hard, so there wasn't much time for them to pry." Yole's father, a successful businessman who had lost his fortune during World War I, had only recently moved to Rome as a professor of applied mathematics at a private technical institute. To supplement his salary, he gave private lessons and Mrs. Cagli worked as an editor of International Red Cross publications.

A quiet reserved woman, very different in temperament from Hannah Zaritsky, Ada Cagli nevertheless resembled her in energy and spirit. Even with five children and a full-time job she found time to write several books, both novels and children's stories (which she published under the pseudonym of Fiducia). Like Hannah, too, she supported her children's diverse ambitions. One of her sons became an admiral in the navy, and the other one, Corrado, an artist. Two of her daughters were educated at the university; the middle daughter married the artist Mirko, and Yole and her youngest sister married mathematicians.

She was happy with Yole's engagement to Zariski, and Prof. Cagli, who would have preferred that his daughter choose a career rather than a husband, was eventually won over. Zariski's reputation had traveled well beyond the university, and neighbors and friends congratulated the Cagli family on having found "a real genius." They were referring, of course, to Zariski's intellectual accomplishments, for only Yole understood that his genius was for life as well as for mathematics. Lively, and curious about the most unlikely things, he would introduce her to the ancient ghettoes of Eastern Europe and later, when they came to the United States, to the Baltimore Orioles.

A few weeks after their engagement, as soon as the term was over, they left together for Kobrin. Yole's parents would have liked for them to marry in Rome, but to do so would have cost a lot of money in bribes because Zariski would have had to send for certain special documents from Poland. As Yole explained, "In Poland anti-Semitism often took the form of money. Jews had to pay bribes for everything."

Yole was eager to see the world, and this visit to Zariski's family would be her first time out of Italy. It would also be her first experience of the acute consciousness of race that Zariski had grown up with. She remembered vividly her first visit to the Jewish quarter in Warsaw: "The Jews in side curls and kaftans made me feel that I was living in two different nations." Equally disquieting was her discovery that she was "more familiar with the Polish part than the Jewish part, because Polish history after all was part of the conventional European history that I'd studied in school."

Like other Italian Jews, she had grown up with "a feeling of being Italian." She had known that her family was "Jewish," but whenever she had asked her grandmother what that meant, her grandmother had smiled and said, "It means that we don't have to go to church." The only time she'd ever heard the word "race" applied to Jews had been at a Zionist meeting of foreign Jews.

"But there in Poland," she explained, "I was suddenly in confrontation with something I could have found in the American South. Jews were recognizable because of their kaftans and dark skins. They were only allowed to sit in certain parks and cafes, very much like southern Blacks. One day as I was walking with my mother-in-law I saw a Jew being thrown down from a streetcar just because he was a Jew."

Even in Kobrin, where Jews constituted a majority, Yole found a self-consciousness that she'd never experienced in Italy. One day, for example, as she paused before a local church thinking to step inside to see the art as she would have in Italy, she felt her sister-in-law's hand on her arm. "Better not go in," she said gently. "You'll just be thrown out." It also seemed unnatural to Yole that Zariski had no friends left in Kobrin, which he'd had to leave when he was only eleven in order to be properly educated. Most disturbing of all to her was "the presence of so many young people, handsome, capable, well-trained and educated, with no work, and no place to go where they could find it."

Their wedding was celebrated in grand style in the gracious garden of the old house in Kobrin on September 11, 1924, or, as their marriage contract read, "On the sixth day after the Sabbath, the thirteenth day of the month of Elul, the year 5684 after the creation of the world according to the count that we use here in Kobrin." Moses was unfortunately on a visit to the United States, but Shepsel was there with his fiancée, as were Zariski's younger sister, Zila, and his father's brothers, whom he hadn't seen in many years, dignified and remote in the long beards and black coats of the Hassidim.

After a ritual bath to please Hannah, with whom she'd formed "a bond of understanding" that would last until Hannah's death, Yole, dressed in white and veiled, was led out to a flowering canopy where a rabbi stood waiting. There was, unfortunately, a slight delay at this point while a search was made for the bridegroom. Yole was amused and not at all surprised when he was found working on a problem.

A few days later, after brief stops in Warsaw and Lodz to visit Zariski's three older sisters, they started back to Rome. Yole had to return to her students at the high school and Zariski to the university for the formal awarding of his doctorate.

5 🎴 "Oscar, you are

not one of us."

Castelnuovo, who had always been aware of Zariski's algebraic tendencies, had chosen a thesis topic for him in the French tradition of solvability by radicals. The question was: When can a polynomial equation be solved, starting from rational functions of its coefficients, taking radicals, then taking more rational functions of these, then taking radicals again, and so on? The early nineteenth century mathematician, Evariste Galois, had discovered large classes of equations that could not be solved in this way and had analyzed the problem in general in terms of the solvability of a key group, now called the Galois group.

"Take a polynomial equation in two variables, x and t," Castelnuovo suggested, "but which is linear in one variable, say in t. So the equation is of the form $f(x) + tg(x) = 0$, where f and g are polynomials in x. If you consider that as an equation in x, then x is an algebraic function of t." What he asked Zariski to do was to find all equations of this type that could be solved for x in radicals, starting from rational functions of t.

The five types that Zariski found formed the basis of his thesis, which generalized results arrived at independently by Chisini and Ritt. The note that announced his results was published in 1924 in the *Atti Accademia Nazionale dei Lincei* [2][19] about six months after he'd begun to work on the problem, and the results were published in full two years later in *Rendiconti del Circolo Matematico di Palermo* [12].

He remained interested in solvability by radicals just long enough to prove a conjecture of Enriques that a general curve of genus 6 cannot be represented by an equation $f(x,y) = 0$, where y can be solved in terms of x by radicals [8]. Even this early in his development we can see his tendency to combine algebraic insights and topological ideas with the synthetic ideas of classical geometry.

Castelnuovo looked to this remarkable ability as a means of rescuing algebraic geometry from the impasse in which it found itself. "Zariski, you are here with us but are not one of us," he once said, referring to Zariski's early doubts about the rigor of their proofs as well as to his algebraic tendencies. On another occasion he was more explicit: "The methods of the Italian School have reached a dead end and are inadequate for further progress in the field of algebraic geometry."

He encouraged Zariski to explore the work of Solomon Lefschetz, a Russian topologist then at Princeton. Many mathematicians were finding topology a promising direction, and several new theorems had recently been proved by topology and analysis rather than by algebraic geometric methods. Although Zariski would find topological methods attractive, as the innovative nature of his work on fundamental groups amply testifies, he would eventually look elsewhere for the tools he needed to restructure the foundations of algebraic geometry.

His search for these tools led him eventually to the algebra of Emmy Noether, and he would always remember his early ignorance of the new developments in algebra, particularly in Göttingen, with regret: "It was a pity that my Italian teachers never told me there was such a tremendous development of the algebra which is connected with algebraic geometry. I only discovered this much later,

---

[19] Numbers in square brackets throughout the text refer the reader to papers in Zariski's bibliography, which will be found in Appendix B.

Zariski (courtesy of MIT Press)

when I came to the United States." But although the lack of contact between Rome and Göttingen was in many ways unfortunate, given the extent of the mathematical achievement in both places, we might wonder more at our current commitment to conferences than at their insularity.[20]

On their return to Rome in the fall of 1924 the Zariskis managed to rent a large room, although it shrank rapidly as their household

---

[20] In his later life Zariski frequently criticized American mathematicians for spending too much time going to conferences and too little time doing mathematics.

grew. That winter Zariski's younger sister Zila came to live near them while she attended the University of Rome, and a few months later, on July 18, 1925, their first child, Raphael, was born. They suffered a shortage of money as well as of space, even though Yole was teaching full-time and Zariski was juggling a number of small jobs.

Having decided not to take Italian citizenship in such a climate of unrest, he had been unable to apply for a university position; he had, however, managed to find work in Yole's school preparing students for university math exams. Severi had also granted him the traditional European title of "assistant," and Enriques had engaged him to translate two important books by Dedekind into Italian for the series he was editing, *Per la Storia e la Filosofia delle Matematiche* [6].

At the further urging of Enriques ("I might say he forced me into it"), he also wrote a number of expository articles on the foundations of set theory [1, 3, 5, 11]. His own work, too, was going well: in the first two years of his marriage he published four papers on the uniformization of algebraic functions [4, 7, 9, 10].

Yole had recently won a national playwriting prize, and for both of them these early married years in Rome were exceptionally happy. As Yole described them, "We felt very free — getting married and having a child without having a thing. We did just what we liked. We spent whole nights talking, baring our souls to each other, and delighting in the contemplation of the panorama of his past life. We were improvident, and we were happy."

But "the war to end all wars" had carried in its wake an enormous energy, a flammable mixture of relief and outrage that would burn through Europe. "Very soon," as Yole said many years afterwards, "everything would begin to go bad." They were, of course, already going bad. Since January 1918 Lenin had ruled Russia with almost dictatorial powers, and in 1919 Bela Kun had seized temporary control of Hungary. The year 1923 had seen the capitulation of King Alphonso of Spain to the military rule of Miguel Primo de Rivera. Before the end of the decade, Marshall Jozef Pilsudski would come to power in Poland and Stalin's dictatorship would be publicly acknowledged.

The situation in Italy, relatively stable since 1922 when King Victor Emmanuel had invited Mussolini to form his cabinet, had worsened dramatically with the disappearance in June 1924 of Giacomo Matteotti, a powerful and articulate Socialist deputy. Many Fascists as well as anti-Fascists had been shocked by the realization that the responsibility for this lay with the highest reaches of the government. Newspapers began to call for Mussolini's resignation, and the opposition withdrew from Parliament in an act of protest.

Feeling threatened, the Fascists called mass rallies and led parades; groups of Black Shirts marched in the streets of Rome. One afternoon on his way to the library, Zariski refused to take his hat off to the Fascists and was thrown to the ground. Violence on both sides intensified after Matteotti's murdered body was found in August, and January 1925 saw the end of constitutional government in Italy.

In the midst of all this political turmoil, the domestic life of the Zariskis flowed on quite peacefully. Shortly after the birth of Raphael, the woman who was renting them part of her apartment was threatened with eviction by her landlord, and rather than becoming involved in lengthy litigation, the Zariskis decided to move in with Yole's parents.

In many ways they were more comfortable: they were given the privacy of the largest bedroom, and Yole's younger sister, Serena, was able to look after Raphael while Yole was at school. The only problem was that Zariski, used to older rather than younger siblings, found it much too noisy to concentrate on mathematics and was forced to rent a room elsewhere.

Most summers Zariski and Yole would travel to Kobrin to see Hannah, but one summer they rented a cottage at the seashore and invited Hannah to visit them. With her usual practicality she solved the problem of living without a kosher kitchen by bringing her own dishes from Poland and not eating meat, and with a practicality that rivaled hers, Zariski left the cream out of his after-dinner coffee. As he said later, "She knew, but there was no point in exhibiting the extremes of not being kosher." Only once during her adventurous weeks in Forte dei Marmi was Hannah upset, and even then it was not with Yole and Zariski but with Zila, whose roommates had eaten ham in front of her—"flaunted it in my face," was how she described it afterwards.

In 1926 Zariski received a fellowship from the Rockefeller Foundation, a generous supporter of international mathematics during the twenties. The stipend of $40 a month, which was what he had asked for, was enough to enable him to give up tutoring and translating. It also brought him for the first time into contact with young mathematicians from abroad, like Szolem Mandelbrojt, Dirk Struik, and André Weil, who had arrived in Rome in the fall of 1925 to study functional calculus with Vito Volterra.

The fellowship was also responsible for his first meeting with G. D. Birkhoff, one of the most distinguished American mathematicians of his generation, and perhaps the only one with a major international reputation. Long interested in the work of Poincaré, Birkhoff had astonished the world, particularly the French (who hadn't believed that Americans were mathematically capable), by proving Poincaré's last "theorem," a conjecture made in a paper written just before his death. (Many years later Birkhoff told a student that he had lost thirty pounds working out that proof.)[21]

A member of the Harvard Mathematics Department, Birkhoff had been asked by the Rockefeller Foundation to stop in Rome to discuss the work of the fellows. As Zariski remembered, however, their meetings were not confined to mathematics:

> "Is it difficult for a Jew to become a student at Harvard?" I asked one evening.
>
> "No, not at all," Birkhoff replied with no trace of embarrassment, "although of course we naturally keep a certain proportion. The Jewish population is about 3, 4, 5% and we admit only 3, 4, 5%."[22]
>
> "Then you must have very large classes," I said, but Birkhoff didn't smile.

Zariski was also curious about the proportion of Jews on the Harvard faculty:

> To me it was amusing that Birkhoff didn't worry about appointing a Spaniard or a Frenchman or a German. I understood that it was different for Jews because there were so many good Jewish mathe-

---

[21] Marshall Stone, personal interview, November 1988.

[22] Zariski seems to have remembered the second set of percentages incorrectly. For while the Jewish population of the U.S. was about 3% in the 1920s, Jewish students made up more than 20% of the Harvard student body. See Rufus Learsi, *The Jews in American History*, Cleveland and New York: World Publishing Co., 1954; and Marcia Graham Synnott, *The Half-Opened Door: Discrimination and Admissions at Harvard, Yale, and Princeton, 1900–1970*, London and Westport, Conn: Greenwood Press, 1979.

A seminar at the University of Rome, 1924. Left to right, front row: Struik, Mrs. Struik, Amaldi; second row: Zariski, Corbellini, (?), Mandelbrojt (courtesy of Yole Zariski)

maticians. I also wasn't very tactful in those days. After all, I came from Russia.

There was also less need for tact in 1926. As Lipman Bers, a Latvian mathematician who arrived in the United States in 1940, put it, "Before the German mass murders anti-Semitism was ugly and small-minded, but it was not a mortal sin."[23]

Zariski grew used to seeing Black Shirts and to hearing the shuffles and shouts of demonstrators, just as he'd grown accustomed in Kiev to students marching with red flags. The Russian Revolution and the rise to power of Mussolini had formed the background of his student life, but mathematics had always played on center stage.

---

[23] "The European Mathematicians' Migration to America," *A Century of Mathematics in America*, part 1, ed. Peter Duren (Providence: American Mathematical Society [AMS], 1988) 235.

The schisms that were rending Europe took on personal significance only insofar as they interfered with the peace and quiet that were essential to his creative work.

"While at the University of Rome I was busy doing work, studying mathematics," he recalled many years later. "That's all I wanted to do. And as long as I wasn't an Italian citizen, Fascism didn't affect me very much." However, since without Italian citizenship he couldn't join the university faculty, by the beginning of 1927 he had begun to explore the possibilities that lay outside of Italy.

Remembering his early loyalty to the Marxist ideals of the Revolution and lacking any real information about the direction it had taken since Lenin's death, he began to dream of contributing something to the "new" Russia, perhaps by becoming a high school teacher in a small town. Yole said nothing to discourage him, although secretly she hoped that his application for a visa would be rejected. For while she shared his sympathy for the ideals of the revolution, she had felt from the first that "Communism had brought a terrible regime to power."

One day in early spring Zariski paid his long-anticipated visit to the Russian consul. "So?" the consul said, peering at him over the papers on his desk. "How come you left Russia?"

"Oh well, I didn't leave Russia. Russia left me."

The consul didn't smile. "What do you mean?"

"Well, the Red Army withdrew from Kobrin."

"Oh? And why didn't you go with them?"

"I just didn't."

"I can see that. It's too bad."

"Really, it was because I wanted to study and I was very very much taken with mathematics. I liked Russian socialism, but at the time mathematics drew me more, and in Russia too much was going on for me to study."

"You make too much of a distinction between science and politics and society. Leonardo da Vinci was a great artist, but he didn't sacrifice his political and social ideals to his art. But you? You sacrificed all your political ideals to mathematics and I don't agree with you. Well, I'll send your application to the center in Moscow. Meanwhile . . . go to America."

Zariski was hardly surprised by the reply he received a few months later: "Your application is rejected."

The rejection would, however, rankle, and the following year he would ask Yole to go to the Russian consulate to try to learn the reason for it. "The denial of my request to return to Russia made me feel badly," he wrote to her from Johns Hopkins, "not for the practical consequences, but for its value as such, the refusal in itself. Time will show if they had reason or not, and I don't despair in the future to get a new *revanche* against my dear bureaucratic Russian friends, showing them that they were wrong."

He applied to Zurich and Jerusalem, but both places were looking for senior mathematicans and hired older men. At last he turned to Castelnuovo for help. "I can't stay in Italy," he said, "and they won't let me go to Russia. There are no jobs in Zurich or Jerusalem. Would it be possible for me to find a place in the States?"

Having hoped for an increased mathematical intimacy between Zariski and Solomon Lefschetz, who had joined the Princeton faculty in 1924, Castelnuovo was enthusiastic. "Since Lefschetz was himself born in Russia, I know he'll understand your problem."

Lefschetz replied immediately with an offer to support Zariski's application for a postgraduate fellowship, called a Johnston Scholarship, at Johns Hopkins University in Baltimore. Yole, who also thought that going to America would be a great adventure, encouraged him to apply, although her father was trying hard to get her to convince Zariski to take Italian citizenship and stay in Italy. "I won't do that," she insisted. "The matter is too important. If he regrets it one day, I will regret it with him."

When Zariski received the news that he had been awarded the scholarship he was delighted: with $1500 a year he and Yole would be almost rich!

At the moment, however, they were faced with the difficulty of raising money for the long voyage to New York. They were able to borrow money for one ticket from one of Zariski's uncles, but more difficult to solve than a lack of money was the problem of a visa for Yole and the baby. As much as she dreaded the separation, Yole had to stay behind in Rome and continue with her teaching job. Of course, for all they knew, he might not even like it in America.

6 ◨ WALKING WITH LEFSCHETZ

BALTIMORE 1927 – 1928

Zariski brought the old world with him to the new. As disarming as Enriques and almost as formidable as Castelnuovo, he carried the high seriousness and broad mathematical culture of the Italians to the quiet shores of Baltimore in 1927.

Johns Hopkins University, whose academic programs had been inaugurated in 1875 with the help of J. J. Sylvester, had played an important role in the development of American mathematics. Although Sylvester, one of the nineteenth century's great mathematicians, had spent only a handful of years in Baltimore, he had managed to establish the *American Journal of Mathematics* and to gather together a lively group of research mathematicians, including Thomas S. Fiske, Charles S. Peirce, and Thomas Craig.[24] Conceived of primarily as a research institute, Hopkins had led the United

---

[24] An English Jew, Sylvester had been unable to obtain a chair (or a degree) at Oxford or Cambridge before the abolition of the "test laws." Like Zariski, he was brought to the United States by an invitation from Hopkins, but unlike Zariski he made the condition that each month Hopkins pay him his salary personally and in gold.

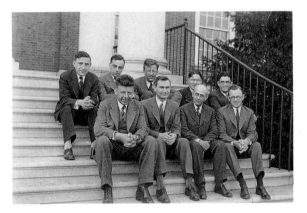

The Johns Hopkins Mathematics Department, 1930. Left to right, front row: Blaschke, Whyburn, Abraham Cohen, Murnaghan; second row: Zariski, Wintner, Williamson, ?, Morrill (courtesy of Yole Zariski)

States in providing doctoral training before the founding of the University of Chicago in 1892.[25] At the time of Zariski's arrival, Hopkins was still one of the few American universities to offer the Ph.D. in mathematics.[26]

It was therefore all the more surprising to Zariski to find himself in the fall of 1927 in a department that seemed to him rather dull. There were only three permanent members: Frank Morley, an English émigré like Sylvester who was serving his last year as chairman; Francis Murnaghan, a young and vigorous man with whom Zariski shared no mathematical interests; and Abraham Cohen, with whom he was able to enjoy an occasional pleasant and lively discussion.

To Yole, with the arrogance of youth and talent, he wrote a checklist of their faults:

---

[25] At Chicago the teaching and research of E. H. Moore had introduced many American mathematicians to the relatively new fields of abstract algebra and topology.

[26] Fewer than 65 Ph.D.s in mathematics were granted each year by American universities in the twenties (compared with nearly 700 in 1989). Describing this period at Harvard, Julian Coolidge wrote, "The number of these men [those who were prepared to take their doctorates] slowly increased from one in two or three years, to three or four a year." Quoted by Garrett Birkhoff in "Mathematics at Harvard, 1836–1944," *A Century of Mathematics in America*, part 2, ed. Peter Duren (AMS, 1989) 19.

The professors here are (1) too old, like Morley, for example, and near retirement or (2) of no creative value or (3) finally, those who represent the matters that I call *"spiccia sbrigativa"* [busy dispatchers] in that they busy themselves with little problems, not particularly illuminated by any high scientific concepts.[27]

One of Zariski's earliest memories of Hopkins is of Morley saying, "You're a geometer and I'm a geometer; we must talk about geometry." Zariski went dutifully to Morley's office every Thursday and listened "without interest" to what he had to say about inversive geometry. He wrote to Yole, "Morley is a very fine person, but he doesn't satisfy me as a mathematician. . . . [He] is too old and is, as well, attached to *'spiccia matematica'* [small change mathematics]."[28]

Fortunately for Zariski, there was a distinguished algebraic geometer, A. B. Coble, visiting for the year from the University of Illinois. Zariski got on very well with Coble, who was in the middle of writing a book on theta functions. "I am the only person with whom he can exchange ideas," Zariski wrote to Yole. "The others work in different fields or truly have little mathematical culture."[29] He and Coble also found themselves in agreement in their criticism of the undergraduate mathematics curriculum. Perhaps echoing Coble,

---

[27] Zariski's first impressions of America are vividly captured in the letters he wrote to Yole during their year of separation. Their daughter, Vera DeCola, has translated them from the original Italian.

[28] Zariski's easy dismissal of Morley, who had supervised 49 Ph.D. theses and served as president of the American Mathematical Society, was to some extent typical of the way European mathematicians saw their American counterparts. The influx of foreign mathematicians during the thirties helped to alter this rather dismal view, and by the middle of the decade, although some Americans still felt slighted by what a Princeton mathematician called "the usual European attitude towards American work," G. H. Hardy was able to say that "now America could produce three mathematicians of rank to every one that could be produced by any other country." See Nathan Reingold, "Refugee Mathematicians in the United States of America 1933–1941: Reception and Reaction," *Century* I, 190–191.

[29] Zariski's feeling that Americans had never learned the deep ideas in mathematics was shared by many Europeans and some Americans. One reason for this might have been that European scholars had a two or three year advantage over their American counterparts as a result of the more intensive training offered by European gymnasiums and universities. According to Garrett Birkhoff, "Even in the 1930s, mathematics concentrators (majors) in many small colleges only got to calculus in their senior year!" ("Some Leaders in American Mathematics, 1891–1941," *The Bicentennial Tribute to American Mathematics,* ed. Dalton Tarwater, Mathematical Association of American [MAA], 1977, 51.)

Zariski explained to Yole that "not the least reason for this deficiency is the lack of competent teachers." He was particularly excited by Coble's vision of "a new kind of department":

> . . . a department made up of gifted young men who are not overburdened with teaching duties so that they can dedicate their time to the formation of a wider mathematical culture and to serious research. . . . The few good students would be carefully tended in order to instill in them an interest in superior concepts and to lead them toward their own research.

This was, of course, much closer to Zariski's experience at the University of Rome than to what he'd found at Hopkins. It was also part of an ongoing struggle between teaching and research within the American mathematics community, a struggle that would intensify in the thirties with the arrival of talented researchers from abroad. Although an increasing number of important mathematicians would come to believe that research was of primary importance, without the support of applied mathematics and government grants it was difficult for any but the most wealthy institutions to reduce the teaching loads of their faculties so that they could "dedicate their time to the formation of a wider mathematical culture and to serious research." [30]

Coble's influence on Zariski during this first year in the United States was almost as important as Lefschetz's. Although it wasn't primarily mathematical, Coble's relationship with Zariski helped him to order and articulate his early impressions of the American mathematics community and to realize his value as a member of a mathematics department. Coble was also directly helpful in negotiating a position for him at Hopkins for the following year:

> Speaking of me, he [Coble] advised Morley not to let me go and to keep me at the university as a useful element, securing my permanency by offering me a less meager stipend. Coble also repeated his general ideals to the president of the university, speaking to him at

---

[30] The growing dependence of major universities on government funds has recently come under attack along with another important source of support for researchers, graduate student teaching assistants. Having long provided another financially viable way for universities to reduce the course loads of research professors, the often overworked and underpaid teaching assistants have begun serious efforts to unionize on several campuses.

the same time about me. The day after this meeting, Morley outlined his intentions to increase the scholarship with the condition that I accept the responsibility of guiding the dissertations of some students. That is all.

As you can see, I owe a lot to Coble and I can only be pleased that it is he, the most capable one here, who appreciates me.

Coble's commitment to his own ideals continued after he returned to Illinois. In 1934, for example, he insisted to a hostile state legislator that he "would hire a foreigner if better than any native prospect."[31] He also remained steadfast in his support of Zariski. As soon as hiring began after the war, he offered Zariski a permanent research professorship at Illinois, and when Harvard invited Zariski the following year Coble wrote, "[Although] we are sorry to lose him . . . it is my feeling that Professor Zariski would rank among the first five mathematicians of the world."[32]

Zariski's eagerness to succeed in this new mathematical environment was inextricably mixed with his longing for his wife and his need for a position that would make it possible for him to bring her and the baby to the United States. Shortly after his arrival in Baltimore he tried to capture for her the exotic flavor of "an American conversation" with a new colleague at Johns Hopkins:

After the mathematical talk we spoke of sports, football in particular, and then seeing a dirigible in the sky we spoke of aviation and then of automobilism, and he advises me to buy a car for $100 and to cross America, going to Niagara Falls and to California. Now you have an idea of what an American conversation is like — in one way it is delectable — could one speak to Professor Castelnuovo with such deep interest about football?

He continued, on a more personal note,

I have had to make a supreme effort to prevent the emptiness of my private life from overwhelming me and destroying my work life. I

---

[31] Coble, letter to R. G. D. Richardson, 30 June 1934 (quoted by Nathan Reingold in "Refugee Mathematicians," *Century* I, 182).

[32] Coble, letter to D. V. Widder, 6 May 1947 (Harvard Math Department files).

have had to definitively divide these two worlds — sad temporary necessity, but a question of life and death for me. . . . I think my work is tied with a very fine but very strong tie to the emotional movement of the soul, and its productivity depends in good part on its strength.

Although he was impatient to go to Princeton to work with Lefschetz, who had repeatedly invited him, he decided to finish his work on an "interesting but difficult problem" because, as he wrote at the beginning of December, "I connect especially to its publication the whole issue of your coming here":

Now I am going through a feverish period. . . . If I will succeed in bringing this research to a good outcome . . . it will be an affirmation of my worth to the professors who have been vitally interested in this problem. I have an extreme need to make such an American coup. Then I will be able to do as I please and dedicate myself exclusively to the study of the work of Lefschetz. . . . You see, once I am recognized I will be more secure about the future and I will be psychologically more tranquil for the coming years.

Two weeks later he wrote to say that he had again postponed the trip to Princeton because of difficulties with this paper:

I have worked intensely and I feel rather tired from the effort. My research has nailed me to the desk, to my papers. . . . I am no longer going to Princeton after Christmas. I have postponed this trip for two reasons: first, I want to finish my work (paper); then I

Eight pictures Zariski took at the Woolworth to send to Yole (courtesy of Yole Zariski)

wish to read more of the papers of Lefschetz in order to be prepared.

At the end of January, he was still at work on the same problem:

> Ah, well, I have had a very bad period. I have gotten stuck on a hard point that I have not been able to overcome for weeks. Now I have had the saving idea and I hope to finish soon. I've been close to despair, even though Prof. Coble consoled me, saying that one must always take these things philosophically and that mathematics is a "slow game." These English and Americans have a sense of humor. I have worked intensely — I hardly left my room.

A month later, he at last wrote of his success, "My most important research is almost finished. I am trying to put some order into the disorder of the first drafts and to organize my work in a methodical fashion. I hope it will be published in the April issue." [33]

In the same letter, referring to a slightly earlier paper, he wrote with pleasure of "a small article which inspired Lefschetz to begin research of his own." This small article, "On a theorem of Severi" [13], was the first that he published in English and marked a transition to what might be called the second phase of his career, his contributions to topology. Although the influence of classical geometry was still quite strong here, looking back after more than fifty years, Zariski would be pleased to find that at last he'd

---

[33] This was perhaps "On hyperelliptic 0-functions with rational characteristics" [14].

begun "to think a little topologically" about algebraic varieties, particularly of the fundamental group.

Using techniques that he described as "refreshingly vigorous," he presented an ingenious correction for an error in an incomplete proof of Severi that the Jacobian of a generic curve of genus g has no nontrivial endomorphisms. His remedy did not, unfortunately, please his old professor, and Severi published his own correction independently in the *Atti Accademia Nazionale dei Lincei* early in 1928. That February, Zariski wrote anxiously to Yole: "I don't know if he [Severi] remembered that I called his attention to the fact that one of his old theorems is not true. And that furthermore, he had advised me to publish a note about it."

Zariski continued to find topology attractive, not only because of its rigor, but also because of the personal influence of Solomon Lefschetz. "Besides our both being mathematicians," he wrote to Yole from Princeton, "we are both European and more especially, Russian, and even more especially, both of us are Jews. This creates a communion of ideas and a possibility of frank discussion that neither one of us can have very often in the American milieu."

Born in Russia and educated in France, Lefschetz had worked for six years as an engineer (during which he lost both hands in an industrial accident) before realizing that what he called his "true path" lay in mathematics. In 1911 he took his doctorate at Clark University under W. E. Story and accepted a teaching position at the University of Nebraska. From Nebraska he moved to the University of Kansas, and finally, two years before Zariski's arrival at Hopkins, he joined the Princeton faculty as associate professor.

One of the first mathematicians to apply topology to algebraic geometry, Lefschetz had found that many questions, particularly in the complex domain, could be phrased in topological language, and that here, as Zariski put it, "he couldn't afford to be just intuitive and leave the proofs hanging because topology had already developed very rigorously." Lefschetz might, for example, take a very special kind of "pencil" with a special kind of singularity, so that from the algebraic point of view it would be rather simple, but topologically very interesting. His research eventually pushed topology to its limits, where it became clear that topological methods

Solomon Lefschetz (courtesy of Springer-Verlag Archives)

couldn't contribute as much to the understanding of geometry as algebra could. As Zariski would later say, "We don't call it 'topological geometry,' we call it 'algebraic geometry.'"

With common roots in the tradition of the Italian algebraic geometers, they shared an awareness of the need for more rigorous methods, although their notions of "rigor" diverged. Gian-Carlo Rota, who took his doctorate at Princeton in the early fifties, described Lefschetz as "a purely intuitive mathematician": "It was said of him that he had never given a completely correct proof, but had never made a wrong guess either."[34]

---

[34] Gian-Carlo Rota, "Fine Hall in its golden age: Remembrances of Princeton in the early fifties," *Century* II, 235.

While Marshall Stone remembered Lefschetz as a charming man "filled with ideas that would bubble over," others found him rude and abrasive.[35] Describing a meeting between Lefschetz and Zariski in the late fifties, Rota wrote, "After exchanging with Zariski warm and loud Jewish greetings (in Russian), he proceeded to proclaim loudly (in English) his skepticism on the possibility of resolving singularities for all algebraic varieties. 'Ninety percent proved is zero percent proved!' he retorted to Zariski's protestations, as a conversation stopper."[36]

Lefschetz, whose quick appreciation of the work of others helped make Princeton into a world center of topology,[37] was very excited by Zariski's early work in topology and urged him to talk at the university whenever he had a new result. "I communicated with Lefschetz regarding the results of some of my most recent research," Zariski wrote to Yole. "He answered me enthusiastically, perhaps too much so (he exaggerates), saying that my results are the most important conquests made in this field in recent times."

Lefschetz also brought him to several conferences, which he seems to have found more stimulating socially than intellectually. At the beginning of November he wrote to Yole about a meeting at Columbia University, where he found the talks "not particularly interesting:"[38]

I didn't bother to listen to all of them, but preferred walking with Lefschetz along the magnificent avenues of the university, every once in a while stopping to converse with new people. . . . I spent many hours with Lefschetz, who introduced me to the professors at Princeton University (Alexander and Veblen) and also to a Russian, Alexandrov (Jewish), a Professor at the University of Moscow, and to a German Professor, Hopf, both at Princeton this year with a Rockefeller Institute stipend.[39]

---

[35] Stone, personal interview, November 1988.

Hassler Whitney, for example, wrote of the "considerable rivalry" between Lefschetz and W. V. D. Hodge, and of Alexander's becoming "increasingly wary" of Lefschetz ("Moscow 1935: Topology Moving Toward America," *Century* I, 105–106).

[36] Rota, "Fine Hall," *Century* II, 234.

[37] Rota remembered Lefschetz referring to Rome as "the Princeton of its time" *(Ibid.).*

[38] R. P. Boas reminds us that "one reason for going to meetings was that photocopying hadn't been invented" ("Memories of Bygone Meetings," *Century* I, 94).

[39] Emmy Noether, who had become interested in topology as a result of seminars given in Göttingen by Heinz Hopf and P. S. Alexandrov, had arranged for their visits to the United States through Hermann Weyl.

He also described his meeting with a "very ambitious" American mathematician:

> I have met Professor Ritt. He and the Italian mathematician Chisini once investigated the question that was the topic of my doctoral thesis; I generalized their results. They arrived independently at the same result — Chisini, however, 4 years prior to Ritt. I made a reference to this circumstance in my notes to the *Accademia dei Lincei.*
>
> As soon as he heard my name, Ritt attacked me because I didn't point out in my notes that he had succeeded, in effect, in going beyond Chisini.
>
> Lefschetz defended me as well as he could. This Ritt is very ambitious.[40]

Of an April AMS meeting he wrote, "I give very little importance to these communications that last ten minutes and follow one another as in a kaleidoscope, making one dizzy. The best thing one can do during these meetings is to walk outside with a friend, talk and smoke . . . and then to meet people."

Again, a month later, he wrote to Yole from Annapolis to say that he "didn't pay much attention to the meeting. . . . I preferred to tour the city, admire the sea, visit the great naval academy for which this city is famous, and to watch a baseball game between the Naval Academy and the University of Virginia." On a very different note, he added, "But unfortunately, American society leaves me dissatisfied. They are too much alike and of this standardization they almost make a virtue."

Princeton, however, where he finally settled down for his long-awaited month-long visit in April, was everything he had hoped for. He was particularly looking forward to a conference on "Analysis Situs — a mathematical theory cultivated especially at Princeton."[41] He wrote to Yole from Princeton in high spirits:

> One works very well here — it is a town made for study, totally occupied by university buildings of beautiful architecture. The appearance of the town is attractive, it offers a variety of colors and vistas and finally my eyes find repose after the annoying monotony of the Baltimore streets. Lefschetz treated me very very well and we have

---

[40] Joseph Fels Ritt, one of the founders of the Columbia University Mathematics Department, was at this time an associate professor. He chaired the department from 1942 to 1945, served as vice president of the AMS, and was elected to the National Academy of Sciences.

[41] "Analysis Situs" was the old name for topology.

really become friends. . . . He invited me to his house various evenings to listen to music and pass the time. . . .

I have in him a very secure support that will help me in my work
and in my achieving success and in eventually establishing myself
within the American university system. . . . I know that he has
written to Coble, expressing a very favorable judgment of me, the
purpose of his letter being that Coble should show it to the rector,
making my candidacy stronger. Castelnuovo writes to me, besides,
that Lefschetz always writes to him with esteem and sympathy for
me.

How is it that I have such good fortune with people? I don't do
anything on purpose, I just act naturally, sometimes even awkwardly
and without diplomacy.

The efforts of Lefschetz and Coble to secure a permanent position
for Zariski helped him to bear his long separation from Yole and the
baby. With a confidence born of his mathematical successes, he had
written to her in February, "It is time for you to prepare your va-
lises," and the following month he invited her to consider the full
reality of leaving Italy:

Despite my contentment, there is a certain added ingredient of
preoccupation that gives me food for thought. I am sorry after all to
take you away from your Italian ambience for only one reason: I am
afraid that this distance might harm the development of your writing
abilities. I can't deny that life in the midst of a population that speaks
Italian is very beneficial to one who wishes to be creative in that
language.

I would like to speak with you frankly about this subject: to know
what you think regarding this matter. . . . I ask you as a sincere
friend to whom your intellectual interests are very dear. Certainly a
partial remedy would be many return visits to Italy. . . . And we will
make these trips, Yolusia, every time that we have the slightest possibility.

Having at last received a definite offer for the following year from
Hopkins, he was optimistic but cautious about her application to the
American consul in Naples: "Let's hope with all our hearts for a
happy ending. Today is the first of April, the 4th or 5th of April I will
be with you with all my thoughts when you arrive in Naples, and
remember this, Yolusia mine, while in Naples you will be put, per-
force, in contact with all the bureaucracies in the world."

But there was to be no happy ending at this point. Yole had gone to Naples and applied for a student visa, but her English was bad, the secretary was rude, Raphael was fussy, and she'd never even been allowed to see the consul. She sent a sorrowful telegram to Zariski, who returned an equally sorrowful reply:

> Many days have passed since receiving your telegram and I haven't as yet completely freed myself from the first immediate depression. And still it is necessary that I take hold of myself and find again my equilibrium because nothing can threaten our eventual reunion more than a prostration that paralyzes, taking away every energy and so every possibility of success.

He went on to say that he'd managed to write to Morley "that only the hope that my separation from you two would not last long gives me strength to work." He'd also written to Coble for advice, and spoken to Lefschetz, who "put the whole problem in a philosophical context, saying that 'life is ugly' and one must have patience."

By May he'd made up his mind to see Yole that summer, no matter what happened with their visas:

> There is a tempest of joy in my heart that has suffered so much during all these long months and there is a sense of liberation in my soul that has fought so hard against this suffering in order that it not interfere with my work.
>
> And, while I write, nature herself is stormy, with many thunderings and lightnings. I have opened the windows because I feel in this moment so close in spirit with this storm.

The indifference of the American consul to Yole's situation only hints at the jingoism that contributed to the shaping of American foreign policy after World War I. In a frenzy of nationalism, not unlike what was being experienced on the Continent, foreigners were being blamed for everything that troubled the United States, from the rise of Bolshevism and anarchist attacks to a mysterious phenomenon popularly referred to as the "hybridization of America." In 1921 Congress had passed the first quota law, and the more restrictive National Origin Act would become effective in 1929.

These efforts to limit immigration did not, however, extend to intellectuals, thanks to the specific exemption of university teachers in Section (4)d of the Immigration Act of 1924. This fortunate loophole helps to explain why the period between the wars was marked by both an increased hostility to foreigners and a wonderful expansion of America's artistic and intellectual life.

In early June Zariski wrote to Yole of his discovery that he could become eligible for a nonquota visa that would allow him to bring her and the baby to the United States if he could prove to the American consul in Naples that he held a professorship in the States and that he had been a professor in Italy for the two preceding years.

The University of Rome offered to help by giving him a certificate that said that he had been a professor for the two years during which he had coached mathematics students for their exams. President Frank Goodnow wrote from Hopkins to say that Zariski had been appointed associate professor,[42] and that he had been sent as their representative to the International Mathematics Congress in Bologna.

Once in Italy, Zariski waited several days to see the consul. When at last they met by accident in the street outside the consulate, they talked for an hour, mostly about baseball. Zariski, already experienced in these American conversations, said that he often went to watch the Orioles play. Smiling, the consul said, "It's quite clear to me that you will be a good American."

The woman who had refused to see Yole and the screaming Raphael now stamped her passport so that she would be able to work as soon as she reached Baltimore. "It was something that had seemed impossible," Yole would remember. "We were so careless and so lucky at the same time."

The Zariskis would arrive together in the United States at the very beginning of what would become, in the thirties and early forties, an unprecedented infusion of talent to this country.

---

[42] This was an untenured position, the equivalent of what we currently call assistant professor.

7 ▦ A Voyage of Discovery

1928 – 1932

Zariski left Rome for the International Congress in Bologna somewhat reluctantly because he didn't want to separate from Yole again and there was no money for her to accompany him. Traveling out of Rome was also difficult for him that fall because of a duodenal ulcer he had developed on the way to the States the year before.

He had kept his stomach-aches a secret from Yole while he was in Baltimore, but she discovered them as soon as he arrived in Rome. The doctor to whom she brought him recommended a special diet, which he followed for many years (without, however, relinquishing the cigarettes that accompanied his work), and his ulcer gave him no serious problems until another trip to Rome in 1953.

His letters to Yole from Bologna were ebullient: he was pleased to see his Italian teachers again and to renew his friendships with old acquaintances like Mandelbrojt. He was also delighted by the attention given to his recent results. Just before leaving the States, he had written to Yole about Lefschetz's response to his "most recent research":

He insists that I publish these results immediately, that I announce them in some way because he would like to mention them in the lecture that he will give at the Congress in Bologna. But I will not publish anything. They are unfinished and I don't like to do things hastily. We will find a way to make them known at the conference, these partial results, without precipitous publication.

They were made known in a particularly dramatic way, which he described to Yole:

Today Castelnuovo gave a lecture; it was the best so far and it made a great impression on everyone, both for its content and for its elegant style. It was a real work of art. He did me the great honor of interrupting his lecture at a certain point . . . in order to announce to the audience my upcoming communication to the Congress, in which, according to him, I have made an important step toward the solution of a fundamental problem which is still unresolved. . . . Since there are hundreds of these brief reports given at the Congress, you can well understand how significant a sign of recognition this was.

Severi, too, said, "Very good, Zariski, yours is a very original and elegant topic. Keep on working." And Professor Hadamard, "the great French mathematician," paid him the compliment of pointing out that Descartes had "posited an analogous question without dreaming of being able to solve it. It was superior," Zariski explained modestly to Yole, "not to his abilities, but to the scientific tools available at that time. Well, to have a spiritual predecessor in Descartes can only give one great pleasure."

In his first year away from the Italian algebraic geometers, as he had fallen more deeply under the influence of Lefschetz, Zariski had begun to look at many old problems in a new way. The ten years from 1927 to 1937, consisting of a stubborn attack on topological problems in algebraic geometry, form what might be called the second phase of his career. The Bologna paper [15], which used a theorem of Severi in order to prove that an irreducible plane curve possessing only nodal singularities was an abelian (and, since its generators were known to be conjugate, cyclic) Poincaré group, was the first of a large and important series of papers on fundamental groups [17–20, 22, 28, 29, 31].[43]

---

[43] It was published in English the following year [16], but the assertion remained unproved for a long time because Severi's proof was subsequently found to have an error. Zariski addressed this issue in his final piece of research [98].

His interest in groups led him on a fantastic voyage of discovery into a territory that remains largely unexplored, and introduced ideas that are still important in knot theory, deformation theory, monodromy, and the geometry of the discriminant locus.

Zariski's "American coup" was a triumph in Bologna and made a fitting end to his first year in America. In spite of his initial fears of not being able to work without Yole, he had found a fruitful area of exploration in fundamental groups and written three interesting papers that demonstrated his increasing mastery of topological methods; he had established himself as a protégé of Lefschetz; and he had obtained a permanent position on the faculty of Johns Hopkins so that he was able to realize his dream of bringing Yole and Raphael to the United States.

Yole adapted as quickly to life in Baltimore as Zariski had. Eight days after her arrival in the States she saw an advertisement for a teacher in the newspaper and made up her mind to go for an interview. Although Zariski's $3,000 a year as "associate" was more than sufficient for their daily needs,[44] she was anxious to repay the money they had had to borrow for transportation from Zariski's uncle in New York, from her own cousin in Rome, and also from a Jewish organization in Baltimore.

Afraid of taking a streetcar to the interview because she didn't know what or how to pay, she walked across the city to the school with Raphael, who was only three. She was immediately hired to teach French; Raphael was admitted to the nursery school; and the next day she found herself in front of her first class of American students.

With two American salaries they soon found themselves, for the first time in their marriage, with enough money. Zariski learned to drive and in 1930 they bought their first car, which Zariski christened "Irrational π." Two years later, when she was pregnant with Vera, Yole also learned to drive, although she never grew to like driving as much as Zariski did.

---

[44] The standard entry level salary for university teaching in the late twenties was less than $2,000.

Baltimore was not as cosmopolitan as Rome, but they enjoyed American films and the occasional play that previewed on its way to New York. They also went to concerts as often as they could. Yole played the violin, and Zariski, who had always liked to sing, began to take piano lessons. He eventually became good enough to play duets with her, but he stopped his lessons when he realized that he had begun too late ever to be more than an amateur musician — as if in music, as in mathematics, nothing less than excellence could bring him pleasure.

They lived for the first year in a furnished apartment on the third floor of the house of a Jewish family in a Jewish neighborhood, which was, Yole remembered, "like living twice in a foreign country." The following year they moved into an unfurnished apartment closer to the university, on 33rd and Calvert Street, where Zariski introduced Raphael to baseball and lacrosse.

They were used to moving, since their frequent summer visits back to Italy meant giving up their apartment, putting their furniture in storage, and going apartment-hunting as soon as they returned in the fall. From 33rd Street they moved to St. Paul Street, and from there to a row house on Guilford Avenue, near the corner of 29th Street. Looking back on this "system," which had seemed so practical at the time, Yole laughed. "I simply took the difficulties for granted," she said. She hired someone to help her with the housework and learned to cook, Italian food as well as American, since she had found books more interesting than cooking before her marriage. She occasionally wrote articles and short stories for an Italian magazine in Rome until 1936, when the political climate of Italy became so fascistic that she felt "doubly alienated" from her country.

"In many ways," she said, looking back at those early years in the United States, "it was nicer here for us. Our marriage was on a more equal footing. We were both starting life in a new country rather than just Oscar making adjustments to the country where I belonged." [45]

---

[45] In commenting upon the speed with which intellectual immigrants became "Americanized," Laura Fermi suggests that "the very traits and education that had shaped the intellectuals rendered them curious about their new environment." See *Illustrious Immigrants*, Chicago: University of Chicago Press, 1971, 5.

Zariski also felt in many ways more at home in Baltimore than he had felt in Rome, in spite of his disappointment with the mathematics department at Hopkins. His knowledge of English as well as of baseball had grown rapidly; only three months after his arrival in the States he had written to Yole that his seminar at Hopkins was going very well. "I spoke an English that astonished everyone," he'd said rather ambiguously. He was also working hard to master written English:

> I am now writing a much longer work. It will require quite some time before it is ready for publication. I wrote in Italian because I tried to write directly in English and I had to stop. . . . It was too hard. After having written it in Italian, I will translate it into English with the help of some acquaintance.

His adjustment to the United States was also made easier by his discovery of a large Russian Jewish community where he could speak Russian. "Not many of those people used English," he later remembered, "because in America they were used to people coming from abroad and settling down in their own neighborhoods." His first student, Jacob Yerushalmi, was drawn from this community. Because he finished his degree during the Depression, Yerushalmi had difficulty finding a job in mathematics; he later earned a doctorate in Public Health and settled at the University of California at Berkeley.

The fall of 1929 saw important changes in the mathematics department at Hopkins. Coble had, to Zariski's "great sorrow," returned to Illinois, which had offered him a professorship at one of the highest salaries in the United States. Frank Morley had become *emeritus,* and the young and energetic Francis Murnaghan had succeeded him as chairman. Robust and ruddy, with pale freckles and bright blue eyes, Murnaghan brought new life to the math department, and the whole Zariski family looked forward to evenings at his house.

One of the first things Murnaghan did as chairman was to go to Europe to recruit young mathematicians. From Scotland he brought John Williamson, who soon became a close friend of Zariski's, even though they shared no common mathematical interests. Williamson offered to teach Zariski to play bridge, saying, "If you want to stay here you'll have to learn it." "And he was right," Zariski later

A PICTURE, LIKE A TENSOR, IS WORTH TEN THOUSAND WORDS.

Zariski and Murnaghan, 1931, with caption by Zariski (courtesy of Yole Zariski)

remembered. "There was no habit of spending an evening there just talking. If you didn't play bridge, other people were kind of bored with you."

Murnaghan also hired an Italian, Enrico Bompiani, and a young analyst named Aurel Wintner, a Hungarian who had studied in Germany. With Wintner, too, Zariski had nothing in common mathematically; he also found Wintner abrasive, and their relationship remained one of studied indifference.

Most valuable to Zariski was the hiring of E. R. van Kampen, a gifted topologist from Holland. Warm and charming, part Indonesian, he shared with Zariski a lively interest in fundamental groups.

When Zariski published *Algebraic Surfaces* and began using the algebra of Noether and Krull — "When," as Zariski himself put it, "I started real algebraic geometry" — van Kampen's enthusiasm was boundless. "That is really mathematics!" he said after one lecture. And again, "Boy, I'd like to work on this thing myself!" He died a few years later, in his early thirties, of a brain tumor.

In 1931 Zariski's topological work was recognized with an offer from the University of Chicago to teach in the summer school. In those days when academics traveled little, such an offer, especially to a young man who'd come so recently from abroad, was considered a great honor. When two weeks before he was supposed to be in Chicago he was rushed to the hospital with an emergency appendectomy, the president of Johns Hopkins, Joseph Ames, went to the hospital to congratulate him on the offer and to express his hope that he would be well in time to go. Fortunately, Zariski did recover in time to meet his classes in Chicago, although he gave his first lectures in a wheelchair.

The University of Chicago Summer School, 1932. Left to right: Zariski, Mrs. Hille, Bliss, Hille, Mrs. Mendel, Mendel (courtesy of Yole Zariski)

Zariski with Raphael on the family's first trip back to Europe, 1931 (courtesy of Yole Zariski)

Although the Zariskis were pleased by the offer from Chicago, they regretted not being able to go to Europe that summer, especially since they had not seen Hannah since her visit to them in Forte dei Marmi three years ago. The following summer, however, shortly before the birth of their daughter Vera in 1932, they did manage to make the trip. Crossing the frontier into Italy, they watched anxiously as the special police of the Fascists examined and sometimes confiscated the books of passengers. In Rome, where Mussolini was now occupying the huge Palazzo Venezia in the very heart of the city, they were struck by a new show of religion. "I found out that a crucifix hung on the wall of my younger sister's classroom," Yole remembered, "while I myself was brought up in schools in which there was no crucifix, no cross on the wall. I'd never had to be excused for a class in religious education."

When Yole asked her younger sister, "Doesn't all this upset you terribly?" her sister answered that she simply never saw it.

8 ◫ "The Algebra Which Sheds Light on Geometry"

1932–1935

From 1932 to 1935 Zariski published nothing. In 1932 he was promoted to associate professor with tenure, and that winter he began work on *Algebraic Surfaces* [25], a definitive account of the classical theory of algebraic surfaces that would convince him of the need to rewrite the entire foundations of algebraic geometry. In the preface to the first edition, dated June 12, 1934, he wrote, "The aim of the present monograph is to give a systematic exposition of the theory of algebraic surfaces emphasizing the interrelations between the various aspects of the theory: algebro-geometric, topological and transcendental."[46]

Although writing this book altered his perception of his Italian teachers and gave a new urgency to his search for other methods, he spoke with characteristic simplicity of his discovery "that in this domain the methods employed are at least as important as the formal accounts of results." One of the classics of mathematics,

---

[46] *Algebraic Surfaces* (New York: Springer-Verlag, 1971). The first edition was published in 1935 as Band III, Heft 5, of the series *Ergebnisse der Mathematik und ihrer Grenzgebiete.*

Algebraic Surfaces provides an important link between classical and modern theories and serves as a landmark in the history of algebraic geometry.[47]

More than forty years later, in the preface to his *Collected Papers,* Zariski is more explicit:

> In my *Ergebnisse* monograph I tried my best to present the underlying ideas of the ingenious geometric methods and proofs with which the Italian geometers were handling these deeper aspects of the whole theory of surfaces, and in all probability I succeeded, but at a price. The price was my own personal loss of the geometric paradise in which I so happily had been living. I began to feel distinctly unhappy about the rigor of the original proofs I was trying to sketch (without losing in the least my admiration for the imaginative geometric spirit that permeated these proofs); I became convinced that the whole structure must be done over again by purely algebraic methods. (I, xi)

Near the end of his life he remembered that "working on that book took all my time because as I worked I became more and more disgusted with the kind of proofs that the Italian geometers were giving, and I started studying algebra seriously. I found I didn't even know the elementary facts of modern algebra. If somebody had asked me, 'What's a ring?' I couldn't have defined it. I spent the next couple of years just studying modern algebra."

He studied alone for the most part, the way he had worked in Kiev and the way he had learned the theory of functions of complex variables in Rome. He began with the books of two algebraists who had been deeply influenced by Emmy Noether in Göttingen, B. L. van der Waerden's *Modern Algebra* and Wolfgang Krull's *The Theory of Ideals.* He was particularly struck by Krull's findings on local rings, and through Crelle's *Journal* he discovered a third source that would help him, namely, an 1882 paper by Dedekind and Weber on the algebraic functions of one variable treated by purely algebraic methods. Characteristically, he felt no need for personal contact with van der Waerden or Krull, although he occasionally wrote to them with a discovery of his own.

When asked about the genesis of the work that had permanently

---

[47] This book is the principle source for the work of the Italian School for almost all algebraic geometers today.

Zariski in Wyman Park, Baltimore, 1933 (courtesy of Yole Zariski)

altered the foundations of algebraic geometry, he simply said, "These are the three things on which I built." [48]

One morning in 1934 President Ames stopped by his office to ask him why he had stopped publishing. Zariski did his best to explain what he had discovered while writing *Algebraic Surfaces* and how

---

[48] Although both van der Waerden and Krull had grasped the potential usefulness of abstract algebra for geometry, it was Zariski who used it to explore what his student Joseph Lipman has called "the deeper questions which lie at the heart of the subject."

he'd decided to learn the new algebra, but even as he heard himself talking, he knew that the president had already decided that all these words were just excuses.

Perhaps the president felt skeptical about such enthusiasm for research because he knew that Zariski was overworked without it. He was teaching eleven hours a week in the day school, and to compensate for the salary cut that Hopkins had asked all faculty members to accept because of the Depression, he was teaching another three hours at night.

The increased teaching load and decreased salary were typical of the Depression. By 1932 the incomes of most colleges and universities had dropped sharply, making retrenchment essential. Many junior faculty members lost their jobs, and in 1934 almost half of the nearly two hundred mathematicians seeking professional positions failed to find them. During this same period the American mathematics community, responding to the worsening political situation abroad, was also struggling to find places for an increasing number of European mathematicians.

Zariski's search for a quiet place in which to do mathematics had brought him to the United States early enough to avoid the serious difficulties of finding a job during the Depression, just as it had carried him out of Russia and then Italy before the violence had entrapped him. Never having been motivated by political astuteness or personal fear, he had always simply called his choices "luck."

He liked to tease Yole by pointing out that his Marxist principles had protected them from the more serious consequences of the Crash; she, however, would smilingly remind him that they'd had no money to lose.

They were living in the red brick row house on Guilford Avenue, where the old wooden stadium of the Baltimore Orioles still stood in those days. Zariski never accepted morning classes that began before ten because he worked until very late at night, every night, at least until two. Sometimes he would also steal an hour in the morning or a few hours during an afternoon on which Yole took Raphael and Vera to the park.

He never learned to do research in a university office: "I go there to teach, but to work on my own work, I want my own room. It is the European habit." He couldn't concentrate with anyone else in the room, and as he had discovered in Rome when he had tried to work in

Zariski with Raphael, 1934 (courtesy of Yole Zariski)

the apartment of Yole's family, he preferred an empty house. He made notes and drafted his papers on yellow legal pads with pens that were quickly exhausted. He never ate or even drank coffee while he worked, but he smoked cigarettes almost continuously.

His work was the secret heart of the family, and it was taken for granted that Yole and the children would adapt themselves to its demands. Yole provided him with hot lunches and long uninterrupted hours, and they all did their best to accommodate his changing moods. "You could always tell when he'd hit what he called a 'snag,'" Yole remembered. "He'd spend weeks and weeks just banging his head against the wall, growing more and more irritable. 'Children,' I'd say, 'Your father has hit a snag so be quiet!' Poor children, they remember that better than I do. For me, although at

Yole with Raphael, 1934 (courtesy of Yole Zariski)

the time I complained the loudest, the tension always evaporated like smoke because I understood."

"You were moody," Yole once reminded him, "especially when you were working on a difficult problem. I wouldn't call it bad, but you were sometimes not very easy to live with. And that affected your relationship with the children and me in many ways. But," she added, smiling, "you always had some very good moments, which compensated for the not so very good ones."

The children, too, remembered many "very good moments" with him. He often took his son, Raphael, now a sturdy English-speaking boy nicknamed Ray, to cheer the Baltimore Orioles. "He was very attached to us," Ray explained many years later. "He had a strong sense of family, and we went everywhere together, not just on summer vacations. He wanted to settle in a big house so that we could all go on living there together.

"But when I was eight or nine, Oscar (he always encouraged me to call him by his first name) was thinking about *Algebraic Surfaces* and working hard so we couldn't go to the games quite so much. At the time I felt upset, but looking back I can see that he handled himself rather well, given the pressure he was under." (Yole pointed out that not going didn't stop Ray from following the night games from his bedroom window, even on school nights when it wasn't allowed, since the ballpark was only a block away.)

Given the eagerness with which he was pursuing his ideas and the pressures he was under to earn a living, it is easy to imagine the delight Zariski must have felt when he received an invitation from the newly formed Institute for Advanced Study at Princeton for the 1934–35 academic year. Although the matter was never discussed, he always assumed that it had been Lefschetz who had found this way to free him from irrelevant matters during the important period that followed the completion of *Algebraic Surfaces.* "I know that he looks for a means of establishing me in the system, writing here and there and recommending me without my knowing it," he had written to Yole in 1928.

The Institute had, of course, been designed to serve just such a purpose. Its founder and director, Abraham Flexner, had long dreamed of a place where "scholars should enjoy complete intellectual liberty and be absolutely free from administrative responsibilities or concerns." [49] In 1930 Flexner received enough money to open the first of what would be several schools and immediately began to recruit scholars. [50] In 1932 he invited Albert Einstein to leave Germany, and in 1933 the school of mathematics began functioning with Einstein as its head.

---

[49] Abraham Flexner, *I Remember: The Autobiography of Abraham Flexner* (New York: Simon and Schuster, 1940).

[50] A school of economics was soon opened and, later, a school of humanistic studies.

John von Neumann, who contributed fundamental work to many areas of pure mathematics and is regarded as one of the founders of modern computer science; Hermann Weyl, a scholar and philosopher who had worked in Göttingen in both pure and applied mathematics; and two distinguished American topologists, James Alexander and Oswald Veblen, were invited to serve with Einstein as a permanent nucleus to attract visiting scholars. Well aware of America's growing anxiety about opening her doors to Europeans, Flexner was careful to balance émigrés with Americans, and during the difficult war years the Institute succeeded in helping many foreign scholars to get to the United States.

The friendliness of Einstein, Veblen, and Weyl helped to give the Institute a separate identity that it might otherwise have lacked, since visiting members were simply assigned offices in the Princeton mathematics department in Fine Hall, and members and their families were left to find their own apartments in town. Weyl and Veblen often gave dinner parties, very formal affairs in the English style. After a dinner of several courses served by a maid, the women would leave the dining room for half an hour, ostensibly so the men could smoke although, as Yole laughingly pointed out, the women smoked more than the men did.

Zariski's visit to the Institute was important to his mathematical development not only because it allowed him time to work out his ideas, but also because it gave him the opportunity to make the acquaintance of two algebraists from Göttingen. Richard Brauer, who had recently arrived to serve as Weyl's assistant, became a close friend and, later, colleague; and Emmy Noether, who gave a series of talks at the Institute that winter, encouraged Zariski's deepening interest in modern algebra.

Zariski's contact with Noether was undoubtedly the single most important aspect of that year for him. Essential to the creation of abstract axiomatic algebra, her work on the foundations of the general theory of ideals had also formed a crucial link between Dedekind and Krull, the two algebraists whose work had been of such particular importance to him.

Her warmth and enthusiasm as a teacher and colleague in Göttingen and, later, at Bryn Mawr, helped to make her a central figure in the development of modern algebra. She was a good friend of Emil

Artin and Richard Brauer and in close contact with many other important mathematicians, including Hermann Weyl, Claude Chevalley, P. S. Alexandrov, and Heinz Hopf. Born in Germany and for many years an instructor in Göttingen, she had accepted a visiting professorship at Bryn Mawr College for reasons of personal safety. But her already formidable reputation had apparently not yet reached the States, for in the winter of 1933–34 she had held a seminar on the work of van der Waerden and Hecke and found only three students and one professor in attendance.[51]

The next year, however, "more than sixty professors and aspiring professors" came to hear her lecture not, as she wrote, at the "men's university where nothing female is admitted," but at the Institute for Advanced Study. Von Neumann was there, and Weyl and Brauer, her friends from Göttingen, and, needless to say, Zariski. "I have started with representation modules, groups with operators," she wrote to a colleague in Germany. "Princeton will receive its first algebraic treatment this winter, and a thorough one at that."[52]

Remembering her seminar many years later, Zariski would say:

> She spoke about ideal theory in algebraic number theory. She was always talking about spots (Oh my, spots!) and a good deal of it was like Chinese to me.[53] But she was very enthusiastic and I was trying to learn ideal theory, so I went faithfully even if I didn't understand everything. Just watching her was fun, and of course, I felt that here is a person who gets enthusiastic about algebra, so there is probably a good deal to get enthusiastic about.
>
> Once, for example, when she was lecturing, her slip came down. She bent down, pulled off the slip, threw it into the corridor, and kept on lecturing.
>
> I was especially glad that she was so happy about my conversion to algebra. She must have thought, "Here is an algebraic geometer like my father [Max Noether], but who's converted to pure algebra." She even came to hear me lecture in Philadelphia, like a mother. She was

---

[51] One of those students was Vera Widder, who remembered that the first thing Noether did when she stepped off the boat from Göttingen was to remove her hat. Widder, like Zariski, was struck by her enthusiasm in the lecture hall: Noether would be so eager to get her thoughts down that "she would write across a wet blackboard, leaving her students to wait patiently for it to dry so they could read it" (Vera Widder, personal interview, January 1989).

[52] Auguste Dick, *Emmy Noether* (Boston: Birkhauser, 1981) 81.

[53] These "spots" were later called "places."

very motherly to me, although I didn't learn ideal theory from her, but from her papers.

Zariski's conversion to algebra was, of course, more apparent than real, as André Weil has suggested. "I wouldn't underestimate the influence of algebra," Zariski once warned, "but I wouldn't exaggerate the influence of Emmy Noether. I'm a very faithful man . . . also in my mathematical tastes. I was always interested in the algebra which throws light on geometry, and I never did develop the sense for pure algebra. Never. I'm not mentally made for purely formal algebra, formal mathematics. I have too much contact with real life, and that's geometry.

"Geometry is the real life."

9 ◩

A CITIZEN OF THE

WORLD OF MATHEMATICS

1935–1937

In May 1935 Zariski left the Institute with Yole and the children. In what would be their last trip to Europe until after the war, they visited Yole's family in Rome, and in what would be their final trip to Kobrin, they spent the summer with Hannah and Moses and Zariski's three older sisters. Shepsel and Zila had already settled in Israel, but the older sisters, who had also bought land in Israel, had stayed behind, hoping to convince Hannah to go with them.

Zariski and Yole also did their best to convince her to leave Kobrin; although they had no intuition of the horror that lay ahead, they repeated their longstanding invitation to visit America. With her usual strongmindedness, however, Hannah cleaved to the place where she'd raised her children and buried both her husbands.

At the beginning of September, having received permission to return late to Johns Hopkins, Zariski traveled from Kobrin to Moscow for the International Conference in Topology. The first large international conference on a specialized branch of mathematics, the Moscow meeting afforded him a glimpse of the future of topology as well as an opportunity to renew his acquaintance with a number of younger mathematicians.[54]

Lefschetz, whose *Topology* (1930) had already become a basic reference, had been a major organizer of the conference, and with him from Princeton were Alexander and von Neumann, whom Zariski had met during his year at the Institute. Alexandrov and Hopf, who'd been at Princeton with Lefschetz when Zariski made his first visit there in 1927, had recently completed their first volume of *Topologie* and were scheduled to give papers. Zariski was especially happy to find André Weil, whom he hadn't seen since their year together in Rome.

The Zariskis were lodged in a boarding house that had been set aside for aged scientists, but they were given their main meal in the sumptuous old Grand Hotel, where the price of a cup of coffee exceeded the price of a meal. They were served by an ancient waiter who worried that Yole wasn't eating enough. When he brought her food he would mutter, "My God, my God." One day Zariski interrupted him. "We're not supposed to have God here," he said, and he never forgot the old man's simple reply: "God exists and I will not renounce Him."

Finikov, a differential geometer they had met in Italy, often invited them to his apartment, and occasionally they visited an art gallery or the theater, but most of their afternoons and evenings were taken up with elaborate formal dinners. Although they were not assigned an "escort," they often felt that they were being watched. Remembering those weeks in Moscow, Yole said, "I loved the country, I loved the people I came into contact with, but I had a feeling of fear and was always thinking: I hope I will be able to get out of here and see my children in Rome."

One evening Pontryagin and another young mathematician, Kolmogorov, were putting forward the Marxist view that only applied mathematics had any importance. With his usual forthrightness, Zariski broke in to ask why they then wrote about abstract things. "Don't you find it difficult to write about topology," he asked, "since it has no obvious applications?"

Skillfully sidestepping the issue, Kolmogorov answered, "You must take the term 'application' in a wide sense, you know. Not

---

[54] Hassler Whitney, one of Harvard's delegates to the conference, described it as having marked "the true birth of cohomology theory" ("Moscow 1935," *Century* I, 109).

everything must be applied immediately. Almost every view of mathematics is useful for the development of technology, but that doesn't mean that every time you do mathematics you must work on a machine."

After the conference finished, Weil and Zariski (who had not been an official delegate) were invited by the mathematics department at the University of Moscow to give a series of lectures on some topic in algebraic geometry. Welcoming the opportunity to renew their friendship, they attended each other's talks and often spent their evenings together. Zariski chose to talk about his recently completed work on the Riemann-Roch theorem, in which he used the topology of the n-fold symmetric product $C(n)$ of a curve to study the linear systems on C [27]. Four or five hundred students and professors gathered in a huge conference hall to hear him, but afterwards, according to Zariski, "There was a real revolt. Finikov and some other geometers of the old school who'd not been very much exposed to algebraic geometry rose up to complain: 'Is this algebraic geometry? What is the matter? We've never seen such geometry!'"[55]

Zariski went on to describe the revolt in detail:

> Pontryagin, Sobolev, and the other younger men tried to defend me, but it was no use. They were just getting wilder. I don't know what I finally told them, but to the younger men I said that I didn't think that I could lecture to the older ones again. I mean, they didn't like me or my subject — the strange way of talking about the Riemann – Roch theorem, this topology, this algebra.
>
> So Pontryagin, Sobolov and the others told me, "Look, let's forget these lectures. We will tell them you don't give lectures anymore. We'll make a secret seminar. You'll just have a few of us who are interested."
>
> And that I did. I lectured for six weeks in Russian, which I very much enjoyed, to a group of maybe thirty or forty people. I gave them all the theory of algebraic surfaces. There was no public announcement, not even something on the bulletin board. We used a small seminar room.

Shortly after leaving Moscow, Zariski wrote an expository article in Russian, giving the foundation of the theory of linear and continuous systems of plane curves [33].[56]

---

[55] Hassler Whitney also refers to the "explosive" character of the conference itself.

[56] Thirty years later, on a visit to the Institut des Hautes Etudes, Zariski met the Russian

During his last six weeks in Russia, Zariski enjoyed the company of a number of friends from his gymnasium whom he hadn't seen since 1921. They sat up late over endless cups of coffee discussing the political situation, with half his friends defending the Communists, and the other half attacking them. One young man cautioned Zariski not to blame Stalin for having become so dictatorial. "You must know," he said, "that the Russian people for centuries were used to not having it soft. That's why they cannot be persuaded on the basis of Marxist principles but must have the equivalent of the czarist power."

Zariski, however, did not need to hear Stalin defended because in 1935 he was still very much a socialist. Even when his stepbrother, the boy who'd left Kobrin so enthusiastically to offer his services as an engineer for the revolutionary cause, came, bitter and disillusioned, to see him in his Moscow hotel room, he took it upon himself to defend what had already become Stalin's personal dictatorship. He argued that Russia was surrounded by enemies and therefore needed a strong center. He excused the secret police for their interrogation of his gymnasium friends after they had seen him. He pointed out that his having been invited by the authorities to lecture in Moscow was itself a good sign.

The purges began a few months later, and Zariski never saw or heard from his stepbrother again. Looking back, he would one day speak as bitterly as the young engineer had of Stalin's "blindness." "Rather than creating a strong center," he would say, "Stalin's ruthlessness completely weakened Russia."

He returned with his family to Johns Hopkins in November 1935. In the next two years he published three more papers that continue his exploration of topological methods [28, 29, 31] and a short note

---

algebraic geometer Manin and told him, with some embarrassment, that he hadn't known the Russian equivalents of many of the technical terms he needed when he wrote that paper (his only one in Russian) and that he'd simply made them up. Manin replied that at the time there had been no equivalents and that Zariski's terminology had become standard Russian usage (Steven L. Kleiman, letter to the author, 4 February 1990).

Zariski and a visiting friend from Kobrin, Maurice Goldberg (left), who brought them both Russian shirts (courtesy of Yole Zariski)

announcing the algebraic concept of the integral closure of a ring [34]. This note, in which we find him "changing the method from intuition to algebra," as his students liked to joke, was the first step in what would eventually become the total transformation of classical geometry into modern geometry.

On April 13, 1936, he and Yole became U.S. citizens. "I knew by then that I was going to spend my life here," Zariski remembered. "I had no Russian patriotism left in me. And why should I be a Polish citizen? I live with human beings. . . . What difference does it make whether they call themselves American? I enjoy people for what they are, not for the nationality that they belong to. Being Jewish doesn't keep me from adapting. On the contrary, if you are a Jew you can become anything."

Zariski with Raphael in "Irrational Pi," his first car (courtesy of Yole Zariski)

And indeed, he seems to have adapted to the informality of social relationships in Baltimore just as readily as he had adapted to the formality in Rome. He and Yole enjoyed an unusually wide circle of friends, which included not only Murnaghan and Williamson and other members of the mathematics department, but also Wilson Shaffer, a professor of psychology and later a dean, and Professor Singleton, a teacher of Italian whom they would be pleased to find at Harvard after the war. Norbert Wiener visited them one weekend and spent his spare time practicing his Chinese on Zariski; and the Liebers, their corner grocers, sometimes stopped by for an evening.

He applied himself to American literature with the passion and thoroughness that he brought to everything he did.[57] He took pleasure in rereading Jack London and Mark Twain in English, and thanks to Yole he made the happy discovery of Willa Cather and Edith Wharton. Faulkner's style gave him trouble and Hemingway's sensibility was not congenial, but he enjoyed the social realism of Sinclair Lewis and Theodore Dreiser.

---

[57] His daughter remembered that one year on a visit to France he became so interested in the French Revolution that he read not only all the books and journals he could find, but also all the accounts from the newspapers of 1789.

He continued to make time for chess and bridge and an occasional baseball game, but what he enjoyed most of all was the old world habit of walking. He walked when he was sad, he walked when he had hit a "snag," and he walked just for the pleasure of it. During the late thirties in Baltimore he was accompanied on his way to and from the university twice a day by his daughter, Vera, who had begun nursery school at Hopkins. As they strolled along he often told her stories about his boyhood in Kobrin — "sometimes sad and sometimes mischievous, depending on his mood." Vera remembered being particularly disappointed on the days when he was quiet and preoccupied. She was so fond of these walks that one morning when she had no school she decided to go alone and meet him anyway. At the crossing of a wide and busy street, two plainclothes policemen in a car stopped to ask her where she was going. "I'm going to meet my father at the university," she said proudly, and was not at all happy when they took her home.

Ray described his father as "cosmopolitan," and while it is true that Zariski's tastes and habits were a potpourri of many nationalities, he had at an early age found a permanent home in mathematics. Unlike Hannah, who repeatedly chose to remain in Kobrin for the sake of the store, he had always chosen to move on for the sake of mathematics. Having given up Yiddish for Russian, and Russian for Italian, he gave up Italian for English when Vera grew old enough to complain that she didn't understand Italian.

But the apparent ease with which he left Kobrin for the Russian world of the gymnasium, and Kiev for Rome, and Italy for America, can hardly hide the unusual amount of personal loss these moves must have entailed, even for a citizen of the world of mathematics.

In 1937 he was promoted to full professor. His salary was still low and his teaching load high, but his own work was going well. His teaching, too, continued to give him pleasure, although he was increasingly bothered by the paucity of good graduate students. He later felt that in his eighteen years at Hopkins he'd trained only three exceptionally talented mathematicians: Irvin S. Cohen, H. T. Muhly, and Abraham Seidenberg. Muhly settled at the University of Iowa, and Seidenberg, who married Yole's sister Ebe on the day he took his degree, joined the mathematics department at the University of California at Berkeley. Cohen, the most algebraic of the three, left Hopkins for the Institute for Advanced Study, and from there he accepted a position at MIT.

A small man with big anxious eyes, Cohen died unexpectedly in February 1955, while on leave as visiting associate professor at Columbia. A week before his death he had gone up to Cambridge to see Zariski, and many years later Zariski spoke of his death in relation to his work:

> Many things are necessary to make a good scientist, a creative man, and left on his own Cohen found himself unproductive. Highly critical of himself and others, he believed that nothing he ever wrote was as good as his thesis.[58] He became increasingly involved with abstract algebra until he found himself at a certain point without ground under his feet. He became disappointed in his work and, finally, fatally, in his own ability.

Most of the very few joint papers that Zariski published were written with his students — one with Cohen [68], two with Muhly [38, 57], and one with Peter Falb [76]. An early paper characterizing irreducible curves of the first kind was written with S. F. Barber, a young visitor to Hopkins [26]; and in 1938, with O. F. G. Schilling, a young German algebraist visiting Hopkins on scholarship, Zariski applied the results of a previous paper [36].

André Weil, who was then at the University of Strasbourg, became especially close to the Zariskis during the semester he spent as a visiting member of the Institute for Advanced Study in the spring of 1937. Although he was still motivated by number theory and sought to extend certain very specific constructions from nineteenth century algebraic geometry onto characteristic p, Weil was attracted by Zariski's use of the new algebra to rework the foundations of algebraic geometry. This common interest was to draw the two men together and engage them in a spirited interchange of ideas for several decades.

Early that summer, Weil stopped to visit the Zariskis on his way to Mexico. What Weil later remembered most vividly about "the very good time" they had together that weekend was Yole's eager

---

[58] Cohen worked out the structure theory for complete local rings, a major accomplishment in the area of abstract algebra.

insistence that he be well-dressed for his holiday in Mexico. As soon as she could steal him away from his conversations with Zariski she took him out and bought him "what was then known as a Palm Beach Suit."[59]

These conversations, though they revealed very different goals and instincts as to what constituted deep mathematics, joined the two men in laboring on the same fundamental problem: the rebuilding of algebraic geometry on a purely algebraic basis, without explicit use of or reliance on geometric intuition.

---

[59] André Weil, personal interview, May 1988.

10 ▧   THE RESOLUTION OF

SOME SINGULARITIES

In the fifteen years that followed the writing of *Algebraic Surfaces,* Zariski's work was marked by an extraordinary outpouring of original and creative ideas. Having discovered that many of the classical Italian "proofs" were incomplete and imprecise, he set to work to develop an abstract theory of algebraic geometry valid over an arbitrary ground field. Abandoning topological and analytical methods, he turned wholeheartedly to the new algebra as a means of elucidating basic geometric ideas.

Armed with two powerful ideas of commutative algebra — the concept of integral closure and Krull's general valuation rings — he mounted a major attack on the longstanding problem of the resolution of singularities of surfaces and higher dimensional varieties.

Many important mathematicians, including Max Noether, Jung, Albanese, and Walker, had worked on the problem, but results had been obtained only in the domain of complex numbers and were partial and incomplete. Looking back after forty years Zariski said, "I didn't quite go to pieces, but the problem of the resolution of singularities led me into a lot of work. In 1938 I spent days at my desk just applying ideal theories and valuation theories to the problem, valuations I got from Krull. He had said in his paper that these crazy valuations have very few applications, but I wrote to him that this is not true. These are important valuations and they have to be used, too. It became obvious to me that there were many connections with algebraic geometry."

After introducing the general concept of valuation to give an ideal-theoretic treatment of the Italian concept of the base conditions imposed by infinitely near points [35], Zariski applied these results to give an algebraic proof of the theorem that an irrational pencil on an algebraic surface X can have base points only at the singularities of X [36]. He was able to find several different ways in which valuation rings, which had until then been explored purely algebraically, could be used in beautiful ways geometrically to study the local properties of algebraic varieties.

"At the same time," he recalls in the preface to his *Collected Works*, "I noticed some promising connections between integral closure and complete linear systems; a systematic study of these latter connections later led me to the notions of normal varieties and normalization" [40, 41]. He introduced the notion of integral closure in "Some results in the arithmetic theory of algebraic varieties" [37], although he had announced it in a note two years earlier [34].

Many years later he would remember how delighted he had been to discover the power of the notion of normalization, which eliminated all but isolated singularities from surfaces and rendered the reduction of singularities of curves trivial [38, 39]:

> From there on, I gradually began to look at the problem of reduction of singularities not merely as something to get, but as a godsend because it gave me ideas in general about many things: for instance, the local uniformization which I needed [that you can find a birational model of the variety in which the center of a given valuation is a simple point]. From that I concluded that given any point in the complex domain, there exists a covering of the whole neighborhood of that point by subsets which are uniformized.
>
> Well, I wanted to prove that the whole variety can be covered by a finite number of such subsets. That led me to the Riemann surface of the field and to the notion of Zariski topology and the fact that "compact" in that topology is not "compact" in the ordinary topology. So there was a whole drama associated with it.

Part of that drama was the astonishingly subtle yet short proof of a theorem that became known as Zariski's Main Theorem. A stability result that provides a general structure theorem for birational maps, it says roughly that a normal point can't be modified at all without really destroying it. Using an intuition of the Italian geometers, who felt that if you consider the effect of a birational transformation on a simple point and if it corresponds to more than one point, then the transform of the point must be a whole positive dimensional connected set, Zariski made a foundational analysis of birational maps between varieties.

These so-called "maps" were one-to-one and onto outside of a finite set of subvarieties of the range and domain, but they could "blow up" or "blow down" special points. Zariski showed that if there are points P and Q in the range and domain that are isolated corresponding points, i.e., the set of points corresponding to P contains Q but no curve through Q and vice versa, and if, further, P and Q satisfy the algebraic restriction that they are normal points, then in fact Q is the only point corresponding to P and vice versa (slightly stronger: the map is biregular between P and Q) [43, 45].

He also applied the new algebraic concepts to function fields to give a birationally invariant way to describe the set of all places that must be desingularized, an application that culminated in his proof that all algebraic varieties of dimension at most 3 (in characteristic zero) can be resolved, i.e., are birational to nonsingular projective varieties [47]. In dimension 3, this was a problem that had totally eluded the easygoing Italian approach; and even in dimension 2, although some classical proofs were essentially correct, many of the published treatments definitely were not. This startling result proved to the mathematical world the power of the new algebraic ideas, and was regarded for many years as the technically most difficult proof in all algebraic geometry.

Zariski grew increasingly interested in the generalization of algebraic geometry to fields of any characteristic (described by his student David Mumford as a leap from reality to unreality). Although for a short time the fields of characteristic p were beyond the range of both his intellectual curiosity and his newly acquired skills in algebra, as he explains in the preface to his *Collected Papers*, it didn't take him long to make that leap.

Excited by all the new and beautiful phenomena he found in

characteristic p, he became increasingly intent upon discovering the appropriate characteristic p versions of classical notions. By combining the algebraic notion of a regular local ring with the geometric notion of a simple point, he was eventually able to define both normal varieties and simple point in the case of characteristic p [48, 49, 50].

The generalization of algebraic geometry to fields of characteristic p, still an active area of research, never ceased to interest him. Near the end of his life he said, "If one could know how to deal in the case of characteristic p with an equation of the form $z^p = f(x_1, x_2, \ldots, x_n)$, then one could probably have a better chance of solving the general problem of reduction of singularities in characteristic p."

Zariski's interest in extending the concepts of algebraic geometry from the classical case to arbitrary ground fields was shared by André Weil, with whom he again established close contact soon after Weil's permanent arrival in the United States in January 1941. A conscientious objector, Weil had spent some time in jail before being drafted into the French army. "The closest I came to killing someone," he remembered, "was when I carried a box of ammunition to a machine gunner who claimed that he downed a German plane — a claim I didn't believe for a minute!"[60]

Weil had always been a mathematician with extremely broad interests and had studied algebraic geometry; however, his principal interest was number theory, especially the theory of Diophantine equations, that is to say, the theory of solutions of polynomial equations in integers. He had recently become interested in algebraic geometry because he had seen that one way to understand Diophantine equations better was to systematically understand their solutions modulo various prime numbers p first, and he planned to develop the tools to do this by extending algebraic geometry over the complex ground field to finite fields, e.g. the integers modulo p. But

---

[60] Weil, letter to the author, 1 November 1989.

André Weil (reprinted with permission from the American Mathematical Society and Paul R. Halmos)

like Zariski, he realized that there was no way he could do this without rebuilding the foundations of algebraic geometry.[61]

One of Zariski's concerns during this period was whether or not to develop a theory of varieties over nonalgebraically closed fields as well as over algebraically closed fields of arbitrary characteristic. In the late summer of 1942 he wrote to Weil to describe the importance to him of fields that are not algebraically closed:

> I entirely approve of your plan to strike boldly ahead. That was what I myself used to think in all my papers and that's what I intend to do in the future. The fine points may be left out at this stage if they do not concern vitally important fields. However, I cannot afford to disregard fields which are not algebraically closed. These fields are essential in the classical theory and especially in the type of problems I am

---

[61] Mumford, personal interview, February 1990.

working on at present. My papers offer any number of illustrations of
their importance.

As another illustration, I will give you the following new application that concerns reduction of singularity of three dimensional varieties. . . . I find these fields essential because you take a pencil of
surfaces and consider the general surface, defined over $k(t)$, and
reduce its singularities. That is important, although it is a process
over $k(t)$, which turns out actually to be a birational transformation
over k. Therefore, I know that I can, by monoidal and quadratic
transformations, eliminate, by Bertini's theorem, the base points
which are singular, and that is important for me.[62]

When Weil, who was at that time discarding projective models by
introducing abstract varieties, questioned the value of Zariski's approach, Zariski replied by arguing that over an imperfect ground
field k of characteristic p there are really two different concepts of
"simple point": regular in the sense of having a regular local ring,
and smooth in the sense that the usual Jacobian criterion is satisfied.

Weil, for whom this was a very minor matter, felt that Zariski's
use of the concept of simple point would only lead to confusion and
suggested, jokingly, that the former be called "zimple points," or,
more seriously, "uniformized points," giving as a parallel the confusion that took place in topology between the two terms, "compact"
and "bicompact," when it was discovered that the two things were
not the same in general spaces.

Zariski defended himself at some length:

I'm afraid that our discussion on simple points is degenerating into a
dialogue in which each one of us is speaking his own mind without
having full understanding of the arguments of the other fellow. The
topic is, of course, of relative importance, but I for my part must
confess that I do not follow you at all when you say that a more
satisfactory exposition can be achieved by using one definition instead of the other. Let me put the dots on the i's or what look to me
like little dots.

First, the definition of simple points by means of the different is as
old as Santa Claus. It cannot really be attributed to anyone in partic-

---

[62] This and the following excerpts from Zariski's letters to Weil are being quoted from
Zariski's reading of them during an interview in 1981. They have been edited by David
Mumford.

ular. It was used by algebraic geometers in the case of algebraic equations and by function theory men in the case of systems of simultaneous analytical equations. If I am not mistaken, Schmiedler was the first to prove the invariance of simple points in that sense under biregular transformations. He, too, uses the rank of the Jacobian as the defining property of simple points.

The ideal-theoretic definition of simple points by means of uniformizing parameters is essentially new. The recognition that a simple point can be characterized by the property that the prime ideal of non-units in the quotient ring is generated by r elements is not a trivial matter; even though it now appears very natural, it didn't come to me straightaway. Think of the definition of simple points of an algebraic curve which is often given in more geometric and arithmetic expositions, namely a point with only one branch through it and that branch is of order 1. The most immediate translation into arithmetic terms is the following:

> The prime ideal of the point in the ring of non-homogeneous coordinates of the general point of the variety corresponds to a simple point if the extension of the ideal in the integral closure of that ring remains prime.

This is actually the condition which I used in a joint paper with Schilling way back in 1937. It only dawned on me later that it is not necessary to pass to the integral closure, that you can define it by uniformizing parameters.

Now you speak of the equivalence of the two definitions. I have never doubted that they are equivalent in characteristic zero, or in the case in which the coordinates of the point are separable algebraic over the ground field. I have never doubted that they are equivalent for the simple reason that I have proved their equivalence. See my papers [37, 40]. They're there. I have used either property of simple points according to which one was more convenient in any particular question. Therefore, I do not see what sort of a shift you had in mind.

Rereading these letters almost forty years after he'd written them, Zariski remembered his original frustration: "If Weil had said, 'Well, these simple points of yours unfortunately don't have the nice properties which simple points in separable cases have, but it's an interesting concept and has some value,' I might have been able to agree with him. But I must say, his ideas were extremely interesting, and this whole discussion was very useful to me."

This discussion also revealed what David Mumford has called "a basic difference" between the two men: "Weil had the idea that there was a 'right' way to define each concept and wanted to find the clean elegant treatment. But the pragmatic Zariski simply enjoyed the curious twists that his beloved geometry revealed to him in this unaccustomed world of characteristic p."[63]

To the generation of algebraic geometers who would profit most from this radical restructuring of the foundations, Zariski and Weil became part of a legend. Although Weil had grown up in a cultured family in the Paris of Poincaré, Goursat, and Borel, whereas Zariski had had to leave home for the world beyond the Pale in order to pursue his education, both men were cosmopolitan, quick-witted and charming, and both held their students and colleagues to the same high standards to which they held themselves. Zariski was more tenacious in his search for solutions and Weil more fierce, but they were equally quick to recognize a fool.

Weil seems to have been as strikingly unsentimental a child as Zariski was. A visitor to his house once told him she thought it charming that at mealtimes "each of his parents would leave for the other what he or she liked the most, thinking that the other also preferred it." The young Weil, however, pointed out that both of them ended up eating what they liked least and no one gained.[64]

Weil was often critical of America and saw Zariski's interest in things like baseball and bridge as misguided and sometimes ridiculous, while Zariski saw Weil's broader intellectual pursuits, which included Hindu culture and Sanskrit, as a kind of snobbery.[65] "Weil never felt any obligation to take into consideration other people who were not in his league," Zariski once complained, "and for the most part he saw students as interfering with his research time."

Although Zariski, too, has often been accused of arrogance (and perhaps, as one colleague put it, "All mathematicians are snobs"[66]) only Weil's arrogance, in the form of his notable wit, has become

---

[63] Mumford, personal interview, February 1990.

[64] Simone Petrément, *Simone Weil: A Life* (New York: Pantheon, 1976) 6.

[65] Zariski also failed to share Weil's interest in the history of mathematics: "I just don't like history of mathematics," he used to say. "I like to *do* mathematics."

[66] Andrew Gleason, personal interview, January 1989.

part of the legend. He had a striking talent for epigram and many of his sayings, like the following, are often quoted: "A good mathematician is one who has proved one theorem in his life; a great mathematician is one who has proved two." [67]

It seems clear that the liveliness of their mathematical relationship more than offset their differences in temperament and background. Near the end of his life Zariski would remember Weil's generosity and his capacity for affection more vividly than his combativeness. "He's not easy to deal with and sometimes I may have gotten angry, but contact with him was always stimulating. A good mathematician, a good mind, and a good man, he always recognizes value when he sees it, regardless of personal feelings."

The extent to which they "agreed to disagree" might be a measure of the intensity of their common interest in the foundations of algebraic geometry. As Zariski put it, "You might just say that we were friends who fought."

---

[67] Mumford, personal interview, July 1987.

11 ◨

A Land of
Intellectual Cannibals

1939–1944

Zariski's work in this fruitful period was recognized with a Guggenheim Fellowship for 1939–40 and an offer from Harvard for the 1940–41 academic year. His position as an intellectual leader of algebraic geometry also brought him invitations to serve as editor of the *American Journal of Mathematics* and associate editor of the *Annals of Mathematics*.

Planning to use the Guggenheim in England in the fall of 1939, he took a year's leave of absence from Hopkins and sublet his apartment in Baltimore. His plans were radically altered one sunny day in early September, however, when he was at the beach with Yole and the children and heard that the Nazis had invaded Poland. In a state of shock they rushed back to the city to find a new apartment for the fall and to begin the desperate wait for news of his family in Kobrin.

Looking back at this painful period, Yole would say, "The war changed him deeply . . . very, very deeply." His daughter would remember him riveted to the radio every morning. He wrote repeatedly to Kobrin, but there was no reply. He contacted his sister Rebecca in Warsaw, who wrote back to ask for help in getting her family out of Poland. He sent money and letters to her through various organizations, but everything always came back.

He decided to spend part of the spring at the California Institute of Technology, and in January he put his family on a train to Pasadena (so the children wouldn't miss the beginning of the second semester) and set off alone by car. He stopped at the Institute for Advanced Study, Harvard, and at the University of Chicago, where he was forced by a severe attack of lumbago to spend several weeks in a hospital.

His back would cause him severe pain, periodically, all his life, although in his usual fashion he would make a virtue of necessity. "Sometimes I have to drag myself to my desk," he once explained to a student, "but those are the times I have my best ideas."[68]

Two math students from Sweden offered to drive him to the West Coast and he reached his family in May. Three months later he left with them for Cambridge, starting up the foggy coast to Portland, then cutting across to Yellowstone National Park. The trip had been designed as something of a holiday, but sitting in the car day after day Yole and the children found themselves increasingly affected by his anxiety about the war. Following the invasion of Poland in September of 1939, the Nazis had continued their offensive with the conquest of Finland, Denmark, Norway, Holland, and Belgium. On June 10 Mussolini had declared war on Britain and France; three days later the Germans had marched into Paris; and that summer saw Britain standing alone against the Nazis. There was no more news from Poland.

"'What's happening?' is what we kept feeling," Yole remembered. "'Is the world coming to an end?'" Plagued by a sense of unreality, they crawled through the vast unfamiliar countryside, periodically pulling over to the side of the road and turning up the radio.

Harvard received Zariski and his family "with great kindness" in the fall of 1940. Zariski renewed his acquaintance with G. D. Birk-

---

[68] Shreeram Abhyankar also remembered that Zariski would refer to his uniformization paper [41] as "my lumbago paper" (CUNY Graduate Center Symposium, 5 May 1989).

hoff and met for the first and last time a number of senior members of the math department, including Edward V. Huntington, who was terminally ill; W. C. Graustein, who died suddenly that spring, and Julian Lowell Coolidge, who had recently retired.[69]

Mrs. Graustein found the Zariskis a house near their apartment, and Graustein insisted on driving them to concerts at Sanders Theater even though they had their own car. Those concerts were very formal affairs in the bitterly cold winter of 1941. Zariski wore a tuxedo and Yole a long dress, although in the large draughty Sanders Theater they never grew quite warm enough to remove their heavy coats.

The formality of the concerts still characterized most aspects of academic life during the war years. R. B. Boas recalled a well-known mathematician who was rebuked by his chairman for not shining his shoes, and divorce or any hint of "immorality" meant an automatic severing of tenure.[70] The faculty was more autocratic and the students more submissive: failed more often than they are now, they accepted it unprotestingly. Graduate students humbly understood that they would forfeit financial aid if they presumed to marry.

Lars Ahlfors, whose first appointment at Harvard was in the late thirties, described the frequent formal dinners, sometimes two or three times a week: "If the invitation didn't say 'informal' you had to go in tuxedos and long dresses and you were given only ice water to drink until the ladies left the table. They say that Coolidge dressed for dinner every night."[71] David Mumford, who joined the department in the early sixties, remembered a formal dinner at the

---

[69] Coolidge, like G. D. Birkhoff, admired Zariski's 1935 *Ergebnisse* monograph, although unlike Birkhoff, he didn't appreciate Zariski's concern for rigor. Harvard's only expert in algebraic geometry, Coolidge had graduated from Harvard *summa cum laude* in mathematics in 1895 and had gone on to study at Oxford and the University of Bonn. He had also studied in Italy with Corrado Segre a generation before Zariski's arrival in Rome; in 1931 he had published a book on algebraic plane curves dedicated to the Italians.

[70] In 1933, a few years before Zariski's arrival, the Harvard Math Department had been scandalized when Professor Osgood ran off with Professor Morse's wife. Coolidge, who was chairman at the time, immediately demanded the resignation of Osgood, who left for China. Morse moved to the Institute for Advanced Study.

[71] Ahlfors, personal interview, 5 August 1989.

Synnott describes Coolidge presiding over a Monday night "high table" during his tenure as first master of Lowell House, an undergraduate residence hall. Seated on a raised platform at one end of the dining hall, he enjoyed his meal in dinner clothes with tutors and selected students and guests (*The Half-Opened Door* 118).

Walshes that included cigars with the after-dinner brandy while the ladies waited in the next room.

Yole found the formality comforting because it reminded her of home:

> One of the things in America that upset me very much in the beginning was that I didn't know how I should dress. Once for a garden party at the Institute for Advanced Study, two other wives and I bought picture hats. When we got to the party, no one else was wearing a hat so we hurried home to change. But when we got back to the party we found that half the people were dressed formally and the other half not. It was very confusing!
>
> That way I found myself more comfortable with the way things were at Harvard. The Birkhoffs entertained on an almost international scale. Mrs. Birkhoff tried very hard to have different sorts of people — historians and so on — mixed in with the mathematicians. One evening I found myself sitting next to Bruning, the former Chancellor of Germany who'd been chased away by Hitler. Mrs. Graustein, too, entertained in this way. It was always dinner, and there was always someone serving at the table. Wine was never served, but after dinner the women left the table.
>
> I myself began to give those formal dinners, since the house we were renting on Shepard Street was very comfortable and hiring someone to serve was not expensive. My only problem was having to ring the bell on the floor under our table when we'd finished a course . . . because I'm so short, I had to work hard to find the bell.

Smiling as he listened to Yole's description of those early days in Cambridge, Zariski explained, "You see, the Harvard people have a certain feeling that if a man has been invited to Harvard, he must be treated nicely. Otherwise, it would reflect badly on THEM."

Harvard was also very selective in issuing its invitations. It had never invited Lefschetz to speak in the colloquium, for example, in spite of the strength of his work. While this might have been a judgment on *Topology* or on the difficulties of his character, Zariski thought it more likely that Harvard's attitude sprang from what he later referred to as "bad blood" between Lefschetz and G. D. Birkhoff.

In May of 1934 Birkhoff had written a strong letter to R. G. D. Richardson to discourage Lefschetz's candidacy for President of the American Mathematical Society:

I have a feeling that Lefschetz will be likely to be less pleasant even than he had been, in that from now on he will try to work strongly and positively for his own race. They are exceedingly confident of their own power and influence in the good old USA. . . . He will get very cocky, very racial and use the Annals as a good deal of racial perquisite. The racial interests will get deeper as Einstein's and all of them do.[72]

In spite of Birkhoff's opposition, however, Lefschetz became the first Jewish president of the AMS in 1934.

Birkhoff's strenuous efforts to preserve the mathematical establishment that he had tried so hard to build were dramatically presented in his address to the AMS in 1938, on the occasion of its celebration of its 50th anniversary. Articulating an anxiety that was by no means unique to him, he described "a sense of increased duty toward our own promising younger American mathematicians," and went on to warn his audience that eminent researchers from abroad were reducing the number of available positions for young Americans, with "the attendant probability that some of them will be forced to become 'hewers of wood and drawers of water.'" His address was rather coldly received, although many mathematicians saw his anxiety in the wider context of his concern for American mathematics.

The influx of European scholars had brought a new urgency to what was already an old debate. Anxiety about hiring foreign mathematicians, whether or not they were Jews, reflected not only the economics of the thirties, but also an ongoing concern with the survival of democracy in an increasingly pluralistic society. Efforts to limit free immigration had been initiated at the end of the nineteeth century, and the ethnic diversity that had been encouraged at Harvard by President Charles W. Eliot in the last half of the century was viewed with alarm by his successor, President A. Lawrence Lowell. Although Lowell's struggle with his faculty to institute formal quotas for entering undergraduates was unsuccessful, his policies resulted in a sizeable reduction of the proportion of Jewish students.[73]

---

[72] G. D. Birkhoff, letter to R. G. D.Richardson, 18 May 1934 (quoted by Reingold, *Century I*, 183).

[73] The percentage of Jewish students at Harvard dropped from 25–27% in the 1920s to

The debate over quotas, like the uneasy alliance of teaching and research, is still very much a part of academic life. Decisions of hiring committees and admissions officers continue to be influenced by things that have more to do with our changing definitions of the essential function of a university than with academic potential. Recent disputes over affirmative action and the recruitment of student athletes suggest that the relationship of a democratic society to its universities is as complex as any other marriage.

Zariski was, as he himself put it, "aware of Birkhoff's limitations." He later remembered a conversation he had had with Birkhoff over tea in the St. Clair's Restaurant during the winter of 1940–41:

> Birkhoff greeted me very warmly and I invited him to sit down and have a cup of tea with me. He spoke at length about a Spaniard, a student of his who could not find a position, and he said, "I think that's very bad because he deserves to be appointed and there aren't many Spanish math students in the U.S. and so we shouldn't be afraid of them. There will not be a rush of Spaniards to come over."
>
> With the Jews it was a different story, and Birkhoff was afraid that if you appointed one, there would be a second and third, and so on, and there probably would be. So that even though he was always kind to me, I knew that he had prejudice.

While Zariski's casual acceptance of what he called Birkhoff's "prejudice" appears a little strange from this side of the Holocaust, it also serves as a reminder of the depth of his allegiance to a world in which being Jewish was no more important than being Russian or American, and not nearly as important as being a good mathematician. He would also have understood the value of the patronage of a man who was, after all, not only a brilliant mathematician, but also a powerful force in American mathematics.[74]

10–16% in the 1930s. (See Synnott, *The Half-Opened Door.*) Harvard's concern over what Lowell termed "the Jewish problem" was unfortunately not unique. When MIT made trouble over the appointment of Norman Levinson to an assistant professorship, G. H. Hardy, who was visiting MIT that year, threatened to publish the news that MIT stood for the Massachusetts Institute of Theology (Peter Lax, "The Bomb, Sputnik, Computers, and European Mathematicians," *Bicentennial Tribute* 134).

[74] Along with his mathematical and administrative activities, Birkhoff had found time to

With the retirement of Coolidge and the death of Graustein, the general consensus of the Harvard Mathematics Department was that Zariski was the most suitable person to provide distinction in geometry. Although there were rumors to the contrary, Birkhoff seems to have been looking forward to the appointment. Before Zariski left for Johns Hopkins that summer, Birkhoff took him aside. "Oscar," he said, "you will probably be at Harvard in the next five years." [75]

"This is a land of intellectual cannibals," Zariski wrote to André Weil in the fall of 1941. Upon his return to Hopkins he had been upset to find that his salary had been frozen, his regular classes swollen by a number of restless new draftees, and, worst of all, that his course load had risen to eighteen hours a week. But his increasing fatigue, like his back pain, seemed to lead him more deeply into his work. Consumed by new ideas, he was at last forced to give up his usual habit of working at night. He began to do his own work in the mornings, leaving the fight to stay awake to his afternoon and evening classes. [76]

After teaching only two courses a term at Harvard, he found returning to the struggle for research time particularly disappointing. He wrote to Coble about a job at Illinois, but it was the middle of

---

supervise the theses of many of Harvard's most distinguished Ph.D.s and to encourage the work of many talented younger mathematicians. See, for example, Stan Ulam's account of Birkhoff in *Adventures of a Mathematician,* New York: Charles Scribner's Sons, 1976.

[75] G. D. Birkhoff did not live to see Zariski's permanent appointment. Because of the freeze on permanent hiring during the war, it was not until Marshall Stone left Harvard in 1946 that a senior position actually became available.

[76] The tensions, fears, and difficult physical conditions of the war also stimulated other mathematicians. Lars Ahlfors, for example, succeeded in his work on metamorphic curves, which he described as technically the hardest thing he ever did, while fearing for his life. David Mumford has suggested that "the isolated secure world of research and the mind offered these people a refuge from the uncertainties around them so that they could channel their emotions into furious intellectual effort when they had no other outlet." As Gian-Carlo Rota put it, "Of all escapes from reality, mathematics is the most successful ever" ("The Lost Cafe," *Los Alamos Science,* Special Issue 1987, 26).

the war and the department had no money for hiring. Although he was tempted by a tentative offer from the Institute for Advanced Study, he eventually discouraged it because of the importance to him of teaching graduate students.

He complained frequently to Lefschetz about the difficult conditions at Hopkins and was puzzled and hurt by Princeton's failure to make him an offer, especially since his research and reputation had by this time reached a level at which most universities would have been eager to offer him a position. "I would very much have liked to go to Princeton," Zariski confessed many years later, "although I never told this to Lefschetz in so many words. My God, I wasn't going to offer myself on a platter. I don't know what was in his mind. It would have been a natural move on his part."

There may well have been internal disputes within the Princeton department that blocked such an offer, because the warmth of Lefschetz's response to an inquiry about Zariski from the Harvard Math Department in April 1947 indicates that he, too, would have regarded it as "a natural move": "I cannot think of a better man to consider for any position anywhere, and if, as I hope, Harvard does annex him, they will do the wisest thing possible. I only regret that it has not been possible for us to do it. If you get him, I envy you a first-rate colleague and one who has been my friend for many years."[77]

Near the end of his life Zariski suggested that perhaps Lefschetz had regarded him as a competitor, offering as evidence Lefschetz's surprise at Harvard's offer of the visiting position for 1940–41. But Lefschetz's surprise might also have sprung from his own experience with anti-Semitism in the Ivy League, which had been administrative as well as personal. "In the late thirties and forties," according to Gian-Carlo Rota, "he [Lefschetz] refused to admit any Jewish graduate students in mathematics [to Princeton]. He claimed that, because of the Depression, it was too difficult to get them jobs after they earned their Ph.D.s."[78]

Zariski grew even moodier as the war continued. He still listened to the news every morning and watched for mail every afternoon,

---

[77] Harvard Math Department files.
[78] "Fine Hall," *Century* II, 235.

but he spoke less and less about the situation in Poland, and finally not at all. He became an air raid warden, and although he was never very fond of gardening, he and Vera planted a Victory Garden and enjoyed a fine crop of tomatoes. In 1943 his son Ray, who'd gone up to Harvard the year before on a National Merit Scholarship, was drafted into the infantry, and two years later he was sent to the front.

But in spite of his intense emotional involvement with the war, Zariski retained enough of his old detachment to distinguish between pro-Nazi and pro-German. Understanding the growing ambivalence of the large German population in Baltimore, he pointed out that Hermann Weyl was "pro-German" but that he had left Germany in protest in 1933 and married a Jew. He saw Charles Lindberg as an isolationist, as part of a reasonable American desire not to get mixed up in European quarrels.

After the Germans invaded Russia he began to subscribe to *The Daily Worker,* and in 1944 he joined the Russian-American Friendship Society. In 1944 he wrote to the Soviet Embassy in Washington, D.C., describing himself as "a friend of Soviet Russia." "To a large extent," he continued, "it's a question of being well-informed in order to be able to dispel information which breeds prejudice."

His devotion to mathematics during these difficult years did not go unrewarded. In 1942 he was elected to the National Academy of Sciences, and in 1944 he received the Cole Prize from the American Mathematical Society. He was invited to serve on the editorial board of the *Transactions* of the AMS and to lecture at an increasing number of conferences and symposia.

12 🔲 "A Superb Audience of

One . . . André Weil"

São Paulo 1945

In January 1945 Zariski left with Yole and Vera for an exchange professorship at the University of São Paulo with a suitcase full of rationed cigarettes, a going-away present from his students at Johns Hopkins. He later remembered that when the State Department had first approached him about going to Brazil, he had thought, "What would be the point in going to such a remote place?" But that when he had found out that André Weil would be joining the department in São Paulo at the same time, he had asked himself, "Why not?"

Weil, who had been invited by Dean Dreyfus of the Faculty of Sciences in São Paulo (whom he'd met through Claude Levi-Strauss), was also looking forward to closer contact with Zariski. In his introduction to *Foundations of Algebraic Geometry* he had written, "The attentive reader will also detect in many places the influence of O. Zariski's recent work; what he cannot easily imagine is how much benefit I have derived, during the whole period of preparation of this book, from personal contacts both with Zariski and with Chevalley, from their freely given advice and suggestions, and from access to their unpublished manuscripts."[79]

Weil was therefore all the more disappointed to find himself denied an exit visa by the State Department. Various people, including Zariski, wrote unsuccessfully on his behalf, but it was only the efforts of F. Aydelotte, who was then Director of the Institute for Advanced Study, that finally got him the visa.

Having suffered what he called his "imprisonment," Weil later told Zariski that it was "paradise" to escape from his American university position at a place he has described as "unmentionable," and where he, like Zariski at Hopkins, had had to fight for research time. He had, however, managed to finish his book, *Foundations of Algebraic Geometry,* which he mailed to the publisher from New Orleans before sailing to Rio with his family in December 1944.

As one of the few countries without a quota system, Brazil had been home to many Europeans — French, German and, especially, Italian — before the war. "I enjoyed myself tremendously," Yole would remember, "because São Paulo was practically founded by Italians. I could speak Portuguese fluently, and I found friends from the time I was a child in Ancona, both Jews and Catholics. It was a great feeling to see again all those people with whom I'd lost touch. I read a lot of Brazilian literature, and Eveline Weil, André's wife, was a good friend of mine."

For Zariski, too, there was a happy sense of reunion. The mathematics department at the University of São Paulo, like the city itself, had been deeply influenced by Italians. Although the newly declared state of war between Italy and Brazil had forced the departure of most Italian professors, the department asked Zariski to lecture in Italian, which he was pleased to do. He was also pleased to be teaching only one course. ("Three hours a week! It was like a vacation!") To complete his pleasure he found himself with "a superlative audience consisting of one person — André Weil — to whom I could speak about these ideas of mine during our frequent walks."

"We talked and we talked," Zariski remembered many years later. ("Oh, they talked and they talked," Yole agreed.) One of the things they talked about was the completion of a ring in an I-adic topology

---

[79] André Weil, *Foundations of Algebraic Geometry* (AMS, 1946) ix.

[in which the powers of the ideal define the topology], a notion that absorbed Zariski during this productive period.[80] While still in São Paulo he wrote and published a paper in which he presented a new concept of certain special rings and their completion (later named "Zariski rings") [49].

Perhaps his most original body of work, which was on the theory of holomorphic functions, had its beginning in this concept of rings [58]. Many years later he would describe the theory as "a natural outgrowth" of his previous work on the resolution of singularities, for it was that larger problem that had led him into such a deep consideration of local rings and their completion.[81]

Weil had Zariski in mind when, in the introduction to his foundations book, he described "makeshift constructions full of rings, ideals and valuations, in which some of us feel in danger of getting lost." Urging a return to the free use of geometric insights and geometric methods, he went on to explain that "the wish and aim" of algebraic geometers should be "to return at the earliest possible moment to the palaces which are ours by birthright."[82]

In support of his view of Zariski as a geometer for whom modern algebra could provide, at best, only a "temporary accommodation," Weil recalled a well-known anecdote about a conversation at a party between Zariski and Claude Chevalley, a French algebraist who had moved to Princeton from France just before the war. The two men were discussing algebra versus geometry in algebraic geometry when at long last, exasperated, Zariski exclaimed, "But when someone says 'an algebraic curve,' surely you see something!" "Yes, of course," Chevalley quietly replied. "I see this: $f(x,y) = 0$."[83]

---

[80] This was another of the concepts from commutative algebra in which Zariski found deep geometric meaning and which he used as a basic tool in his later research.

[81] While normally the term "holomorphic function" applies to certain kinds of complex valued functions that had been investigated for several years before Zariski's work, David Mumford has explained that "Zariski transposed these notions into algebraic geometry in a wholly original way and in doing so created a powerful new tool. Nowadays when algebraic geometers talk of holomorphic functions they are probably referring to Zariski's wholly algebraic version, which was extensively developed by Grothendieck and others."

[82] In the preface to his *Collected Papers* Zariski had similarly mourned "my personal loss of the geometric paradise" (I, xi).

[83] Chevalley had once before shocked Zariski by insisting that he'd arrived at a particular theorem by thinking of the word "ideal." "What?" Zariski exclaimed. "You mean to say that if you think of a word, then you create a theory?" "Yes," Chevalley nodded. "That's mathematics."

Although Zariski shared Weil's vision, he didn't feel that his use of algebraic methods was preventing him from claiming his "birthright." On the contrary, in the introduction to his first algebraic proof of resolution of singularities of an algebraic surface [39] he wrote:

> We should say that the requirement of rigor is to be regarded as trivially satisfied in the present proof. More significant, however, is the clarification of the problem brought about by the use of the methods of modern algebra. . . . What is gained concretely thereby is the center of gravity of the proof is shifted from minute details to underlying concepts.

"Of course," he explained many years later, "one cannot apply a method just formally without developing a sort of sixth sense, which is what you call intuition. I mean, if you want to apply an algebraic method, how do you start? You must have in mind something. Before you have the method, the finished product, you must have a good guess that this algebraic procedure will have to be used. You may be wrong, but if you are right, it means you have developed an algebraic solution."

Heisuke Hironaka, a student of Zariski who proved the existence of a resolution of singularities in all dimensions, explains the way in which Zariski's approach made it possible to "just come to the essence":

> You can see planes and curves and surfaces, and if you just make an analogy or depend on intuition and make a guess in higher dimensions and then use all the tools, topology or anything, you make mistakes, sometimes terrible mistakes. Or you can't really get into things in an essential way, you can't see the essential difficulty. This is what the Italian School did.
>
> But Oscar tried to forget unnecessary things, eliminate unnecessary things, just come to the essence. If you make the problem algebraic, if you formulate it in algebraic terms, then the rest is just purely algebraic reasoning. It's more rigorous and also you get more intuition, which you can call algebraic intuition.
>
> But you don't get algebraic intuition from the geometric intuition. For instance, even if you can see a polynomial of degree 100, then what about degree 101? Now, this intuition is not in the geometry,

you can't visualize it in space, and so for me it was very useful that Oscar discovered these algebraic intuitions.[84]

Zariski's stay in Brazil was clouded by two pieces of news. He and Yole received word that Ray had been wounded at the front, and only after several weeks of anxiety did they get a letter from Italy with the welcome news of his recovery. "My sister opened the door," Yole remembered, "and there was this boy they hadn't seen since he was ten or twelve. It was a very happy reunion."

A few months later a letter arrived from Palestine ending his long and painful suspense about the fate of his family. From the fragmented accounts of survivors, Shepsel and Zila had managed to piece together enough details to confirm the deaths of Hannah and Moses. Hannah, driven from the old stone house in the square, had died of cold and malnutrition. Moses had been shot jumping from a moving deportation train. One of Zariski's older sisters had been glimpsed in a concentration camp. He learned that of the almost 11,000 Jews in Kobrin, fewer than ten had survived.

After receiving the letter from Palestine Zariski left the house without a word to Yole or Vera, and when he returned several hours later they could see that he'd been crying. "I tried for many years to talk to him," Yole remembered, "but he couldn't stand it and wouldn't speak. When he was very old he began to have nightmares about the deaths of Hannah and Moses, and only then could he bear to mention it."

"Maybe it was just as well I wasn't able to get a closer knowledge of what actually happened," he said many years later. "I just tried, at that time and also afterwards, never to think about it. It happened. They were there and they are not there. That's all."

The effects of the ending of the war were just beginning to be felt by universities. There were more students and more money, and the hiring of new faculty, which had been virtually at a standstill, began

---

[84] Hironaka is being quoted from a 1981 conversation with Zariski and Ann Kostant.

in earnest. In the summer of 1945 Zariski received an offer of a research professorship from the University of Illinois at Urbana. Pleased by the prospect of a lower teaching load and a higher salary, and looking forward to closer contact with his friend Coble, who had become chairman of the mathematics department at Illinois, he wrote to President Bowman at Johns Hopkins offering to return only if they could arrange a more comfortable teaching load for him.

When he received a letter refusing his offer, he resigned. Having found passage for Yole and Vera on a boat to New York, he flew to Lima, Peru, to deliver a series of invited lectures. After brief stops in New York and Baltimore he rejoined his family in Urbana in February 1946.

A year later, in March 1947, the California Institute of Technology in Pasadena made him an offer that he found attractive enough to consider, even though he didn't feel very happy about leaving Coble, who had so recently rescued him from the onerous teaching load at Hopkins. In a state of indecision he flew to Princeton to talk the matter over with Chevalley and Lefschetz before the April meeting of the AMS in New York. They were both enthusiastic about CalTech, and their praise of the graduate students convinced him to accept the offer.

The night before the AMS meeting, on his way home from dinner with Lefschetz, he passed an open post office and said to himself, "Well, I'm going to send that wire now." "Accepted," he wrote to CalTech, and he wired Yole that they were moving to California.

The next morning at the meeting George Mackey, then an assistant professor at Harvard, walked up to him and said, "I have a message for you from Harvard. My colleagues have authorized me to tell you that the department has voted to recommend that you be offered a full professorship." It was the offer he had been waiting for since 1941, but an hour too late! Mackey retained a vivid memory of that meeting, "and the expression on Oscar's face when he heard the news."[85]

Zariski rushed a wire to Yole: *"Che vita dura!"* ("What a hard life!") She received it over the phone as "Cevitador," and for a

---

[85] "Oscar Zariski," *Harvard University Gazette,* 6 May 1988.

moment she wondered why he was wiring her about a foreign mathematician.

Having thought the matter over, he decided that it might be possible to go to CalTech for one year and still accept the Harvard offer. He spoke to President Conant and members of the math department at Harvard and wrote to President DuBridge at Cal-Tech, describing the Harvard offer and his decision to honor his commitment to CalTech for one year only.[86] Conant and DuBridge also talked the matter over privately at a meeting of the National Academy of Sciences, and eventually Zariski received a letter releasing him from his commitment to CalTech.

Leaving Urbana was not hard for Zariski, except for saying goodbye to Coble, but for Yole it was a different matter:

> I had made several new friends and loved the flavor and texture of midwestern life, so often misunderstood by Europeans, Easterners, and Californians alike; I was also extremely fond of the beautiful house we'd bought with some financial hardship. It had been built of stucco on concrete by Professor Vanderpool from whom we'd acquired it, and it was perfect, from the beautiful stately rooms to the poetic small garden covered with violets and ivy.
>
> However, I was also fascinated by the prospect of going to Harvard, of meeting new and interesting people, and of exploring another part of the country I had come to love.

That summer Zariski was honored with an invitation from the AMS to deliver the Colloquium Lectures at Yale.

---

[86] Elizabeth Walsh remembered her husband returning from the department unexpectedly one morning with "a man he introduced to me as Professor Zariski. He explained that the Professor had just come to Cambridge to visit, and to make a decision about his offer from Harvard. . . . Before he left I was told he would be accepting the position at Harvard" (letter to the author, 8 March 1990).

13 ▨

NORMAL POINTS

OF A VARIETY

CAMBRIDGE 1947

Zariski remained at Harvard until the end of his life, profoundly influencing algebraic geometry through his training of graduate students as well as through his research. His arrival in Cambridge in July 1947 marked the end of his peregrinations and, as he put it, "the quieting, at least partially, of my nomadic instincts." At Harvard his dream of attracting young people of talent "to continue the work of the Italian School, even though with other methods" would be eminently realized. While Princeton became an international center of topology, founded by Lefschetz, Alexander, and Veblen ("three shining stars," as Zariski put it), Zariski's presence would help make Harvard into the world center of algebraic geometry that Rome had once been.[87]

He found a very different department from the one he'd visited during the war. Coolidge, Graustein, Huntington and G. D. Birkhoff

---

[87] Lefschetz left Princeton for Brown when his interests shifted from topology to dynamical systems, but Princeton's strength in topology was maintained through many decades by Steenrod, Moore, Thurston, Browder, Hsiang, and others.

had died, and Marshall Stone and Saunders Mac Lane had moved to the University of Chicago (where Weil would soon join them). Garrett Birkhoff, Lynn Loomis, George Mackey, John H. van Vleck, Joseph Walsh, Hassler Whitney, and David Widder, who was now chairman, were still there, along with Lars Ahlfors, who'd recently returned from Finland. At forty-eight, Zariski was only four years younger than the oldest member of the department.

The youth of the faculty and a welter of bright new graduate students seems to have inspired the department to minimize rather than dramatize social differences. Long dresses and tuxedos appeared less often at formal dinner parties; "Mr." occasionally replaced "Professor"; and Zariski, who had never called André Weil "André," was surprised by a Harvard custom that put him on a first-name basis with other full department members, some of whom he was meeting for the first time.[88] He was the first Jewish mathematician to be granted tenure by the Harvard Mathematics Department.[89]

The anti-Semitism that had been taken for granted before the war had become intolerable. According to Zariski, at the First International Congress in Cambridge in 1950 Severi (who had been sent with Segre as an official delegate from the Accademia Nazionale dei Lincei) was treated with polite indifference by other mathematicians because of his cooperation with the Fascists.[90] After the Congress he complained bitterly to Zariski, who was amused to find himself in the role of his comforter.

The condescension toward Severi was also a rejection of the known lack of rigor in much of his work, according to Maxwell Rosenlicht, who was at that time studying with Zariski. As a result of the work of Zariski and Weil, algebraic geometers, like poets and

---

[88] Peter Lax tells an amusing anecdote about two newly arrived mathematicians who are uncomfortable with the American first name convention: "In public you must call me Stefan and I will call you Hilde; but of course, when we are among ourselves you will continue calling me Herr Professor and I will call you Frau Professor Doktor" (*Bicentennial Tribute* 133).

[89] In the late 1910s a Jewish geometer named Gabriel Marcus Green had been hired with the expectation that he would be given tenure, but he died before receiving it.

[90] Some time before the Congress Severi had written to André Weil and probably others to defend himself against charges of anti-Semitism. Weil had replied, "I know you to be far too intelligent to have ever believed that anti-Semitic nonsense" (letter to the author, 1 February 1990).

topologists, had begun to pursue "rigor" with the same passion with which they had once embraced "intuition."

Secure in his achievement and on home ground, Zariski seems to have been in unusually high spirits during the Congress. As the first speaker in a session chaired by Hadamard he delivered a grand overview of algebraic geometry [60]. A friend described him dashing out of a waiting car into his newly bought Lancaster Street house to change into a clean shirt for a cocktail party at President Conant's house: "'This is a real Italian!' I thought to myself."[91]

Exhausted by his monumental work on the reduction of singularities, Zariski was happy to turn to problems with a more local frame of reference and spent his first few years in Cambridge continuing his exploration of the analytic properties of normal points of a variety. In "Analytical irreducibility of normal varieties" [52], he introduced a concept of normal varieties in which the local ring of every point is integrally closed. (The Italian geometers, who called a variety "normal" if the system of its hyperplane sections was complete, accused him of misusing their term, but he insisted that *their* use of the word was unfortunate.)

Using results that he had presented in a brief survey of the theory of holomorphic functions [55], in the more elaborate overview that he had prepared for the 1950 Congress [60], and in his famous memoir on holomorphic functions [58], he applied a theorem on the invariance of the ring of holomorphic functions under rational transformations to a "principle of degeneration," thereby extending his Main Theorem [45] to a very general connectedness theorem. His results — for example, that a normal variety is locally everywhere analytically normal — helped to create one of the indispensable tools of modern algebraic geometers [53, 59, 66].

In his first year at Harvard Zariski brought a new emphasis to the traditional two-semester projective geometry course, Introduction

---

[91] Erna Alfors, personal interview, August 1989.

to Higher Geometry, and created two advanced courses: Ideal Theory and Algebraic Varieties, and Algebraic Surfaces, which he conducted like a seminar, inviting his students to use the new algebraic tools. Like other members of the department, he also offered a year-long reading course in his special field to direct the research of his graduate students.

In the next two years he brought other new material, designed to train students in the new methods, into basic courses. "Harvard is unusual in the extent to which standard courses are public property. They might rotate among several members of the department from year to year, and no one objects if a specialist in a totally different area of mathematics takes such a course one year in order to extend his own knowledge." [92]

In 1948 he offered Algebraic Curves and a class on Abelian Integrals, and the following year he taught Introduction to Algebraic Geometry and the course in Modern Higher Algebra that had been introduced into the department by Garrett Birkhoff and Saunders Mac Lane in the late thirties. Except for very occasional excursions, the courses he developed in his first three years at Harvard would be his courses for the next twenty-two years.

The appointment in 1953 of Richard Brauer, who had been at the Institute for Advanced Study with Zariski in 1934–35, completed the introduction of modern ideas in algebra and geometry to Harvard and brought a touch of Europe to those hallowed American halls. Brauer's interest in noncommutative algebra complemented Zariski's interest in commutative algebra; seminars augmented colloquia; and when more and better students were drawn to mathematics during the anxious political climate of the fifties, the traditional undergraduate mathematics curriculum began to give way to the broader mathematical education that Coble and Zariski had envisioned in 1927.

Of course, not everyone was pleased by the changes. While some colleagues felt that Zariski's work was recondite, others feared that it would turn out to be more flashy than profound; although some thought it was too difficult for students, others were alarmed by its

---

[92] Mumford, personal interview, February 1990.

attractiveness and felt that he was seducing students into algebraic geometry.

The power of Zariski's mathematical vision was matched by the force of his personality in the classroom. He immediately attracted a number of graduate students, although only two students from this first group finished their degrees with him—Daniel Gorenstein, who eventually settled at Rutgers, and Maxwell Rosenlicht, who joined the University of California at Berkeley.

Preserving what was most valuable in the two familiar extremes of teaching styles—the well-prepared but boring and the poorly prepared but exciting—Zariski's lectures seemed to combine Castelnuovo's perfection of form with the lively openness of Enriques or G. D. Birkhoff, whose lectures often bewildered even his best students.[93] When Rosenlicht was asked by a professor at Columbia if he would study with Zariski when he went to Harvard, he wondered why he should. "If you go to a place where a great man is doing ballet," he was told, "you do ballet." Skeptical at first, he soon found his interest in algebra transformed into a passion for algebraic geometry because "Zariski made it seem abstruse and fascinating."[94] "He was so creative," Gorenstein remembered. "There was a giant working on the earth."[95]

Many students have confessed to feeling too frightened in his presence to think clearly, and by most accounts he was often intimidating. Yole used to wait with a handkerchief at the foot of the stairs for a young woman from Toronto who cried during her tutorials in Zariski's study. A colleague who was forced to overhear Zariski's students through the thin wall that separated their department offices thought that he must have been "a tough person to work with."[96]

Zariski himself liked to tell the story of his assigned visit to the class of a teaching assistant named Saul Kravetz. Ten minutes late, he was quietly slipping into his seat when Kravetz stopped his lecture and turned to him: "You're late, Prof. Zariski." Zariski stared

[93] Stone, personal interview, November 1988.

[94] Maxwell Rosenlicht, personal interview, October 1989.

[95] CUNY Graduate Center Symposium, 5 May 1989.

[96] Lynn Loomis, personal interview, January 1989.

back over the heads of the students: "I don't think I missed much, Mr. Kravetz."

Forceful and quick-witted, he often startled students even when he intended to be comforting. To an ambitious teaching assistant from India who was teaching freshman calculus as if it were a course in analysis, he said, "You must always remember that the Anglo-Saxon race is incapable of understanding anything abstract." When the student asked for his advice about whether to major in math or physics, he said, "Choose math. It's more useless."[97]

Rosenlicht remembered hearing students complain about Zariski's projective geometry class, which had been expanded to answer complaints made by Rosenlicht and Gorenstein that there was no place where they could learn all the interesting examples of the Italian School. Describing Zariski's high standards, he emphasized Zariski's openness — his evolving tastes and his willingness to re-evaluate his own work: "Gorenstein and I were thrilled by Zariski's paper on the concept of a simple point [50], but all three of us discovered later that it wasn't all that great."[98]

"It wasn't easy to be Zariski's student," Gorenstein remembered. "He didn't like fools. When I'd go to see him with questions he would ask his questions first and then go on talking for an hour. It was pretty demoralizing, but he was so intense about mathematics that he couldn't back off. Because he had such high standards I always felt afterwards, 'Why should I bother writing up *my* ideas?' Many years later he suggested that he'd held me back, but what he'd really done was give me high standards of what math really is."[99]

There is no doubt that Zariski held himself to the same high standards. One of his last students described his "stage fright" as he waited to begin a lecture: "He said, 'Oh God! I've been teaching for, let's see, over fifty years now, if you include my assistantship in Italy. You'd think I could do it in my sleep.'"[100]

Perhaps because he himself had had to work hard to claim the attention of his older brother and his Russian and Italian teachers, he was often impatient with the personal needs of those who were

---

[97] Rohit Parikh, personal interview, December 1988.
[98] Rosenlicht, personal interview, November 1989.
[99] CUNY Symposium, 5 May 1989.
[100] Kleiman, letter to the author, 4 February 1990.

more dependent or less confident than he had been. But the striking achievements of those students who were trained by him are dramatic testimony to the success of his methods. Rosenlicht, a Guggenheim Fellow and winner of the Cole Prize in algebra, has continued to do important research in algebraic geometry. Gorenstein, who was elected to the National Academy of Sciences and the American Academy of Arts and Sciences in 1987, left algebraic geometry in the late fifties for what he called "the more self-contained subject" of finite group theory, where he has made extensive contributions to the classification of the finite simple groups.

During his years at Harvard, Zariski attracted not only graduate students but also a number of established mathematicians who were eager to learn the new methods. Wei-Liang Chow, who'd taken his degree in 1933 in Leipzig with van der Waerden and had spent some time at Princeton with Emil Artin, met with Zariski often during the late forties and early fifties, at Harvard and at Hopkins, where Zariski and van der Waerden had recommended him for the chairmanship of the math department.[101]

In September 1952, Zariski received a note expressing interest in his work from a young mathematician in Kyoto who had already published several papers, Jun-ichi Igusa. Their correspondence over the next few months (which Igusa, who didn't know English, managed through an intermediary) proved of interest to both of them. In November Igusa wrote: "I believe one can solve any problem when one decides firmly to solve and work persistently. I hope that I could get a conviction for the method in future developments of algebraic geometry under your direct leading and suggestions."

Zariski replied immediately with an invitation to Harvard, and Igusa arrived in Cambridge in the fall of 1953. Two years later he accepted a position at Johns Hopkins, where he later became the J. J. Sylvester Professor of Mathematics. An eclectic mathematician, Igusa has made substantial contributions not only to algebraic geometry, but also to number theory and several complex variables.

The ease with which Zariski was able to issue invitations and extend support to those who were interested in working with him

---

[101] "Chow had agreed, with the proviso that he not have to come to the department before 3pm" (Abhyankar, letter to the author, 5 February 1990).

Zariski in front of the Harvard Math Department at 2 Divinity Avenue (courtesy of Jun-ichi Igusa)

arose, in part, from the financing of his work by the Department of Defense.[102] All the branches of the armed forces supported pure mathematics after the war until the passage of the Mansfield Amendment in 1969. Although it was in effect for only a year, its stipulation that D.O.D. money should go only to project-oriented research permanently altered government funding patterns, and since then, pure mathematicians have come increasingly to rely on the National Science Foundation's formula of two months' summer salary and a travel allowance.

---

[102] In his recommendation of Igusa's application for a permanent visa, Zariski wrote, "I have invited him, in 1953, to come to Harvard University and join me as chief collaborator on a research project monitored by the Office of Ordnance Research, U.S. Army."

14 ◨

THE PURE
PLEASURE OF IT

In his domestic habits as well as in his relationship to his students, Zariski revealed his affinity not only with European culture, but also with the traditions of the nineteenth century that had shaped the minds of his Italian teachers. He rented half of a comfortable old duplex on Avon Street for three years, and in 1950, when Ray was already twenty-three and finishing his doctorate in political science and Vera was eighteen and about to begin her first year at Radcliffe, he and Yole bought a house at 27 Lancaster Street in Cambridge.

With its big front porch and mahagony-panelled dining room and, especially, its octagonal study lined with bookshelves on the second floor, the elegant Victorian house would have pleased Enriques or Castelnuovo. Zariski immediately moved his huge oak desk up against the front windows of the study, where twenty-five years of pacing have left their mark upon the floor.

He took lunch and afternoon tea in the wainscotted kitchen every day, and worked in his study until very late at night with only cigarettes for company. Someone gave him a mathematical type-

Zariski with Yole (courtesy of Jun-ichi Igusa)

writer in the sixties and he learned to use it even for rough drafts, but when it broke he happily returned to legal pads. In the late fifties he grew interested in photography and bought a camera in Japan; he especially liked to take slides and to show them on his new projector. Never very fond of gardening, he nevertheless made a visit every fall to the house of his younger colleague Lynn Loomis to bag leaves for mulch for his small backyard. He initiated a weekly game of chess with Loomis and played hard, almost ruthlessly, to win — and usually did.[103] In 1957 he introduced Loomis to the game of GO, which he played with equal intensity.[104]

He bought a bicycle to ride to his office at 2 Divinity Avenue and around the reservoir; he also bought himself a beret and a leather jacket and a cream-colored Mercedes with a red interior. He liked to

---

[103] One of Zariski's students remembered a sailing trip on which Zariski was too preoccupied with a chess problem to talk about mathematics (Kleiman, letter to the author, 4 February 1990).

[104] Lynn Loomis, personal interview, 20 January 1989.

Zariski with Vera (courtesy of Yole Zariski)

have students with him after class when he wheeled his bike home or
stopped at the garage to pick up his car or went on other errands —
"so he could go on talking mathematics, like breathing, for the pure
pleasure of it." [105]

He followed the custom of regular summer holidays at the seashore, from which he would emerge in late September with a host of
new ideas. In love with the sea, which he'd seen for the first time in
Italy, he and Yole rented the same cottage every August for ten years
in Madacket, in what was then a wild area on the western side of
Nantucket. Spartan, sparsely furnished, and surrounded by rag-
weed, the old cottage was relinquished with regret when Yole developed allergies. Zariski found them a replacement with a beautiful
view of the harbor in Monomoy, which they returned to for twelve
summers.

He spent his first summer on Nantucket in a rowboat, as if he were
back on the River Bug. The next summer he rented a sailboat from

---

[105] Kleiman, personal interview, November 1989.

Zariski sailing on Nantucket (by Frank DeCola, courtesy of Vera DeCola)

his landlord, who gave him lessons, and in the early fifties he bought himself a little sailboat named "Catpat," which Yole often helped him crew. By all accounts his sailing, like his driving (and unlike his biking), was not very graceful, but was managed with his characteristic aplomb. Exuberant but controlled, he would glance furtively at his nervous passengers with the smile of someone who is rather pleased with himself. Many of his mathematics department colleagues remember "the fine stately feeling that Oscar expressed in his bicycle riding" and "his wonderful smile,"[106] perhaps the same smile that would inspire Lynn Loomis to call him "that chess pirate."

Yole gave up teaching elementary Italian to "mostly ungifted" students and stayed at home like other faculty wives. "The notion of a working wife was unheard of when I first came, or even of her having interests of her own," according to Lynn Loomis, who had joined Harvard as a graduate student in 1937. "Even the marriages of the younger members like Garrett Birkhoff were under the sway of the Old Regime."[107] Erika Mumford remembered being taken aside by her husband's mother at their engagement party in the late fifties and reminded that she was assuming the grave responsibility of "nurturing his talent."

As Ivan Niven reminds us, ". . . the prevalent lifestyle in America fifty years ago was based on an unwritten but commonly understood contract between husband and wife that it was his responsibility to work outside the home to support the family financially, and her responsibility to manage the household. [This] meant doing everything possible to free the husband for his work, in a very full sense."[108]

Vera Widder, who took her doctorate in mathematics at Bryn Mawr and studied with Emmy Noether, remembered G. D. Birkhoff leaning across the dinner table shortly after her marriage to David Widder in 1939: "I hope you're not planning to continue teaching mathematics," he said authoritatively, peering over his glasses at his wife, Marjorie. "One career in a family is enough."[109]

---

[106] Barry Mazur, personal interview, 20 January 1989.
[107] Loomis, personal interview, 20 January 1989.
[108] *Century* I, 217.
[109] Vera Widder, personal interview, 21 January, 1989.

Zariski on the Harvard campus with, from left to right, his daughter-in-law, Birdine Zariski, Yoshio Igusa, and Vera (courtesy of Yole Zariski)

When Karin Tate, the daughter of Emil Artin, came to Harvard with her husband, John Tate, in 1956, she was welcomed by a close-knit community of faculty wives. Ilse Brauer taught her where to find the best bargains in Boston, and Elizabeth Walsh, a soft-spoken Southern woman who had been a lieutenant colonel in the W.A.C., introduced her to the Faculty Wives Tea, where women met without their husbands and ate watercress sandwiches. Apparently still intent upon their role as the upholders of convention, many wives regarded Karin's choice to write "Karin Tate" rather than "Mrs. John Tate" across her name tag as "provocative."

The youngest faculty wife by almost twenty years, Karin also saw the end of a long-held convention at the weekly colloquia teas at the math department. When Zariski became chairman in 1958 Yole was expected to find one department member's wife to bake cookies and another to pour tea for the men every Thursday afternoon.[110] She asked Karin Tate to take charge of recruiting tea pourers and

---

[110] The Harvard Mathematics Department has never had a tenured woman on its faculty.

Karin, who had always felt rather superfluous at the tea table, simply let the convention lapse. The first few weeks without a wife the men asked the department secretary to pour. "But little by little," Karin remembered, "they learned to pour for themselves."[111]

The frequent social gatherings—the dinners, evening parties, and afternoon teas—dependent as they were on the labor of women, helped to make a community out of a few eccentric and talented men. Most wives, like Yole, made their husband's travel arrangements, packed their bags, and kept the children quiet. Their days were broken into pieces preparing lunch and dinner, and at night they fell asleep alone while their husbands sat up working. Like Yole, they didn't use their talents or their training to pursue careers. Vera Widder taught mathematics without tenure at Tufts, and Ilse Brauer, who had been educated as a physicist in Germany, lectured in mathematics without tenure at Boston University.

However, while the men depended on their wives, their wives depended on the labor of other women. As household help became increasingly expensive and less available after the war, the time for pouring tea and planning parties began to be regarded as a luxury. By the early seventies, political choices had combined with economic changes to make working outside the house seem more attractive.

The turning-away of women from traditional domesticity has altered the character of the Harvard Math Department, and senior members look back fondly on a past in which their relationships with their colleagues were warmer and more intimate. "The respect, warmth, and affection that existed among the families of the senior members of the department in the forties, fifties and early sixties created a golden era. Professor Zariski contributed enormously to that era."[112]

After finishing his doctorate in political science in 1952, Ray lived at home while he looked for a job, partly for convenience but partly because he felt that moving out might hurt his father's feelings: "He liked everybody to be together. He had got that big house on Lan-

---

[111] Karin Tate, personal interview, 4 May 1989.
[112] Elizabeth Walsh, letter to the author, 8 March 1990.

caster Street with the idea that everyone would live there." When
Ray finally found a position and got married and moved out, however, Zariski surprised him by being pleased. Zariski was especially
pleased, as he explained many years later, that his son had chosen an
academic life rather like his own.

"I think my father would also have been glad if I'd tried math
seriously in college," Ray remembered. "He used to give me math
problems to solve for fun when I was small, and sometimes he would
say that it would be nice if I went into math. Other times, though, he
would tell me that it often didn't turn out well for fathers and sons."
Zariski would remind him of a visit that Garrett Birkhoff had made
to them in Baltimore shortly after a friend of his, the son of a
prize-winning chemist, had committed suicide. "Garrett told us that
his friend just couldn't stand the pressure."

Of course, mathematicians suffer from the same ambivalence
about their sons' careers that other parents do. Yole remembered a
visit that Emil Artin made to them in Cambridge in 1947. A student
of Emmy Noether in Göttingen and soon to be "the idol of Princeton
mathematicians," Artin, like Zariski, was known for his toughness
as well as his generosity as a teacher.[113] Having praised Yole's spa-
ghetti and her Italian "double n," he went on to talk at length about
how "very glad" he was that his son Michael was not going to be a
mathematician. When Zariski saw him the following year at a meeting in Paris, however, Artin kept repeating how "very glad" he was
that Michael had decided to be a mathematician.[114]

Ray felt that he had escaped the pressure of having a famous
father because he hadn't known he had one. Never remote and
rarely too busy to appear at the kitchen table for lunch, Zariski's
presence carried with it none of the glamor his young son might have
associated with "fame." Sometimes he would be in a bad mood and
Yole would explain to Ray that his father had hit a "snag," but
usually he was as busy in his study as Hannah had been in the store.

Ray was taken aback the day his thesis advisor exclaimed, "Zariski! He's your father and you never told anyone!" He was even more
surprised when, many years later, after he had become a professor of

---

[113] Rota, "Fine Hall," *Century* II, 230–233.
[114] Michael Artin became Norbert Wiener Professor of Mathematics at MIT in 1988.

political science at the University of Nebraska, he heard his father described as one of the century's great mathematicians.

"Perhaps it was because he was interested in the problems themselves rather than in fellowships or lecture invitations," Ray suggested. "He might try to explain the importance of something he was working on, but the significance of it would be lost on us."

During his years at Harvard, Zariski's political loyalties shifted gradually but steadily to the right, beginning with his relationship to the new state of Israel. In 1917 he had written an article against the Balfour Declaration for the official paper of the Soviet executive committee in Chernigov in which he had called on all Jews to fight against British imperialism. And even in 1948, when Yole told him of the official founding of Israel he had received the news with indifference.

It was only on his first visit to Israel in 1953, on his way home from a semester in Italy on a Fulbright, that he became aware that he was in a country which, as he put it many years later, "gathered in suffering Jews." He was particularly struck by the realization that

Zariski and Yole visiting Lucca during a semester at the University of Pisa on a Fulbright, 1953 (courtesy of Yole Zariski)

the last remnants of his family — his sister and his nephew and their families — depended for their lives on the safety of Israel.

His acute awareness of their vulnerability followed closely upon his own nearness to death that spring in Rome. Yole's father had died suddenly, and when the family reached the cemetery they found that no one knew the Prayer for the Dead. "I asked Oscar if he could say it," Yole recalled, "and I remember him walking beside my father's casket and reciting it. I remember looking back and seeing his face strangely pale and emaciated and realizing how terrible it must be for him. Maybe he was thinking, 'Here's this man who died in his bed, while my mother. . . .' That terrible image has always remained with me."

The next morning the stomach-ache he had had for weeks suddenly worsened, and by the time they reached the hospital his duodenal ulcer had ruptured. Doctors were forced to remove two-thirds of his stomach and he lay near death for several days. In the middle of one of the most critical nights the telephone rang, waking Zariski, who'd just fallen into a half-sleep. "Who is it?" Yole whispered into the receiver, although she'd immediately recognized the familiar demanding tones. "This is Severi! I just heard that Oscar had a serious operation and why wasn't I notified?"

Emotionally as well as physically exhausted by the ordeal, Zariski cancelled his remaining lectures at the University of Rome and left with Yole for Forte dei Marmi, the town on the sea where they had spent so many happy days during the first years of their marriage. A few weeks later they went on to Israel. Still too weak to work on mathematics, he found himself for the first time with no defense against his losses. Upset by the death of Yole's father and the seriousness of his own illness, he grew more depressed than he had ever been before. He mourned, after so many years, the deaths of Hannah and Moses.

He returned to Israel in 1958 to see his sister Zila, his brother Shepsel, and several nephews, and to lecture at the University of Jerusalem. It was not, however, until a visit on the eve of the 1967 war that he became, as he put it, "a real nationalist." The American consul was urging all Americans to leave Israel and his relatives were begging him to go. When with great anxiety and a heart heavy with foreboding he left at last, he felt "the surge of a sentiment which became stronger and stronger with time."

Yole described his response to Israel as "a very deep ethnic, rather than religious, reaction" to the persecution and killing of his family. "He felt his own survival at stake. He was a man of very delicate feelings, and the pain was always there."

Khrushchev's revelations at the Twentieth Congress in 1956 also affected his views, forcing him to understand, as he put it many years later, that "what Stalin had done had had nothing to do with the victory of communism." The revelations were all the more painful to him because, from his stepbrother's divulgences in 1935 through the Hungarian Uprising, he had believed so wholeheartedly in the rightness of the socialist ideals. "I justified Stalin because I saw him as a man who was forced to fight the whole bourgeois world. . . . I did not understand then that you cannot fight it after all."

The weakening of his youthful loyalty to the Soviet Union and the intensification of his ties to Israel gradually altered the way he saw himself and the world. "When I came to America and for many many years afterwards," he remembered, "I was a Marxist. I considered myself more Russian than Jewish; I was proud of my ability to write in Russian." For the first time since the revolution almost forty years before, he found himself identifying with the Jewish rather than the socialist cause.

His new identity was reflected in a new conservatism in his views on American foreign policy. "[In the Korean War] he was still sympathizing with the Koreans and the Chinese," according to his son, "but by the late fifties he was already pro-French and very anti-Arab in everything, whether it was the Middle East or North Africa." Ray remembered their heated arguments about the Algerian War: "He could already see which way the Algerians were going to go, but I thought they were just a bunch of freedom-loving freedom fighters." "While he would never quarrel about mathematics," Ray explained that "in politics he was sometimes governed more by his emotions, and this thing of the Jews was all wrapped up with everything."

His concern for Israel, however, had very little to do with religion. The young student who had made a quick bar mitzvah between classes to pacify his mother had grown into a man who regarded religious orthodoxy with the same disdain with which he viewed psychoanalysis: both seemed to him irrational dependencies. "He was never interested himself," Vera said, "and couldn't understand why anyone would be interested, much less observant." In the late seventies a rabbi at Beth Israel Hospital wrote him a note inviting him to come and talk. After Yole read it to him he pointed to the wastebasket. "Throw it there," he said.

His new conservatism also didn't obscure his appreciation of the Soviet point of view:

> In every Russian there is still a residue of anti-Semitism, just like there is all over the world. But for the communists it's not just blind anti-Semitism, but a view based on what is actually happening as part of the Cold War. They see that Jews all over the world, even many Russian Jews, are allied with what they call the imperialists, both in the United States and in the Middle East. . . . Often a Jew who gets permission to leave Russia on the basis of an invitation from Israel comes instead to America. . . . For every ten Jews in Israel, one goes away.

His new conservatism also never convinced the F.B.I., which refused him clearance in 1953 when Stan Ulam invited him to join the project at Los Alamos, citing, among other things, their observation that at the University of Illinois he had associated with well-known radicals. "I told them," Zariski said, amused to remember the conversation, "'Yes, I even played chess with one of them. I must say, he was a poor chess player, but after all, he was still my colleague.'" The F.B.I. told him he could appeal, but he was still recovering his strength from his operation in Rome the previous spring and didn't feel well enough to make the necessary trip to Washington to defend himself.

In spite of the views of the F.B.I., for many years both the Army and the Air Force continued to support his research interests and his frequent invitations to other mathematicians to visit Harvard, and only once, in 1960, was he asked to do something in return. "Look, you're going to Russia. Could we ask you to keep your eyes open and ears wide? You needn't ask any questions, but just give us a report when you come back." Zariski refused, and could not resist adding, "You may not realize it, but I don't even have clearance from the F.B.I." "Oh yes," they said, to his surprise. "We know all that."

15 🔲   An Attack on the

Theory of Linear Systems

1950 – 1956

W ith the results of his foundational work on varieties and, as he writes in the preface to his *Collected Papers,* "with the conviction, indelibly impressed in my mind by my Italian teachers, that the theory of algebraic surfaces is the apex of algebraic geometry," Zariski decided that working out a complete theory of surfaces would be the real testing ground for his new algebraic tools: "If he could find rigorous proofs of the results in that body of theory and if he could, moreover, extend those results to characteristic p, then it would show that he and Weil had provided proper foundations for the whole theory of algebraic geometry."[115] His work was also an answer to a challenge given by Castelnuovo in 1949: "Will someone come soon to continue the work of the Italian and French School by giving to the theory of algebraic surfaces the perfection that has

---

[115] Mumford, personal interview, November 1989.

been reached in the theory of algebraic curves? I hope so, but I doubt it."[116]

Having developed definitive tools for proving the necessary results, Zariski and Weil were now faced with the question of how to apply these tools. "To do mathematics efficiently one needs not only powerful rigorous techniques but also an intuitive flexible language — that is to say, an array of definitions of technical terms that readily support both your intuition and your analysis."[117] The basic problem was to find a way of doing algebraic geometry that could use all the powerful tools of Weil and Zariski while capturing the intuitive geometric feel of the old Italian School and it remained an important issue throughout the fifties and sixties.

Although other fields of mathematics, including algebra and topology, had developed their basic definitions, their style, and their language during the thirties and forties, in the fifties there was still very little agreement on which of the new foundational languages being offered for algebraic geometry was the most satisfactory. André Weil had used his concept of specializations as the fundamental building block in *Foundations of Algebraic Geometry;* Zariski had developed an approach using generic points and relying heavily on his algebraic techniques in an unpublished AMS Colloquium Lecture manuscript; and Masayoshi Nagata had worked out a ring theoretic approach. This lack of agreement continued to be a major obstacle to research and, especially, to effective communication between research groups for over twenty years.[118]

In the early fifties following the appearance of a book by Enriques on algebraic surfaces, Zariski and his students mounted an attack on the theory of linear systems that lay at the heart of Italian geometry. Recasting the Italian theory from an algebraic point of view, they freed it from all dependence on the complex ground field and extended it to characteristic p; they also extended many of its results from surfaces and curves to higher dimensional varieties.

During this period Zariski also managed to write several hundred pages of a book on commutative algebra that has become a standard

---

[116] Quoted by Zariski in the preface to his *Collected Papers,* and translated from the Italian by Vera DeCola.

[117] Mumford, personal interview, February 1990.

[118] *Ibid.*

reference for algebraists [72, 75].[119] According to his student Joseph Lipman, "His pioneering applications of the methods of abstract commutative algebra to questions in geometry have opened the way for further developments of massive proportions."[120]

He also wrote three survey articles that give a broad overview of the field at that time. The first one, "The fundamental ideas of abstract algebraic geometry" [60], which he presented at the International Congress in 1950, demonstrates how thoroughly he had reworked the foundations. Four years later he wrote an introduction to algebraic geometry from the point of view of valuation theory [64], and in 1956 he published "a lovely careful mathematical introduction" to the startling new work of Jean-Pierre Serre, in which he described two applications that Serre had made to classical problems as "highly encouraging indications of the power and potentialities of the cohomological method in abstract algebraic geometry" [67].[121]

Sheaf theory, which had originated with Cartan and the French School, had already proved its usefulness to topology and the theory of analytic functions when Serre's paper "Faisceaux Algebriques Coherents"[122] introduced the idea of coherent sheaf theory and the cohomology of sheaves into algebraic geometry. Kodaira remembered Zariski's "amazement" at the simplicity of the sheaf-theoretic proof of the lemma of Enriques and Severi, which he had extended in a 1952 paper [61].[123]

---

[119] In a letter to Abhyankar he wrote, "I'm still slaving on my book on commutative algebra, but delivery and freedom are in sight" (2/17/56). Overwhelmed by the proliferation of manuscript pages, he was finally rescued by Pierre Samuel.

[120] "Biographical Sketch" 1973 (unpublished).

[121] Kleiman, letter to the author, 4 February 1990.

[122] Known familiarly to algebraic geometers as "FAC," Serre's paper first appeared in the *Annals of Mathematics,* 61 (1955), 197–278. His work had come to Zariski's attention a year earlier through "a sketchy letter" that was circulated at the second Summer Institute in Algebraic Geometry and Functions of Complex Variables at the University of Colorado in Boulder. Serre's letter had led to an ad hoc seminar, although Zariski, in spite of his interest, does not seem to have attended it regularly (Abhyankar, letter to the author, 5 February 1990).

[123] *Creativity and Inspiration* 23.

This lemma had been the subject of a longstanding controversy between Enriques and Severi. In *Algebraic Surfaces* Zariski, who doubted that either of them had proved it, had correctly attributed the first complete proof to Hodge, who had used the theory of harmonic integrals. (In his persistent loyalty to the Italian School, Lefschetz had dismissed Hodge's results as the work of a crackpot.)

However, although Zariski recognized the power of sheaf theory, he felt that in the last analysis it only reworked and made more intelligible the ideas inherent in the Italian approach. One of Zariski's students has described "the tremendous overlap" between Serre's paper and Zariski's generalization of the lemma: "One of the remarkable things is to see how various theorems were re-expressed in each new generation in different languages. Zariski and Serre were really in fact doing the same thing, but they had a totally different language for it." [124]

A way of dealing systematically with linear systems and other spaces of functions defined by local properties, coherent sheaf theory and the cohomology of sheaves allowed for the naming of intermediate steps in the course of a calculation. (They were called "higher cohomology groups.") By giving them a name and having a notation for them, algebraic geometers could investigate them more easily:

> After Serre, manipulating linear systems was no longer just a black art which only a few people knew how to do, but it became something that any idiot could do because you just plugged in these exact sequences. And I think that in some way Oscar didn't like this so much — he liked it to be a black art.
>
> Although he realized the beauty of Serre's techniques and that they were the best that had been offered, I think what he basically decided was that there was not anything new in it and that these techniques didn't feel natural to him.
>
> But to the next generation, especially after the work of Grothendieck, it seemed infinitely more natural and more powerful, in particular much more efficient when you really had to deal with higher cohomology groups. [125]

In Boulder with Zariski in the summer of 1954 were Zariski's protégé Jun-ichi Igusa and his student Shreeram Abhyankar, who had come from the University of Bombay two years before to study

---

[124] Mumford, personal interview, November 1989.
[125] *Ibid.*

Zariski with Shreeram Abhyankar (courtesy of Y. Abhyankar)

with Garrett Birkhoff but had become so excited by Zariski's class in projective geometry that he had decided to study algebraic geometry instead. His decision to work with Zariski had not, however, been easy. One student had warned him, "If you never want to graduate, take your degree with Zariski."[126]

Abhyankar soon became interested in resolving the singularities of surfaces in characteristic p different from zero and decided to use that as the subject of his dissertation. "I tried myself," Zariski remembered having warned him. "Maybe I didn't know enough about rings of characteristic p different from zero, but it's very difficult." Abhyankar, however, persisted, finishing his degree in only two

---

[126] Interestingly, Abhyankar described his early impression of Zariski with the same image that Zariski had used to describe Castelnuovo: "He looked like the Moses of Michelangelo" (personal interview, May 1989).

years, and going on to extend many of Zariski's results to characteristic *p*.

Zariski was enormously pleased. "What Abhyankar did was extremely difficult. Some of the points are so delicate and so different from what could possibly come up in characteristic zero. And he couldn't use any of the old notions and habits, couldn't interpolate on the basis of what we know from the classical field."

When Abhyankar's results appeared in the *Annals,* Lefschetz failed to appreciate their difficulty: "Look, Zariski," he wrote, "what about this paper? I mean, you already did it for surfaces in characteristic zero. I'm quite sure in a couple of years somebody will do it in characteristic *p* for any dimension." Zariski replied with an angry defense of Abhyankar's work, and almost thirty years later he was happy to point out that "nobody has done it yet."[127]

Abhyankar was as close to Zariski as Zariski had been to Enriques. Calling Zariski and Yole "my other parents," Abhyankar invited them to dinner at his various student apartments, and when Zariski had trouble with his lumbago Abhyankar often brought him his mail from the department and stayed to talk about mathematics.[128] Acknowledging Zariski's warmth and helpfulness, Abhyankar's father wrote from India to thank him: "When keen students are enabled to do a substantial work, the credit for the work in progress is not solely due to the preceptors but to the humanity of the teachers."[129]

After finishing his degree Abhyankar taught at various places, including Columbia and Cornell, and now holds joint appointments at Purdue and the Mathematical Institute in Poona, India, where he serves as director. Although his ideas about the best problems and techniques in algebraic geometry gradually diverged from Zariski's, he continued to send him his work for comments. Zariski was amused by the transformation of Abhyankar's salutations — from

---

[127] In 1966 Abhyankar presented results for dimension 3. His book *Resolution of Singularities of Embedded Algebraic Surfaces* (Academic Press, 1966) is dedicated to his former teacher: "To Zariski: without his blessings, who can resolve the singularities?"

[128] Kleiman remembered finding him "sick in bed discussing mathematics with Abhyankar" (letter to the author, 4 February 1990).

[129] Professor Shankar Abhyankar, letter to Zariski, 10 January 1955.

July 23, 1953

Dear Abhyankar :

    I have received your letter and am glad to 'learn that you have read a good deal during this period and that you have many questions on your mind, and also some ideas about how to go about them. You will soon have to select one of these questions and concentrate your thesis work on that particular question. The problem of local uniformization is perhaps too difficult, but some partial results in the direction of the solution of that problem (not necessarily the full solution itself) would be an acceptal goal for a thesis. I have not followed very well your considerations on local uniformization, and I therefore prefer to discuss them when I am in Cambridge. There may be something fruitful in what you say, and I should like to hear more about it from you viva voce

A letter from Zariski to Abhyankar, 1953 (courtesy of S. Abhyankar)

"My Dear and Respected Professor Zariski" in 1953 to "Dear Professor Zariski" and, finally, "Dear Zariski." [130]

Zariski's "nomadic instincts" had been only partially quieted by his arrival in Cambridge. In 1949 he had attended a summer conference in Paris; in 1953 he had visited Italy and Israel; and in 1954 he gave a series of lectures at the Sorbonne, after which he and Yole

---

[130] They probably reminded him of his own discomfort in his early relationship with Lefschetz. "For a long time," he remembered, "I didn't dare to write anything but 'Dear Professor Lefschetz.' But at last there came a time when I took the courage and wrote only 'Dear Lefschetz.'"

were joined by the Brauers on the first stage of a journey through France, Switzerland, and Italy. In 1956 he set off with Yole for a trip around the world, supported in part by the U.S. Air Force, which flew him on its own planes across the Pacific. Yole made the journey separately on commercial planes, and they met in Tokyo at the end of September. After two weeks of sightseeing, they settled down at Kyoto University, where Zariski lectured on the theory of minimal models of algebraic surfaces once a week, from October 13 through November 15.

He was very impressed by the high quality of Japanese mathematics, particularly by the work of a young mathematician who attended all his lectures in Professor Akizuki's seminar, Heisuke Hironaka. In his memorial address for Zariski Hironaka recounted his memory of those weeks:

> It was in the fall of 1956 in Kyoto that I met Oscar Zariski for the first time. His name was well-known in Japan along with André Weil as

Sendai, Japan, October 1956. From left to right: Masuda, Amai, Kuniyoshi, Kanno, Zariski, Yole, Terada, and Sasaki (courtesy of Yole Zariski)

the twin leaders of the ALGEBRAIC geometry at the time. Zariski was especially a familiar name among the members of Akizuki seminar, such as Matsumura, Nagata, Nakai, Nakano, Nishi and others, including some graduate students like myself, the biggest and perhaps the most active group in those days within the Mathematics Department of Kyoto University. Not only had we in the seminars studied Zariski's research papers such as "Analytical irreducibility," "Bertini's theorems," "Local uniformization" etc., but also we knew that the prominent ex-members of the Akizuki group such as Junichi Igusa and Teruhisa Matsusaka had been in good contact with Oscar Zariski at Harvard University. . . .

When Oscar was staying in Kyoto, he made himself present in the Akizuki seminars and offered his opinions and advice on topics under discussion of algebraic geometry. Most vivid in my memory was the occasion when I was asked to speak on my own research work in the presence of Professor Zariski. I could read and write English modestly, but barely enough for mathematics. . . . But speaking a foreign language I had never done before, whether in mathematics or otherwise. I was indeed petrified before Zariski and could not even speak sentences I prepared beforehand. Oscar often looked perplexed and sometimes even annoyed. . . . I thought that he was completely disappointed with my poor presentation, but to my surprise he recommended my work to be published in an American journal. . . .

To my further surprise and delight, he also suggested that I might qualify for an American scholarship if I wished to come to the Harvard Mathematics Department as a graduate student. Professor Nagata, then my research advisor at Kyoto, had already received an invitation to come there as a visiting professor.[131]

To a young Japanese of those days, coming to America was a case of Dream-Come-True.

For Zariski, too, it would be "a case of Dream-Come-True," for Hironaka's elegant and difficult results would contribute significantly to the foundations of algebraic geometry. Zariski's recognition of the talent of the young mathematician on such brief acquaintance seems a talent in itself, and perhaps helps to account for the exceptional achievements of his students.

But Zariski's enjoyment of Japan does not seem to have been

---

[131] Masayoshi Nagata went to Harvard as a visiting professor in the fall of 1957.

confined to mathematics, judging from the postcard he sent to Igusa, who had accepted a permanent position at Johns Hopkins:

> Dear Igusa,
> Some of your good friends (including me) are now in Ikaho, near your hometown, and we remember you while we drink tea or saki, and while we sing some songs (especially Prof. Akizuki, who is an expert in Gion songs and the songs of third high school). Your brother is very kind, and we were happy to meet his family. Your nephews are very good looking, better looking than you.

("I think you are just as handsome!" Yole wrote across the top.)

After giving invited talks at Osaka, Sendai, Kobe, Hiroshima, and Tokyo, Zariski left Japan for India at the beginning of December. While he lectured at the Tata Institute in Bombay, he and Yole lived what Yole called "a good and lazy life" in the Taj Mahal Hotel in Colaba, directly across a beautiful little park from the Yacht Club in which the institute was then housed. To his student Abhyankar he wrote at the beginning of January, "India is a very interesting country, but I have seen only a small part of it (Delhi, Gwalior, Agra and Bombay). At present I am conducting a small seminar on sheaf theory at the Tata Institute. The students are very bright."

His lectures were followed by a group of about ten students, including one "good but not typical algebraic geometer named Seshadri."[132] Exhausted by the hard work he had done in Japan, he was, as he put it, "in no mood for adventure" during his six weeks in India. He and Yole did manage, however, to pay their long-promised visit to Abhyankar's father in Gwalior.

The Abhyankars and most of Gwalior, in fact, welcomed them warmly.[133] Mr. Abhyankar had arranged for Zariski to visit the college of which he was the principal, and when Zariski said that he was too tired to give a lecture or even a speech, he had explained, "The only thing you have to do is to give *darshan* — to show yourself

---

[132] C. S. Seshadri, a Fellow of the Royal Society, is currently on the faculty of the SPIC Science Foundation in Madras.

[133] To Zariski's chagrin, they were later told that the Maharajah had invited them to stay with him in the palace but that Abhyankar had told his father that Zariski wasn't interested in wordly things and wouldn't want to stay with a maharajah.

and allow yourself to be garlanded." Zariski agreed reluctantly. "I felt ill at ease and tried to provoke them to ask me some questions," he remembered, "but I had to just sit there like a mummy or a god."

The Zariskis left India on January 11 for Italy and France, stopping briefly in Turkey and Greece, and for a longer time in Spain, where Zariski lectured at the University of Madrid. Before settling down for the summer at Forte dei Marmi, they returned to Rome. Yole visited her family and friends, and Zariski gave a series of talks in the old familiar lecture halls of the University of Rome.

16 ▧   Tying Bells on

Characteristic Zero

1957 – 1961

Upon his return to Harvard in September of 1957, Zariski initiated what would later fondly be called his "famous seminar." Using work that he had done in Japan, he led a small group of students on a forced march through what remained of unexplored territory in the older "real" world of characteristic zero, extending each result into the treacherous new world of characteristic p. ("He was tying bells on characteristic zero" is the way David Mumford remembered it.) Never shirking the slog through the swamp of characteristic p, he guided his students through questions of the existence of minimal nonsingular models in each birational equivalence class of surfaces.

They moved swiftly. Each student was required to prepare a seminar paper each week on a topic that had been announced only the previous week, although Zariski chose the actual speaker only at the last minute. Some fell by the wayside; others, like Michael Artin, Heisuke Hironaka, and David Mumford, were permanently converted to algebraic geometry.

Artin wrote his thesis on Enriques surfaces; Hironaka gave an analysis of birational maps between 3-dimensional varieties; and Mumford's thesis gave the first algebraic construction of the moduli space of curves, valid also in characteristic p. Zariski himself continued his reexamination of Castelnuovo's criterion of rationality.

Gorenstein had called his classes with Zariski "inspiring," Rosenlicht had remembered them as "abstruse and fascinating," and many of these later students described Zariski's lectures in almost mystical terms. "When Zariski talked," Hironaka and Mumford have written, "you didn't even have to know what his words meant to believe at once that these were not dry abstractions, but came from a world which lived and breathed, which glowed with promise and with secrets."[134]

"He was incredibly influential on all of us," Michael Artin remembered. "What attracted me to algebraic geometry was his dynamic personality in class."[135] "Perhaps everything he said seemed so important because he believed in what he said himself," Joseph Lipman suggested, and Robin Hartshorne has described the unusual clarity of Zariski's class in projective geometry, which deeply influenced his own teaching and writing.[136]

David Mumford vividly recalled Zariski's lecture style:

> Zariski's style was unlike that of any other mathematician I know. He didn't lay out the proof of a theorem as a mere sequence of logical steps, nor did he spend a lot of time on what people call the philosophy of a result, building intuition through analogies. No.
>
> What he did was to lay seige to the theorem. He spread out his forces carefully and lovingly, making sure that you knew every one of their names and exactly what their uses were. He would make preliminary skirmishes to the main result, cutting off points of retreat for the opponent and probing its weak points.

---

[134] "Oscar Zariski," *Harvard University Gazette,* 6 May 1988.

[135] Michael Artin, personal interview, July 1989.

[136] Hartshorne, who describes himself as "an honorary student" because he took his degree formally at Princeton, enjoyed a long and close association with Zariski. He met Zariski when he arrived at Harvard as an undergraduate in 1955 and he attended his seminar as a graduate student. Zariski proposed him as a junior fellow, after which he remained on the Harvard faculty until 1972 (Hartshorne, personal interview, July 1989).

Then he would go for the heart. His writing on the blackboard would get extremely small. The audience literally held its breath. He paused for emphasis.

Then the key steps, which cut the ground away from under the theorem. Now his writing got large again. The theorem had yielded to his forces. The result was his and he raised his QED proudly over the territory.[137]

The nurturing of his later students — Artin, Falb, Hartshorne, Hironaka, Kleiman, Lipman, and Mumford — seems to have been easier for him than the training of his earlier students. Confronted by Hartshorne's interest in a topic he himself didn't care about, he simply said, "If you're interested, go and do it." [138] Kleiman remembered that "as a matter of explicit policy he wouldn't describe a problem as 'hard' in order not to discourage anyone." Kleiman also described Zariski's "active helpfulness":

> One time during the summer before my last year, Zariski asked me how my work was going. I replied that I had no results to report, but I had heard that Griffiths was currently doing some work that might help me. Griffiths was around at the time, and Zariski immediately responded, "Let's get him in here and find out." And we did speak to him right away.[139]

He was, however, still formidable. The late-afternoon teas that John Tate introduced into the department from Princeton, designed to bring faculty and students together informally, were not his favorite way to interact:

> What he would do is come out of his office to get a cup of tea and then see which of his students was around. Then he'd say, "Come into my office with me."
>
> And you'd go and he'd sit you down and grill you: What were you doing? What were your ideas about this? You always felt that he was testing you and your ideas and whether or not you understood what he was doing. He would ask you to go to the board and show you this and that.
>
> He always liked to put a frame around any conversation. So he

---

[137] "Oscar Zariski and His Work," invited address to the AMS-MAA, 7 January 1988.

[138] Hartshorne, personal interview, July 1989.

[139] Kleiman, personal interview, November 1989.

would make a point of lighting up. . . . He'd just had a stomach operation and would meticulously cut a cigarette.[140]

Some of Zariski's students found the high standards he set in algebraic geometry too daunting even after they had received their doctorates, and they moved into other fields: Gorenstein into group theory, Rosenlicht into differential fields, and Falb into control theory. Artin has suggested that "if someone didn't have confidence it might be hard for him." Kleiman remembered that when his thesis work was going well Zariski was more friendly to him. Joseph Lipman saw his face "like a stone cliff," and David Mumford never forgot the intensity of their sessions in Zariski's "lair" at 2 Divinity Avenue. "Zariski was not always kind, but he was never vicious or deliberately cruel," is the way Peter Falb put it. "You knew that he was measuring himself against the same high standards that he applied to you." [141]

The intensity of his relationships with his students continued to be manifest in his lively personal interest and concern for their welfare. When Lipman, a Canadian, found himself unable to return to Harvard for his thesis defense because of visa problems, it was Zariski who rescued him by means of a letter to McGeorge Bundy, who was then in the State Department.

He was "mildly hurt" when Kleiman didn't call him immediately to tell him of his daughter's birth. "But a year and a half later when my son was born, I let the Zariskis know right away, and he and Yole made a point of being among the first to come by and see him." When Kleiman was offered at job at Columbia and worried about graduating on time, Zariski said, "Just pad the thesis." [142]

Lipman, whose research interests remained close to Zariski's, settled at Purdue, where he'd gone to work with Abhyankar; and

---

[140] Mumford, personal interview, November 1989.

Many students remember Zariski's meticulous division of his cigarettes with a special cutting tool. Kleiman also recalled Zariski's description of his doctor's warning: "He told me that smoking was Russian Roulette, and I said, 'Well, after all I'm Russian.'"

[141] Peter Falb, personal interview, July 1989.

[142] That spring Kleiman proved some important results, including a conjecture of Chevalley.

Hartshorne, who was awarded the Steele Prize by the AMS, joined the department at Berkeley. Zariski's other students remained near him — Artin, a member of the National Academy of Sciences, holds a chair at MIT, and Kleiman, who was recently awarded an honorary degree by the University of Copenhagen, is also at MIT; Falb, who developed a successful investing firm, is at Brown; and Hironaka and Mumford, who both went on to win Field Medals, hold chairs at Harvard.

Hironaka, who has received many prizes, including the Japanese Order of Culture Award (elevating him to a position known as a "National Treasure" in Japan) and an honorary degree from the University of Madrid, has served as Director of the Research Institute for Mathematical Sciences at Kyoto University; and Mumford, who was elected to the National Academy of Sciences in 1975 and holds an honorary degree from the University of Warwick, is currently a MacArthur Foundation Fellow and is working on computer vision.

As a group Zariski's later students seem to have been more confident and independent than his earlier ones, and perhaps he too had changed. This is not to say that his legendary egotism had given way to self-effacement. When someone likened Michael Artin's relationship with him to his relationship with his Italian teachers, he suggested that even though Artin is now interested in noncommutative algebra, what he is really trying to do is to extend Zariski's Main Theorem.

Zariski took a deep pleasure in sharing the bountiful harvest of his earlier labors. Mumford has described him as "gathering many students together and inviting them to use his new algebraic tools," and whether drawn by the quality of his published work or seduced by his lectures, the students he trained have made fundamental contributions to many areas of mathematics and been recognized by the highest academic honors.

Near the end of his life Zariski was amazed to hear his years at Harvard referred to as "dessert." "Dessert!" he'd exclaimed. "The main course was not good?" [143]

---

[143] Mumford, invited address, 7 January 1988.

The Harvard Mathematics Department has always been small, and by tradition everyone serves on committees and takes a three-year turn as chairman. Zariski, who was very involved with his own work, dreaded taking on that responsibility when his time came in 1958. He was also just recovering from the removal of his gall bladder — or, as he put it, "It seems that the doctors have, by this operation, resolved a nasty singularity in my 3-dimensional inner variety."[144] He therefore fought very hard for a two year term with McGeorge Bundy, who was then Dean of Arts and Sciences, arguing that, for one thing, he had joined the faculty at an older age than most of his colleagues. Bundy replied that he'd argued his case so well and so vigorously that it was clear that Harvard needed him as chairman for a full three years.[145]

Zariski did eventually manage to negotiate a two-year term, but he found to his surprise that he enjoyed being chairman because it enabled him "to do things." He developed a reputation for being agreeable with his colleagues and implacable with the administration, and was sometimes criticized for not being sufficiently aware of the need to please alumni. When the college's appointment rules fit with what he wanted, he used them; when they didn't, he feigned ignorance.[146] It was perhaps this pragmatism that led Dean Bundy to refer to him as "that Italian bandit."

As chairman he strengthened the department, particularly the algebraic geometry group, through his appointments. Because the department simply talks until it reaches a consensus before it votes unanimously *pro forma* to send a recommendation to the ad hoc committee on hiring, his forceful personality made him a formidable ally.[147]

---

[144] Letter to Abhyankar, 24 July 1958.

[145] Mumford, personal interview, February 1990.

[146] These rules, known as the Graustein Plan because W. C. Graustein had devised them, set a fixed time schedule for tenure appointments. They were designed to monitor the tenure positions available in each department in order to achieve a roughly uniform age distribution.

[147] "A standard procedure at Harvard is that every department member writes the dean about every appointment. The dean then appoints a so-called ad hoc committee with three or

Very impressed with Raoul Bott's flair and brilliance, he decided that Bott was just the man to liven up what often seemed to him a rather stodgy department, and as with Igusa and Hironaka, his judgment was excellent. As Mumford remembered it, "Raoul would come into parties and clap his hands and say, 'Why is everybody whispering? Where am I? At Harvard?'" Bott and John Tate, who were good friends, were being courted by many places, but with the aid of Brauer and Mackey Zariski succeeded in keeping one and hiring the other. He also helped to recruit Schlomo Sternberg.

As chairman Zariski further strengthened the algebraic geometry group by extending enthusiastic invitations to those who were doing new work. He welcomed Alexander Grothendieck to Harvard three years in a row even though Grothendieck's radical techniques in algebraic geometry threatened to replace his own.[148]

Continuing in the algebraic direction initiated by Zariski, Grothendieck's work would push algebraic geometry hard and far and fast, radically altering the language and permanently transforming the field. "After Grothendieck's great generalization of the field," Zariski said many years later, "what I myself had called abstract turned out to be a very very concrete brand of mathematics." Obsessed by mathematics, working twelve hours a day in an unheated study at the top of his house and emerging with 3,000 page manuscripts, Grothendieck, like Zariski, must have seen birds "whirling like numbers."

One of the many important results of Grothendieck that affected classical questions involved the incomplete proofs of Enriques and Severi of a fundamental fact in the theory of algebraic surfaces called the lemma of the completeness of the characteristic linear

---

so outside people and they look over all the letters, interview the chairman, etc., so that everyone is invited to express dissent, but I know of no appointment that has been publicly opposed by a member of the math department. Because there is a general atmosphere of respect, if 90% of the department endorses an appointment, the others have sufficient respect for them to endorse it, too" (Mumford, personal interview, November 1989).

[148] Grothendieck, who was very eager to work with Zariski, was radical in more than mathematics. As Mumford remembered, "Since his own beliefs did not allow him to swear the loyalty oath required in those dismal days, he wrote to ask Zariski to investigate the feasibility of his continuing his mathematical work from a Cambridge jail cell. He wondered, in particular, how many books and visitors he would be allowed."

Tata Institute, Bombay, 1968. From left to right: Alexander Grothendieck, Armand Borel, C. S. Seshadri (standing), and Phillip Griffiths (courtesy of David Mumford)

system of a complete continuous system.[149] Mumford has described how Grothendieck was finally able to analyze this controversial lemma with purely algebraic methods:

> It was a standard idea from the Italians and from lots of geometers that you could analyze infinitesimal deformations. You'd try to move something and you'd say, "Let's just move it the tiniest bit." (This goes back to Leibnitz and the calculus.) So you could analyze geometrically the effect of an infinitesimal motion, and this had worked its way in its own form into algebraic geometry.
>
> What it corresponds to algebraically is dealing with deformations that have a parameter in them which you could call t. But for all your calculations, assuming that t was already so small that t^2 was negligi-

---

[149] See Chapter 15 for a discussion of Serre's contributions to this lemma.

ble, you could say that t^2 is equal to zero, and that would give you a way of calculating with infinitesimals.

On the other hand, it was also known that you could deal with power series in t, which gave what people called the "analytic" approach to algebraic geometry.

But what Grothendieck pointed out and no one had dreamed of was that you could also calculate in t and let t^3 be zero, or say that t^3 is measurable but t^4 is so small you can forget about it, etc. This whole calculation with what were called "nilpotent" rings was an absolutely new idea, and it was precisely the tool necessary to analyze this old Italian problem.

When Grothendieck would lecture on anything in algebraic geometry, someone might raise his hand and say, "But that's absurd, such and such," and Grothendieck would always say, "Ah, but the ring might have nilpotent elements in it." Once John Tate made out a little card that said, "There may be nilpotent elements in it," and Grothendieck carried it in his breast pocket and every time this came up he would pull it out.

Three of Zariski's best students — Artin, Mumford, and Hironaka — were attracted to the work of Grothendieck and Serre and used the new techniques to prove outstanding problems. Artin worked with Grothendieck to develop étale cohomology. Mumford used Grothendieck's language and the ideas of Kodaira to give a purely algebraic proof of the controversial Enriques-Severi lemma in characteristic zero and was able to explain exactly why it was false and when it would be false in characteristic p; his thesis, "Existence of the moduli scheme for curves of any genus," was written entirely in Grothendieck's language.[150] The concept of flatness, which Serre had introduced into algebraic geometry, was an essential tool for Hironaka when he proved his fundamental theorem on the resolution of singularities in characteristic zero (over an arbitrary ground field k for any dimension).

In his report on Hironaka's paper for the *Annals* Zariski wrote, "The transition to arbitrary dimension is achieved by Hironaka in

---

[150] In the preface to the first edition of *Geometric Invariant Theory*, which was based on his thesis, Mumford wrote, "It is my pleasure to acknowledge at this point the great encouragement and stimulation I have had from Oscar Zariski, John Tate and Alexander Grothendieck" (New York: Springer-Verlag, 1965) iv.

Zariski giving a guest lecture (courtesy of Yeshiva University Office of Photographic Services)

part by the introduction of some conceptually new devices, but in good part by a relentless and awe-inspiring technical breakthrough, in which he both extends the technical gadgets of my own proofs and introduces new technical tools which go beyond those which I have already applied myself." [151]

Hironaka, who was teaching at Brandeis that year, remembered that when he'd told Zariski that he was reconsidering the problem of

---

[151] *Annals of Mathematics*, 1964.

resolution of singularities, Zariski had said, "You need strong teeth to bite in." He also remembered Zariski's cautioning him to "check all the details" when he called him one night to say that he thought he had a proof:

> After the telephone conversation with Zariski, I began writing my proof step by step from the beginning. Every night till late, I kept writing and rewriting the manuscript. . . . Often I worked till dawn, and just before I went to bed, my wife woke up and counted the number of new pages I had written during the night. (She was supposed to take my handwritten manuscripts to a personally hired typist every day so that a typewritten manuscript would be completed as quickly as possible.)
>
> I often got stuck with minor points which I had thought were obvious, and each time I had to stop writing and think hard for a few days. However, the main track of the proof was so clear in my head that I never lost confidence that it was only a matter of time. The final manuscript grew to about 300 typewritten pages, and meanwhile I often had to go back to earlier pages, change definitions and rewrite subsequent paragraphs so that the logical consistency of the whole was assured.
>
> I refrained from seeing Zariski during these months of manuscript preparation and when he would see me on the street he would ask me smilingly, "Is your resolution still a theorem?" [152]

"It was perhaps this time more than any other when Oscar really felt that one of his students had done something that he would have liked to do," Mumford recalled. "But one can see in retrospect that it would have been hard for him to carry out the general case with the tools he had at the time. He had developed half of the abstract tools needed but then stopped short in other directions. And as with Grothendieck's work, once he saw that Hei could do it with these techniques, he was very pleased, but he himself pulled back." [153]

---

[152] From a letter of February 1977 written by Hironaka to Haruhiko Hagimoto and published in *Yawarakana Kokorowo Motsu (Having Soft Heart)*, a book made up of a series of conversations between Seiji Ozawa of the Boston Symphony and Heisuke Hironaka. Translated by Hironaka.

[153] "The first year that I was assistant professor I thought I would show Oscar how great the new ideas of Grothendieck really were. So I said I'd give a course on these new ideas and the climax would be proving how they clarified this whole question of surfaces. I thought that Oscar would be really intrigued, but unfortunately he wasn't. He never even came to the class" (Mumford, personal interview, November 1989).

Zariski after the lecture (courtesy of Yeshiva University Office of Photographic Services)

Kleiman pointed out that "learning to use new mathematical tools is not as easy as learning to drive a new car: it requires a lot of time and a serious intellectual investment. Zariski had many other demands on his time, and his own research was going well enough with the tools he already had."[154]

Zariski's belief that the real goal of mathematics was to find new techniques and new concepts as well as good theorems and proofs

---

[154] Letter to the author, 4 February 1990.

made it possible for him to welcome his students' interest in the work of Grothendieck and Serre with only a trace of envy and frustration.[155] When Kleiman asked if he could study Serre's notes in a reading course, he simply sighed, "Then you'll know more than I do."[156] A younger colleague remembered his saying that Grothendieck was paying him back for what he did to his Italian teachers.

The first time Hironaka used a cohomology group in his seminar Zariski raised his eyebrows and said, "Hironaka, you are using cohomology." Hei said, "Yes, Professor Zariski," and Zariski growled, "All right."[157] But a few years later, in his course on algebraic functions in the fall of 1962, he spent half the term developing and using cohomology groups.[158]

He also had an unusually deep sense of what he had to offer his students, as was revealed one day in a remark he made to Kleiman. Objecting to Kleiman's suggestion that some of his students were only "nominally" his because they worked on their own, "Zariski pointed out that they had acquired their taste and direction in mathematics from him."[159]

Still peering through the eyes of that "darling old lady," he saw the shift toward greater generality not as personal competition, but as part of an ongoing search for a deeper truth.

The importance of his work continued to be recognized. Holy Cross University awarded him an honorary degree in 1959, and the year after his chairmanship he was invited back to the Institute for

---

[155] "About 1975 Briancon and Speder found a counterexample showing that topological triviality did not imply the Whitney conditions. Zariski had worked on the question and was very interested in it. So was Bernard Teissier. . . . Zariski asked me if Teissier was disappointed by the counterexample. I said that I thought Teissier was happy to have the issue settled, and Zariski replied that that was the right way to react" (Kleiman, letter to the author, 4 February 1990).

[156] Kleiman also recalled Zariski's (often repeated) description of the Tate children playing in their backyard: "Flinging his arm as if to throw something down, Oscar would say, 'Let's throw away the Zariski topology.'"

[157] Mumford, personal interview, November 1989.

[158] Kleiman, letter to the author, 4 February 1990.

[159] *Ibid.*

Zariski at Princeton, 1959 (courtesy of Jun-ichi Igusa)

Advanced Study in Princeton. He spent the spring of 1961 as a visiting member of the Institute des Hautes Etudes in Paris, and returned to Harvard in the fall of 1961 as the Dwight Parker Robinson Professor of Mathematics.

The speakers he brought to the mathematics colloquium helped to make Harvard into an international center of algebraic geometry. He welcomed many prominent algebraic geometers to the university, including Hodge, Kodaira, Nagata, Serre, Weil and, of course, Grothendieck.

To augment his courses he sometimes gave a seminar of his own in which he talked about his ideas at greater length:

A lot of people can give you the gist of their ideas in an hour, but Oscar really liked to have space and time enough. He wanted to *develop* the idea with its own beauty. He would give you definitions. He would sort of lick his lips telling you the lemmas and the properties and laying it all out. He hated to talk for just an hour; he would much prefer to give four talks.[160]

He also encouraged his students to begin a weekly seminar on algebraic geometry, which eventually became the main algebraic geometry seminar in the Boston area. Having grown from one hour to two, from after tea to before and after tea, the Tuesday seminar gradually expanded to include dinner, and sometimes dinner followed by beer and pretzels at Zariski's house.

He and Yole often gave parties for visiting colloquium speakers, and he was by all accounts a particularly charming host. Erna Ahlfors remembered "one time when Oscar was not supposed to drink because of his ulcer. He was holding a glass and had become so animated and so gay and was talking and talking. Yole went up to him and said, 'Oscar, don't you remember you're not allowed to drink.' And he said, 'Well, what I'm drinking is water.'"[161]

Many mathematicians have tried to evoke the intensity of those evenings:

His Lancaster Street parties would have ten or twenty people scattered about, eating and drinking and talking. I remember once Auslander, Mumford, and Tate worked out a theorem standing in the kitchen: they laughed and said it should be attributed to Zariski. Those evenings were half party, half math. It was a wonderful atmosphere.[162]

He'd get a twinkle in his eyes. He'd come up to you and you could tell that you had his full attention. He'd ask you questions, trying to find out what was animating you. It was the same way as when he was lecturing. It was like he was flirting.[163]

Punctuating his remarks with the hand that held his cigarette and leaning toward a guest, he might have been back in the Caffe Greco, sketching out a proof for Beniamino Segre.

---

[160] Mumford, personal interview, November 1989.

[161] Erna Ahlfors, personal interview, August 1989.

[162] Hartshorne, personal interview, July 1989.

[163] Mumford, personal interview, August 1989.

17 ▨   A FEELING OF AWE

1962 – 1974

W hen he and the century were in their early sixties, Zariski returned to the problem of singularities with an attack on what he called "the elusive concept of equisingularity." [164] Alternating fierce skirmishes with strategic reexaminations of territory and method, he sought a natural way of stratifying any algebraic or complex analytic variety so that its singularities at the point of each stratum would be equivalent in some convincing sense [80, 86, 88, 91, 95].

Underlying this attack was his feeling that there was a strong link between the singularities and their "generic branch loci," an intuition already present in his early work on fundamental groups [16–20, 28, 29]. His mastery of topological methods was also helpful to him here, for finding it necessary to capture algebraically the topo-

---

[164] Lipman has pointed out that "there is no definitive notion of what equisingularity should mean. There are only several different plausible stratifying conditions; deep and fascinating problems arise when one looks for relationships among them."

logical type in situations more general than that of plane curves [81, 83], he was able to devise the notion of the saturation of a local ring [85, 89, 90, 91, 93].[165] He completed his work on equisingularity when he was eighty with the publication of "Foundations of a general theory of equisingularity" [97, 97a].

His many insights into equisingularity helped him to give new proofs for results in his general theory of surfaces [96]. As Lipman and Teissier point out,"[He discovered] many different criteria for equisingularity in codimension one — of algebro-geometric, differential-geometric, or topological nature [78, 84, 92] — and each of these provided him with a theme for further development in a higher codimension."

There, however, some of the striking interconnections among the criteria vanished. For example, the theory in codimension one did not exhaust all plausible notions of nonvariation of singularity type. The theory also didn't work, as Abhyankar showed, for varieties over fields of characteristic p. And while the singularities of an equisingular family of plane curves could be simultaneously resolved by monoidal transformations [82], he was unable to discover any canonical process for resolving singularities of higher dimensions.

His exploration of this area during the last two decades of his mathematical career aroused the interest of many algebraic geometers, including Joseph Lipman and a group of mathematicians at the École Polytechnique: J. P. Henry, Dũng Tráng Lê, Monique Lejeune-Jalabert, Frederic Pham, Jean-Jacques Risler, and Bernard Teissier. The conjunction of the ideas of the discriminant locus and topology provided the basis for many connections between his work and the more recent work of others on monodromy, singularities of differentiable mappings, and analysis on singular varieties.

Teissier described Zariski's attacks on the resolution problem as "a thing of great beauty":

> Oscar introduced the conceptual approach, through valuations and the local uniformization theorem, which do not give much food to geometric intuition. He also used, for surfaces, the more intuitive

---

[165] During this period he wrote to Lipman: "I labored hard on the 3rd paper on the general theory of saturation, but I now have it under full control" (14 December 1972).

approach via discriminant loci. After Hironaka's proof, he developed this into a full scale attack based on the concept of equisingularity. Because equisingularity is more directed towards understanding the structure of the resolution processes, it was a natural thing to turn to after resolution had been proved.

However, the depth and energy with which Oscar attacked equisingularity also brought to light new connections between the structure of discriminants (one of the most important objects in algebraic geometry and algebraic number theory), the topological structure of singularities, and the structure of resolutions. This is far from being completely understood yet; in fact, we may not even have developed the language in which to express what goes on, but I hope that within the next ten years we will understand much more, in part thanks to the recent progress in the study of algebraic threefolds.

Oscar's work on resolution is like a cathedral: beauty locally everywhere, directed towards a single global purpose, and a feeling of awe.[166]

"And beyond the large theories for which he's famous — the basic lore, the facts of life — there is much more, much deeper thought. People haven't explored these deeper things yet, but they will." [167]

When Zariski turned 65 in April 1964, he was asked by the university to stay on for five more years. He agreed, with the stipulation that he be put formally on half-time, and he spent the spring semester of 1964 at the University of Rome.

The following summer, shortly after his election to the National Academy of Sciences, he organized a conference on algebraic geometry at Woods Hole, Massachusetts. Like the summer institute at Boulder ten years before, it was devoted to a specific topic and sponsored by the American Mathematical Society. It marked the beginning of the AMS sponsorship of what has become a tradition of summer institutes on a specific area of mathematics.

---

[166] Teissier, letters to the author, 30 March 1990 and 9 April 1990.
[167] Barry Mazur, personal interview, January 1989.

Zariski at his 65th birthday party with, from left to right: Michael Artin, Shreeram Abhyankar, David Mumford, and Peter Falb (courtesy of David Mumford)

A seminal conference, it brought algebraic geometers from all over the world together for the first time during a very exciting period. Among Zariski's own students, Hironaka had recently proved new results on resolution, Mumford had results on the theory of moduli, and Artin was finding interesting results on étale cohomology.

The table of contents of the proceedings demonstrates how thoroughly Zariski's influence pervaded what was still, in those days, a very small field.[168] Abhyankar, Hironaka, and Zariski gave all three of the papers presented on the theory of singularities.[169] Of the six

---

[168] American Mathematical Society, "Lecture Notes Prepared in Connection With the Summer Institute on Algebraic Geometry held at the Whitney Estate, Woods Hole, Massachusetts" (July 6–July 31, 1964). The 1964 proceedings were not published.

[169] Abhyankar, in his report on "The Current Status of the Resolution Problem," explained why after a lapse of eight years he had come back to the resolution problem: "The primary reason was that the fall of 1963 was the first time after 1955 when I got an opportunity to be in Zariski's neighbourhood (not a Zariski neighbourhood); it is a theorem that to resolve singularities it is necessary to be near Zariski; the resolution problem consists of proving the sufficiency of this condition."

lectures on the classification of surfaces and moduli, two are attributed to Zariski's students, Mumford and Rosenlicht, and two to his
protégés, Igusa and Nagata; and of the three papers on Grothendieck cohomology, one is by Artin and one is by Zariski's Harvard
colleague, John Tate.

Many major problems would be solved during the next decade
using the tools that Zariski and Weil and Grothendieck had developed for algebraic geometry. "The summer institute gave us the idea
that algebraic geometry was now a real subject, and no longer simply
a mass of iffy results with a few valiant people like Zariski and Weil
struggling to make order in this Augean Stable."[170]

In 1965 Zariski received an honorary degree from Brandeis University and a National Medal of Science from President Johnson,
and that spring he gave a series of lectures at the University of Pisa
where, as Yole put it, "he was still resistant to the charms of the
city." In his last three years of half-retirement he spent three semesters at Purdue, where his students Abhyankar and Lipman had
settled, giving courses on his emerging theory of equisaturation, "in
his customary dynamic style."[171]

He also enjoyed two semesters at the University of California at
Berkeley, where he found Hartshorne, Rosenlicht, Seidenberg, and
an old mathematical friend, Gerhardt Hochschild, whom he and
Yole had first met at Hopkins. They had been delighted to discover
that Hochschild was a visiting professor at Harvard in 1947 and had
celebrated their first Thanksgiving in Cambridge with him.

In 1967, two years before Zariski became *emeritus,* he returned for
a few weeks to the Institut des Hautes Etudes. He went regularly to
Grothendieck's seminar, where (perhaps because his hearing was
beginning to fail) he always asked questions in English even though
everyone there spoke French and his own French was "superb, although Italian accented."[172] As Bernard Teissier remembered that
visit, "I was at that time a beginning graduate student fresh out of
the Ecole Polytechnique, mostly interested in number theory. Zariski gave a colloquium lecture on his theory of saturation, and the

---

[170] Mumford, personal interview, November 1989.
[171] Lipman, personal interview, July 1989.
[172] Kleiman, letter to the author, 4 February 1990.

Zariski, 1966 (courtesy of David Mumford)

mixture of geometry and algebra, expounded with Zariski's lively style, intoxicated me."[173]

In 1970 Teissier and Monique Lejeune-Jalabert went to Harvard as research fellows. They attended Zariski's seminar, where Teissier was surprised to learn that Zariski had a reputation for being stern and demanding with students:

---

[173] This lecture also caught the interest of Dũng Tráng Lê (Lê, letters to the author, September 1990).

In one lecture I gave a proof that I privately thought quite neat, and Oscar's reaction was "This is nice, but only a sketch of a proof!" I learned much from him through such remarks, and also by discussing many dreams about equisingularity. He had a large collection of examples carefully written in exercise books, and many an optimistic question would last only the time it took him to find the right page.[174]

They also enjoyed weekly lunches with Zariski and Hironaka at the faculty club. Teissier, who always had to borrow a necktie from the cloakroom, recalled Zariski's sense of the absurdity of the faculty club rules: "In 1970 the Harvard Faculty Club held a referendum about whether it should lift the obligation of wearing a tie. . . . Despite the fact that I was not on the faculty, Oscar encouraged me to vote in the register, knowing full well what my vote would be. (He jokingly refused to tell what his was.)"[175]

When the social and political upheavals of the late sixties brought unrest to the university and conflict to the halls of the math department, Zariski found himself basically out of sympathy with the protest movement. "It seemed to me not such a bad idea not to let the North Vietnamese take over by force a country which was not communist." He described with horror a math conference during which Roger Godement spent four hours attacking George Mackey's relatively conservative views (which rather coincided with his own). A lifelong liberal, he had become "not so much anti-communist as anti-Russian Communist."

As president elect of the AMS in 1968 and president in 1969–70, he faced what AMS secretary Everett Pitcher remembered as "a heavy overlay of emotional politics." Confronted by requests for the society to take a stand on issues like draft deferment and govern-

---

[174] Teissier, letter to the author, 20 January, 1990.

[175] The faculty club's requirement had once caused Zariski some embarrassment. Having invited Hochschild to lunch and remembering his disdain for neckties only at the last minute, he'd taken him to the Ambassador Hotel instead of to the faculty club. They were in the middle of one of their interesting conversations when the check came and Zariski suddenly realized that having expected to sign for lunch at the club, he had brought no money at all!

Zariski in Harvard Square, 1968 (taken by Frank DeCola, courtesy of Vera DeCola)

ment funding of war-related work, he made an effort to separate the Society from politics. There was a referendum that approved this position ("the Society shall not speak with one voice"), but according to Pitcher it had little effect. Unable to control the political subject matter, Zariski went to barely a third of the joint meetings of the executive committee and board of trustees, and attended and presided over only three of the six meetings of the council.[176]

But his distaste for the mixture of mathematics and politics did not interfere with his passion for political discussion. He had many lively conversations during this period with Lê, who remembers that Zariski's understanding of the situation in Vietnam extended well beyond the artificial boundaries of North and South.

---

[176] Everett Pitcher, letter to the author, 19 March 1990.

When Zariski became professor *emeritus* on July 1, 1969, he was a member of a very different department from the one he had joined twenty-two years before. Since 1947 it had not only doubled in size, it had also changed in spirit from a genteel but rather provincial enclave to an active center of research with an international faculty, a transformation to which he had made a significant contribution.

His retirement dinner on April 24 of that year seemed to his students different from other retirement dinners because "he was still so much in charge,"[177] and his seventieth birthday, celebrated with a party at Hironaka's house, was marked by invitations to speak from universities all over the world. The Institut des Hautes Etudes published a volume of papers written by his former students and "affectionately dedicated to him in warm appreciation of his pioneering achievements, deep insight, encouraging conversations, and inspiring teaching."[178]

Late that summer he left for his last visit to Israel, where he spent the fall semester lecturing at the University of Tel Aviv. Just after Christmas he flew with Yole to Italy, and after lecturing at the University of Rome and the Institut in Paris, he returned to the United States to spend the remainder of his first year of full retirement at Purdue.

His hearing had worsened, and the hearing aid he now wore provided him with only temporary relief because of the tinnitus that would plague his final decade. A steady ringing in his ears disturbed his solitude, and an increasing sensitivity to noise forced him to avoid the social gatherings to which he had once brought so much warmth and wit. He began to dread the lectures he used to find enlivening, and he would often accept invitations and make preparations only to ask Yole to cancel at the last minute.

---

[177] Mumford, personal interview, November 1989.

[178] This volume includes papers by Shreeram Abhyankar, Michael Artin, Peter Falb, Daniel Gorenstein, Robin Hartshorne, Heisuke Hironaka, Steven L. Kleiman, Joseph Lipman, David Mumford, Maxwell Rosenlicht, and Abraham Seidenberg (*Publications Mathematiques,* No. 36, 1969).

He spent what Yole described as a difficult five months at Cambridge University in the spring of 1972. In May he wrote to Teissier, Lejeune-Jalabert, and Lê that he was "making no progress at all" on the general theory of saturation "because I lecture too much and travel too much. Very stupid of me!" He went on to say that he'd declined three invitations to speak and had reduced his lecture schedule in Cambridge, and added in a postscript, "I wish all this lecturing was over so I can start working in earnest."[179]

The following summer he attended a conference on singularities in Corsica, where he prudently refused invitations to parties and large dinners, and the lectures he gave at the Ecole Polytechnique in the fall of 1973 (published as *Le probleme des modules pour les branches planes*" [92]) cost him an even greater effort. Having always taken pleasure in every nuance of a student's question, he now found himself unable to make out simple words.

In spite of his advancing age and diminished hearing, he was still, as many students have pointed out, faster and more creative than most younger mathematicians. His course on moduli of plane branches gave, as Teissier put it, "a new impetus to a subject that had lain dormant," and Lipman remembered the quickness with which he answered a question about algebraic curves of genus 2 during his visit to Cambridge: "What was so impressive about his instant answer was that he didn't have to go shuffling through his mental filing cabinet: whatever was needed rose instantly to the surface."

His letters to Lipman and Teissier during this period convey not only mathematical ideas, but also a persistent desire to encourage the work of younger mathematicians. Before deciding on the subject of the lectures that he had agreed to give at the Ecole Polytechnique in the fall of 1973 he had written to Teissier for advice:

> Another possibility is for me to lecture on the <u>problem</u> of the moduli space of plane analytic branches. I have <u>some new</u> results on that, which I did not have at the time I lectured on this topic at Harvard (the year you and Monique Lejeune were here), but the question is still 99% an unsolved problem, and I would hope that my lectures could stimulate some younger men to work on it.[180]

---

[179] Letter to Teissier, Lejeune-Jalabert, and Lê, 8 May 1972.
[180] Letter to Teissier, 24 May 1973.

Two years later he wrote to Teissier that he was "very much interested" in his ideas of simultaneous resolution of singularities." He went on to say that "I am also thinking along these lines, but so far I have only conjectures and some vague ideas. Still, what I have in mind may present good problems for younger men to solve." [181]

Aware of his advancing age, he turned hopefully to the younger generation. In 1976 he wrote to Teissier:

> So far I was not able to prove some critical points of the theory I had in mind, and so the elusive concept of equisingularity still remains elusive. I think that Lipman is also interested in this problem, and I hope that either you or Lipman will in time obtain a complete theory of equisingularity, leading to a good stratification of the hypersurfaces, with strata which are maximal sets of equisingularity.[182]

He made the last of several visits to Purdue in 1973 to receive an honorary degree and found that his tinnitus had worsened dramatically. Exhausted by the effort that contact with others now demanded, he came so near to emotional collapse that Yole cancelled a visit to their son in Nebraska and hurried with him back to Cambridge. She was particularly troubled to find him strangely confused and irritable. Although by the end of the summer he was almost back to normal, he decided not to give his usual seminar at Harvard that fall but rather to devote himself to finishing his work on equisingularity.

He resumed the weekly lunches with Mumford, Hironaka, and other algebraic geometers that he had initiated in the early sixties "to stay in touch." When his hearing had worsened, Hironaka had found a private room in the faculty club, and because that, too, now came to seem distracting, they began to bring sandwiches into Zariski's office, which was even quieter. "Then gradually it became more painstaking," Mumford recalled. "We'd go over things sentence by sentence because it was hard for him to hear almost everything, and he'd sort of piece things out as we said them to him." [183]

He grew increasingly depressed. Yole remembered that he went to the celebrations of his seventy-fifth birthday "as if he was going to a

---

[181] Letter to Teissier, 4 August 1975.

[182] Letter to Teissier, 6 January 1976.

[183] Mumford, personal interview, November 1989.

funeral," although his mood improved once they got there. Former students came from all over the world to a party sponsored by the Harvard Math Department. Speeches were given and a bronze bust of Zariski was unveiled in the Commons Room.[184] Later that night there was a supper in his honor at Mumford's house, where a separate room had been prepared for him to receive the congratulations of his friends and colleagues.

---

[184] This bust had been proposed by Mumford and Hironaka and commissioned by all of Zariski's students.

18 ⬚   THE DEPTH OF

HIS ATTACHMENT

A year younger than the century, Yole was herself now over seventy, and as Zariski's tinnitus worsened and his moods more often darkened into depression, she found it increasingly difficult to cope with the old three-story house on Lancaster Street. In spite of Zariski's objections she began to search for a smaller, more manageable dwelling, and in 1975 they sold the house that they were both so fond of and moved across the river to an apartment in Brookline — "a very tiring and time consuming process," as Zariski wrote to Teissier.[185]

After the move his memory began to fail, but he found refuge from the encroaching silence and the darkening of his mind for the few hours each day that he was able to concentrate on mathematics. Intensely aware of the weakening of his creative power, he tried to work in areas where it was still possible for him to accomplish something; he focused his efforts on giving a coherent sequence of

---

[185] 30 April 1975.

results that would at last put the theory of equisingularity on a solid basis. Working on "Foundations of a general theory of equisingularity" [97] took all his energy, but as he said one day during the writing of it, "The more active the mind is, the happier one feels."

His letters to Lipman and Teissier during this period show a very active mind. In February 1975 he sent Teissier a six-page proof giving "the correct answer to question 1 on p.490 of my AMS Bulletin note 'Some open questions in the theory of singularities'" [88]. In June he described his busy spring:

Dear Lipman,

Many thanks for your interesting letter of May 14 and apologies for my late reply. These have been very busy and hectic months, what with 1. moving to our new house (a condominium) 2. the reading (finally) of the galley sheets of my 3rd paper on the general theory of saturation (which is due to appear in the summer issue of the Journal) in which also your two articles will appear,[186] and 3. the final revision of the semi-final French version of my lectures (at the Ecole Polytechnique) on the space of moduli of plane algebroid branches (about 130 typed pages).

The following March he wrote Lipman a seven-page letter presenting his recent progress on the problem of equisingular stratification: "I have both a local treatment (for algebroid hypersurfaces) and a global treatment for algebraic hypersurfaces. I have yet no proof that my local definition of equisingularity is equivalent to my global definition. I shall outline my global treatment."

In January of 1976 he wrote to Teissier, "While I cannot say that I have read your manuscripts in all detail and thoroughly, I have an impression of a very valuable addition to the notes [of his course of lectures at the Ecole Polytechnique]. The most valuable aspect of your appendix is the greater generality with which you approach the whole problem."

He went on to explain, "There were two reasons why I have not been able to read carefully your appendix," one of which had to do

---

[186] Lipman has described both these papers as directly inspired by Zariski during his visits to Purdue in the late sixties.

with his trip to Rome and the other with his involvement with his own work.

But one by one familiar things were lost. The cigarettes that had been his company while working had at last been given up entirely the year before they sold the house. His brother-in-law, the artist Corrado Cagli, died suddenly in 1976, and the following year his friend and colleague Richard Brauer died. The old corner office at 2 Divinity Avenue that had seen so many students through their dissertations had been replaced by a shiny new one in the Science Center, which he never quite moved into. He gave his sailboat to the Boy's Club on Martha's Vineyard, and although he could no longer drive he mourned his cream-colored Mercedes. Impatient with his increasing ineptitude, he stopped taking photographs and showing slides.

He could still speak both English and Italian, but he lost the ability to concentrate and retain information over a span of time. He quoted Pushkin, but he was unable to read novels or short stories; his reading of the newspaper was at best perfunctory. All the characters on television looked alike to him.

The most painful and irremediable loss was his ability to do mathematics. Referring to his devotion to geometry, he had often called himself a "faithful man," and he remained committed to research mathematics even when he could no longer work. His struggle to remain in touch was aided by the occasional teas with algebraic geometers that Yole arranged at home for him when he could no longer go to his office.

The failed efforts of his family and friends to distract him from what he couldn't do by finding what he could were painful testaments to the depth of his attachment to research mathematics. The Hironakas proposed the idea for this book in 1981, and although he agreed to be interviewed he never really became interested. Remembering facts could not evoke the feelings, nor could it lead him back into the mathematical world that had fascinated him for almost eighty years.

One day, encouraging him to eat, Vera said, "But look, you're losing weight." "What difference does it make?" he answered. "I've lost so many things."

Describing the family's experience, Vera wrote, "His diminution as a human being in terms of intelligence, emotional and rational

*Zariski receiving an honorary degree from Harvard, with Heisuke Hironaka, 1981
(courtesy of Yole Zariski)*

consciousness and interaction was gradual and insidious but also
erratic, so that it was very difficult for me (and I think for my brother
and even my mother) to understand that a very physical erosion of
the brain (as the CAT scans eventually showed) was taking place.
Unfortunately, the doctors were vague and non-communicative
when they should have been articulate and explicit."

He was barely cognizant of the many honors bestowed upon him
during his last years. His eightieth birthday was celebrated at the
house of Michael Artin, who had arranged to present him with an
advance copy of a special volume written by his students and colleagues.[187] In 1981 Harvard awarded him an honorary Doctor of
Science degree: "In a long and remarkable career he has applied his
strong will and penetrating mind to rejuvenating a branch of pure

---

[187] *Contributions to Algebraic Geometry: in honor of Oscar Zariski*, ed. by Michael Artin and
David Mumford (Baltimore: Johns Hopkins University Press, 1979). Zariski's final work on
equisingularity was published along with these papers in two volumes of the *American Journal of Mathematics*, Vol.100 (1978) and Vol.101 (1979).

Zariski celebrating the honorary degree with Yole and his students, from left to right: Hironaka, Mumford, Kleiman, and Artin (courtesy of Yole Zariski)

mathematics and enhancing the international outlook of a great department." The following year Israel honored him with the Wolf Prize, for "harnessing the power of modern algebra to serve the needs of algebraic geometry." [188]

During this darkening period he was still able to take refuge in mathematics for a short time each week. In June of 1980 he wrote to Lipman:

> I was glad to receive your letter of May 30. You certainly have had a busy year administratively, but this — as I can see from the rest of your letter — did not prevent you from being active and very successful in your research. . . .

---

[188] On May 26, 1982, his signature rather surprisingly appears (with Lipman Bers and others) on a letter in *The New York Times* sponsored by the Committee of Concerned Scientists on behalf of an imprisoned Polish scientist, Dr. Ryszard Herczynski.

Zariski, 1979 (courtesy of Nan White)

I must confess that at my age (81) one finds it very difficult to read mathematical papers. I have devoted the last few months to a paper dealing with the old but still open problem of proving that the <u>irreducible</u> plane algebraic curves of a given order n and a a given number of nodes belong to a single maximal irreducible algebraic system.

He went on to explain that

Severi's "proof" . . . is trivially erroneous and shows nothing. It is this failure of Severi's proof that has rendered incomplete my old proof that the Poincaré group of the residual space of any plane <u>nodal</u> is abelian.

Zariski attempted to prove Severi's 1921 assertion of the irreducibility of these families of plane curves in his final paper [98]. The basis of some of his own work, as he wrote to Lipman, the theorem's unsatisfactory proof had bothered him for several years. (Kleiman remembered that after dinner in the late seventies and early eighties Zariski would take him aside and try to "recruit" him into working on it.) The solution, recently discovered by Joseph Harris,[189] shows that even though Zariski was no longer able to hold the complexities in his mind simultaneously for more than a few minutes at a time, he had managed to work out the correct approach.

When he lost his hold on these few remaining periods of brightness, he slipped behind a wall of confusion and silence into an overwhelming anxiety that made it impossible for him to let Yole out of his sight. He had nightmares about the deaths of Hannah and Moses and sang himself to sleep with Russian songs. He became obsessed with death. Although he was totally dependent on Yole for almost four years, it was only in the last months of his life that he was diagnosed with Alzheimer's disease.

On the morning of July 4, 1986, he refused to eat or drink his orange juice. Knowing how much he hated the hospital, his family kept him home, and Yole and Vera and the doctor were with him when he died. "Yole," he said, "you have been very good to me."

He was buried in Mt. Auburn Cemetery in Cambridge, and services were held in the Bigelow Chapel for the family and close friends. Ray and Vera read from Pushkin and Lermontov, and Michael Artin, Barry Mazur and David Mumford recalled how deeply his work and personality had influenced their lives. That September mathematicians came from all over the world to a special memorial service, to honor him.

---

[189] Joseph Harris, "On the Severi Problem," *Invent. math.* 84 (1986): 445–461.

◪ APPENDIX A ◪

A DISCUSSION OF

ZARISKI'S WORK

Zariski's Topological and
Other Early Papers

⊠ Michael Artin and Barry Mazur

Zariski describes three phases of his mathematical career in his preface to his collected works — his early years in Rome, the ten years from 1927 to 1937 when his interest centered on topology, and the subsequent period during which he worked on algebraic foundations. They are marked by abrupt transitions in his published work. The second phase began soon after he left Rome for the United States and consisted in an energetic attack on topological problems in algebraic geometry — the fundamental group, mainly. He worked on these problems with unbroken concentration for ten years; many of the ideas he pioneered were innovations in topology as well as in algebraic geometry and have developed independently in the two fields since then.

Zariski's impetus towards topology was brought on, in part, by a presentiment shared by his Italian teachers that further advances in algebraic geometry required new methods. This thrust ended abruptly around 1937, when Zariski was struck by the realization that the classical language was inadequate and that a thorough reconsideration of the field in terms of the new commutative algebra was needed.

This discussion describes his early papers, all of his articles on the topology of varieties, and two preliminary forays into the algebraic foundations, which occupied him fully later on. It also describes

several important later papers whose subject matter did not fit into
any of the major categories considered later. We discuss the articles
under thematic headings, leaving Zariski's work on the fundamental
group for last.

1. Survey Articles [60,64,67]

It may be worthwhile to say a word about the three surveys
[60,64,67]. Paper [60] is Zariski's address at the international congress in 1950 and shows his view of the whole field at that time. His
introduction [64] to algebraic geometry from the viewpoint of valuation theory can be recommended especially to algebraic geometers
trained in the modern way who have never learned about valuations.
The exposition begins at an elementary level, but he gets far enough
to state without proof some of his most important contributions.
Paper [67] is Zariski's report on a seminar at an A.M.S. summer
institute, whose topic was Serre's theory of coherent sheaves. This
seminar was held just after Serre had done his work and before his
paper *Faisceaux algébriques cohérents* had appeared.[55] The report is
notable for its clarity and for the frequent connections Zariski
makes with his own work. It is still one of the best places to get an
introduction to algebraic sheaf theory.

2. Solvability by Radicals [2,8,12]

In these papers Zariski considers the following question: Let us call
a non-constant map of curves $\pi: X \to \mathbf{P}^1$, or a fixed-point free g_n^1 on
X, solvable if the corresponding field extension $K(X)$ or $k(t)$ is
solvable by radicals. In [8] Zariski proves a conjecture of Enriques
that no solvable g_n^1 exists when X is the general curve of genus $p > 6$.
He also remarks that a curve of genus $p \le 6$ carries a g_4^1, which is
always solvable. (Actually, the existence of such special g_n^1's was not
proved completely until much later and has been the subject of
recent work. See for instance reference 32.)

In [2,12] he considers the case $X = \mathbf{P}^1$. Chisini[15] and Ritt[52] showed
that there are five types of solvable g_n^1 of prime degree n; Zariski
generalizes their elegant result to arbitrary degree. He classifies
maps π having the familiar property that all points of $\pi^{-1}(p)$ can be

expressed rationally in terms of any pair. The key point is that the Galois covering of $\mathbf{P}^1$ determined by X is either a rational or an elliptic curve ([12], p. 17).

3. Uniformization of Algebraic Functions [4,7,9,10]

The problem considered in [4,7] is the following: Let D be a plane domain bounded by Jordan curves $\gamma_1, \ldots, \gamma_m$, and let $y = f(x)$ be an n-valued analytic or algebraic function of x, defined on D. The function y is allowed to have some critical points (branch points) in the interior of D. In analogy with Puiseux series one may wish to write y as a single-valued function of a variable z, where z is algebraic and of degree n over x.

Zariski begins by noting that the condition for the existence of such a z is purely topological. Namely, let D' be the n-sheeted covering of D defined by y, and let S' be the compact Riemann surface obtained by spanning discs into the boundary curves of D'. One may arrange S' as an n-sheeted branched covering of the x-sphere; then the Riemann existence theorem asserts that S' has a unique algebraic structure. Thus z exists if and only if S' is a topological sphere. Zariski goes on to give an explicit description of y as a sum of Laurent series in z, applying Runge's theorem, and in [7,9,10] he applies the theory to various interesting special cases.

4. A Paper on Correspondences on Curves [13]

This is the paper closest in style to classical Italian geometry, though its use of monodromy recalls Zariski's first studies of solvable extensions and leads into his work on fundamental groups. In it Zariski takes up an idea of Severi and corrects an error in one of Severi's papers.[57] The main theorem proved is that the general curve of a linear system $|C|$ on a regular surface F has no singular correspondence, provided that $|C|$ is sufficiently nondegenerate. We recall that a correspondence $T \subset C \times C$ is singular if its cohomology class is not a rational linear combination of the classes of $p \times C$, $C \times p$, and Δ. An assertion equivalent to the theorem is that the Jacobian of C has no nontrivial endomorphisms.

In his fundamental work[29] on algebraic correspondences, Hurwitz defined the notion of singular correspondence and exhibited the quadratic relations that the existence of such correspondences impose on the periods of a curve. He asserted that they could exist only on special curves C. Severi[57] undertook to prove this assertion, that is, to show that the generic curve of genus g has no singular correspondence. He based his argument on families of plane curves with nodes, and this led him to study correspondences on curves varying in a linear system on an arbitrary regular surface F.

In the first sections of his paper, Severi considers the monodromy action on a correspondence T, which varies with the curves C in a pencil Σ. He assumes that the only degenerate members of Σ are curves with a single node, that is, that Σ is a "Lefschetz pencil,"[33] and computes the local monodromy actions on $H^1 \otimes H^1$ explicitly in terms of the Picard-Lefschetz transformations (cf. ref. 30, pp. 321–326). Using these computations, he proves that the cohomology class of T is *invariant*. The following theorem is an easy consequence of this fact:

> (*) Some multiple of T is algebraically equivalent to a correspondence T' defined rationally as a function of the parameter of Σ.

At this point the logical sequence of Severi's reasoning becomes obscure. He seems to say that his results do not suffice to prove the main theorem but that a geometric proof will be given in later sections of the paper. These later sections unfortunately contain errors. His second proof of (*) (ref. 57, pars. 15–18) is not convincing, and there is an error in paragraph 19 as well.

This last point is the one which Zariski addresses in [13]. He starts with Severi's reasoning and adds an ingenious argument, to conclude that the main theorem holds provided that the rational map from F to projective space defined by $|C|$ is birational. In the proof he uses the result (*) of Severi, which is correctly established only for Lefschetz pencils, so it seems to us that the condition that a generic pencil of $|C|$ be a Lefschetz pencil must be added to the hypotheses of theorem III. This will, for instance, be true if $|C|$ is very ample (cf. ref. 30).

It is not difficult to verify this extra condition in the cases of plane curves with nodes that Zariski considers at the end of his paper, and so a proof of the fact that the general curve of genus p has no singular correspondence can be distilled from the two papers of Severi and Zariski. These questions have been taken up in a recent paper of Mori.[39]

5. Symmetric Products of Curves [27]

In *A Topological proof of the Riemann-Roch theorem* [27] Zariski uses the topology of the n-fold symmetric product $C(n)$ of a curve to study the linear systems on C. He exhibits a basis for the homology of $C(n)$ modulo torsion in the first section of the paper. A linear system g_n^r is represented by a subscheme of $C(n)$ isomorphic to projective space $\mathbf{P}^r$ and thus has a class in the homology ring. By calculations in this homology ring, Zariski proves the following:

(i) Clifford's theorem: If a linear system $|\mathfrak{a}| = g_n^r$ is special, then $n \geq 2r$.

(ii) Assuming the Riemann inequality $r \geq n - p$ and the existence of some $g_{2p-2}^{r-1} = |k|$, every special linear system $|\mathfrak{a}| = g_n^r$ is partially contained in $|k|$.

The Riemann-Roch formula $i(\mathfrak{a}) = \dim k - \mathfrak{a}| + 1$ follows easily from (ii).

In a footnote to his paper, Zariski posed the problem of determining the torsion of $C(n)$. This was not solved until 1962 when Macdonald[34] showed that $H^i(C(n), \mathbf{Z})$ is torsion-free. More recently, Deligne[18] has proved a general symmetric Künneth formula.

The use of the rich geometry of symmetric products was revived around 1960 by Mattuck[35] and has been continued actively since then in the work of Macdonald,[34] Schwartzenberger,[53] Kempf,[31] Kleiman and Laksov,[32] and others. In this work various bundles and cycles on $C(n)$ are related to problems in the classical theory of curves, and theorems are proved using calculations in the rational equivalence ring or in the homology ring of $C(n)$.

Mattuck and Mayer[38] have given a proof of the Riemann-Roch theorem, based on symmetric products, in which $i(\mathfrak{a})$ is exhibited explicitly as the dimension of the space of regular differentials vanishing on the divisor $\mathfrak{a}$. Their proof is based on a natural $1-1$ correspondence between regular differentials on C and on $C(n)$, in which a differential ω on C, such that $(\omega) \geq \mathfrak{a}$, corresponds to a ω' on $C(n)$ vanishing at the *point* $\mathfrak{a}$.

6. Purity of the Branch Locus [73]

Zariski's theorem on purity of the branch locus [73] has been the basis of continued work up to the present time, and though his own proof may be considered definitive in terms of elegance and simplicity, the result has continued to intrigue people, and several other proofs have been proposed.

In its simplest form, the theorem asserts that a finite map π: $Y \to X$ of normal algebraic varieties of dimension n is everywhere unramified if its ramification locus has codimension >1 and X is smooth. The proof in characteristic zero takes a few lines in Zariski's paper, and we will repeat it here: Let $x_1, \ldots, x_n$ be local parameters at a point $p \in X$, and let $q \in Y$ be a point lying over p. The derivations $\partial/\partial x_i$ extend uniquely to the function field $K(Y)$. If f is a regular function at q, then the fact that π is unramified at all points of codimension 1 implies that the partial derivatives $\partial f/\partial x_i$ have no polar divisor passing through q, and therefore since Y is normal, they are regular functions at q. So f may be expanded in a Taylor series at q with respect to $x_1, \ldots, x_n$. We may view the Taylor expansion as a homomorphism $\mathcal{O}_{Y,q} \to k[[x_1, \ldots, x_n]]$. Since $\mathcal{O}_{Y,q}$ is normal and n-dimensional (analytic normality [59]), the induced homomorphism

$$\mathcal{O}_{Y,q} \to k[[x_1, \ldots, x_n]] = \mathcal{O}_{X,p},$$

which is obviously injective, is an isomorphism. It follows that π is unramified at q, and so the theorem is proved. As Grothendieck has observed,[24] the appeal to analytic normality can be avoided by basing the theorem on the depth of Y instead.

Zariski goes on to extend his proof to the case of a perfect ground field of characteristic p, and Nagata[41] treats the imperfect case. More recently Altman and Kleiman[5] have taken Zariski's idea up again, replacing derivations by the algebra of principal parts, to prove the purity theorem over an arbitrary base.

We will review briefly the ideas involved in some other proofs. If Y

is flat over X, so that θ_Y is a locally free θ_X-module, then the condition that Y be étale can be expressed as non-degeneracy of the bilinear form trace $(y \cdot y')$, and the zeros of the discriminant of this form must have pure codimension 1. Since every reflexive module over a regular local ring of dimension ≤ 2 is free, flatness is automatic when dim $X \leq 2$, and so the theorem follows in that case (cf. Auslander and Buchsbaum[9]). Using a local Bertini theorem of Chow, Nagata[42] reduced the general theorem to the case of dimension 2 and concluded his proof by appealing to Auslander and Buchsbaum's result. Grothendieck[24] made a similar argument, replacing Chow's theorem by his local Lefschetz theory to reduce to dimension 2. His method also shows that purity holds for complete intersections of dimension ≥ 3. Finally, Auslander[8] has given an entirely different proof based on the structure of the endomorphism ring $\text{Hom}_{\theta_X}(\mathcal{O}_Y, \mathcal{O}_Y)$.

The purity theorem has an obvious topological analog in the classical case: If $Z \subset X$ is a closed set of codimension > 1, then $\pi_1(X - Z) \approx \pi_1(X)$. This fact explains the importance of the theorem to algebraic geometry. Together with Abhyankar's lemma, it is one of the main tools in the study of the algebraic fundamental group, and its generalizations to higher cohomology groups for the étale topology are closely analogous to classical ones (cf. Artin,[7] Raynaud[50]).

Other generalizations of the purity theorem are to maps of relative dimension > 0. Lang conjectured that an analog of the purity theorem should hold for maps smooth on an open set. Such theorems have been proved by Grothendieck[25] for abelian schemes and by Dolgačev[19] and Ramanujan[48] for families of curves. An example showing that the most naive generalization is false was given by Mumford,[40] and other examples are furnished by deformations of cones over rational space curves (cf. Pinkham[45]).

7. The Fundamental Group

The papers included under this heading are [15–20,22,28,29,31]. Some general surveys of the topics dealt with in these papers are:

a) Chapter VIII of Zariski's *Algebraic surfaces* [25];
b) Brieskorn's lectures in Arcata: *Special singularities — resolution, deformation, and monodromy* [12] (especially 2.1.5);
c) Serre's Bourbaki report.[56]

Although the papers range broadly and introduce ideas that are now important in knot theory, deformation theory, monodromy, and the geometry of the discriminant locus, there is one problem at the forefront, which will serve as a focus.

The Central Problem

Let $C \subset \mathbf{P}^2$ be a plane curve defined over the complex numbers. The curve C may be reducible and possess singularities of various sorts. What can be said about its *Poincaré group G*, that is, the fundamental group of the complement of C in $\mathbf{P}^2$?

This problem is stated in terms of curves, but it lies at the heart of an understanding of the fundamental group of the complement of a hypersurface of any dimension in projective space. In fact the main theorem of [29] asserts:

Theorem: Let $V \subset \mathbf{P}^N$ be a hypersurface, and let H be a generic hyperplane. If $N \geq 3$, the map $\pi_1(H - H \cap V) \to \pi_1(\mathbf{P}^N - V)$ is an isomorphism.

By induction the Poincaré group of V is isomorphic to the Poincaré group of the plane curve C obtained by intersecting V with a generic linear space of dimension two. We shall refer to this fact as the *plane section theorem.*

Zariski's proof [29] requires amplification at certain points. A complete proof along the same lines has been given by Varchenko.[60] Another proof [28] uses stratifications in the sense of Whitney and Mather, and there is a third proof [14] which is Morse-theoretic in nature. There seems to be no algebraic proof yet, but see Raynaud.[50]

As Zariski noted in the introduction to [28], the usefulness of the theorem we have just quoted is not just that it "reduces the study of the fundamental group of the complement of a hypersurface of general dimension to that of a curve in $\mathbf{P}^2$." Indeed, it is extremely fruitful to go the other way:

The advantage of transforming the plane problem into a problem in a space of higher dimension seems due to the fact that if a curve C is a generic plane section of V_{n-1}, then, everything else being equal, the hypersurface V_{n-1} supplies a more intrinsic picture of the Poincaré group of C than C itself. The essential features of the Poincaré group of C should be revealed best on the hypersurface V_{n-1} lying in a space of the highest possible dimension.

This idea is still being vigorously pursued in various forms; it pervades the current study of deformation of singularities and of universal unfolding (cf. ref. 12).

The chronology of his papers suggests that Zariski's first interest in this problem came from a study of the branch loci of algebraic functions of two variables. Enriques[20] began this study by his extension of the classical Riemann existence theorem to $\mathbf{P}^2$. As Zariski remarks in chapter VIII, [25], Enriques' theory provides information about *finite quotient groups* of G and guarantees the existence of *algebraic* finite coverings corresponding to any finite quotient group of G.

The Riemann-Enriques existence theorem has subsequently been generalized to the case where $\mathbf{P}^2$ is replaced by an arbitrary variety (Grauert-Remmert[22] and Grothendieck[23]). A study of these finite topological coverings, or equivalently of the associated finite algebraic coverings of $\mathbf{P}^2$, whose branch locus is contained in C, could lead to a systematic understanding of the profinite completion $\hat{G}$ of G. (By definition $\hat{G}$ is the projective limit of the finite quotient groups of G.) But one needs more topological techniques to obtain information about G itself.

At this point it is perhaps worth mentioning that if we attempt to generalize our central question from the complex numbers to an arbitrary field k, the natural object of study would be the so-called *algebraic* fundamental group of $\mathbf{P}^2 - C$, which, by definition, the projective limit of the system of Galois groups of connected base-pointed finite Galois coverings of $\mathbf{P}^2$, whose branch locus is contained in C and which are defined over k. When $k = \mathbf{C}$, the algebraic fundamental group is then $\hat{G}$. This is an interesting area of study, but the extremely topological flavor of Zariski's approach and the extra information one obtains about unramified infinite coverings of $\mathbf{P}^2 - C$ make it reasonable to regard the case $k = \mathbf{C}$ as having special and separate status. For modern developments concerning the algebraic fundamental group, see references 1,26,47.

Examples

As an indication of the richness and difficulty of the central problem, we consider three examples:

1. The general surface of degree n in $\mathbf{P}^3$: Consider the projection to $\mathbf{P}^2$ of the general surface of degree n in $\mathbf{P}^3$, and let $C_n \subset \mathbf{P}^2$ denote the branch locus of this projection. Let G_n be the Poincaré group of C_n in $\mathbf{P}^2$. It can be shown that G_n admits a surjective homomorphism to the symmetric group of n letters and, therefore, the G_n is non-abelian if $n \geq 3$.

The first interesting case to consider is the case $n = 3$, which is studied in detail in [28]. The curve C_3 is a sextic with six cusps lying on a conic, and the group G_3 is a free product of a cyclic group of order 2 with a cyclic group of order 3.

The group-theoretic structure of G_n for general n has not been worked out and may be difficult. Moreover, even for $n = 3$ one is tempted to ask more delicate questions concerning this instructive example. For example, let U denote a convenient open sub-scheme in the projective space of all cubic surfaces in $\mathbf{P}^3$. One has a monodromy homomorphism $\pi_3(U) \rightarrow \mathrm{Aut}(G_1)$, and one might like to understand the image of that homomorphism.

2. The discriminant locus: Viewing $\mathbf{P}^n$ as the space of all nonzero polynomials in the variable X of degree $\leq n$, up to scalar multiplication, one may consider the hypersurface $D_n \subset \mathbf{P}^n$ that is the locus of zeroes of the discriminant form. Let Γ_n denote the fundamental group of the complement of D_n in $\mathbf{P}^n$. The group Γ_n has been studied closely by Zariski; it is essentially the *nth braid group* defined by Artin[6] and may also be interpreted as the group of homotopy classes of automorphisms of the sphere with n holes (cf. [28]).

By the plane section theorem, Γ_n is the Poincaré group of the curve $C_n = D_n \cap \pi$, where π is a general plane in $\mathbf{P}^n$. This is an important example for understanding current work on the topology of the discriminant locus and Zariski's analysis of plane curves.

3. The case of an abelian Poincaré group: We consider this case under its own heading since it occurs quite often and could be regarded as the *unextraordinary* situation. When G is abelian, it is isomorphic to the first homology group of $\mathbf{P}^2 - C$ and, therefore, can be computed quite easily using the Alexander duality theorem in elementary topology: If C is a union of r irreducible curves whose

degrees are given by the numbers $d_1, \ldots, d_r$, then $H_1(\mathbf{P}^2 - C, Z)$ is isomorphic to the quotient of Z^r by the group generated by $(d_1, \ldots, d_r)$.

Cyclic Multiple Planes and Knot Theory

Whether or not G is abelian, there are certain cyclic coverings of $\mathbf{P}^2$ whose branch loci are contained in C and that deserve to be studied in their own right. Let C be the locus of zeros of the inhomogeneous polynomial $f(x,y)$. For any d one may consider the hypersurface H_d in $\mathbf{P}^3$ given by

$$z^d - f(x,y) = 0.$$

These hypersurfaces H_d, which are called *cyclic multiple planes* by Zariski, need not be irreducible, and their normalizations need not be nonsingular. In the special case that the group G is *cyclic*, these coverings H_d provide models of every finite (irreducible) covering of $\mathbf{P}^2$ branched on C. As Zariski remarks [20], the case that G is cyclic is analogous to the situation in knot-theory in which the sphere Σ is unknotted.

Let us consider, briefly, this analog in classical knot theory. In the latter one forms, for any integer d, the compact 3-manifold M_d, which is a cyclic d-fold covering of S^3, ramified precisely along Σ. (The idea of considering these manifolds and their invariants goes back to Reidemeister.[51]) The algebraic-geometric and the knot-theoretic situations come together in the following important construction:

Consider a curve $C \subset \mathbf{P}^2$ ($f(x,y) = 0$) and a *singular* point $s = (0,0) \in C$. Suppose for simplicity that C has only one branch at S. Draw the three sphere S^3 of points in $\mathbf{P}^2$ that are a distance ϵ from s, for a suitably small $\epsilon > 0$. Then S^3 will intersect C in a one-sphere knot $\Sigma \subset S^3$.

The fundamental group of this knot Σ maps homomorphically to the Poincaré group G, and one obtains a relationship between the cyclic multiple planes H_d, considered above, and the manifolds M_d associated with Σ. The above construction was initiated by Brauner[10] and is studied further by Zariski in [22]. The knots one obtains from such algebraic singularities are among a special class of knot called *compound toroidal knots* (or Schlauchknoten), and their topological type is determined by numbers arising from the Puiseux expansion of y as a series in x. Brauner[10] gave a description of these knots and a presentation of their fundamental group. In [22]* Zariski rederives a presentation of the fundamental groups of such knots by working directly with the algebraic singularity. Moreover, Burau[13] and Zariski [22] independently prove that if two algebraic singularities, each having a single formal branch, are inequivalent algebraically, in the sense that they have different *characteristic terms* (cf. [22]) of their Puiseux expansions, then the fundamental groups of the associated knots are nonisomorphic.

This last result is a model for a type of question that was raised only much later in higher dimensions. In particular, Mumford[40] showed that a point s on a normal surface S is a nonsingular if and only if the maniford Z, obtained by interesecting S with a small sphere about s, is simply connected; this had been conjectured by Abhyankar. Working in a more general dimension, Brieskorn[11] showed that the differential topology of the analogous manifolds Z constructed about isolated singular points could be quite subtle. First, Z could be diffeomorphic to a sphere even though $s \in S$ is singular. Second, for the appropriate choice of complete intersection S one may obtain as manifold Z *any* exotic Milnor sphere that bounds a parallelizable manifold.

The 3-manifolds M_d are intimately connected with the so-called *Alexander polynomial* of the knot Σ; this was pointed out by Alexander[3] in the paper in which he introduced this notion. In [22] Zariski showed that, for compound torus knots, the first Betti number of M_d is the number of zeros (counted with multiplicity) of the Alexander polynomial that are located at dth roots of unity. Zariski raised the question of whether this relationship holds for general knots; Goeritz[21] answered Zariski's question affirmatively. Later knot-theoretic developments showed that most of the salient invariants (the 1-dimensional torsion number and the self-linking invariants of Seifert[54]) of the manifolds M_d can be determined from the Alexander matrix of the knot.

Let us return to the cyclic multiple planes H_d. Although they play a role in the study of the Poincaré group G of a plane curve C similar

---

* See also Errata for paper [22] on p. 231 of Zariski's Collected Works, Vol. 3.

to the role played by the M_d in the study of Σ, there are some differences. The first striking one is that the *singularities* of the normalization of H_d may be difficult to analyze and it is important to have some understanding of them before a fine study of the H_d can be undertaken. These singularities depend on the nature of the singularities of C (and, at times, on the manner of intersection of C with the line at infinity). In the important case where C has only nodes and cusps (and, if necessary, is arranged to have transversal intersection with the line at infinity), the singularities of H_d are easily described [20]. In [20] Zariski embarked on a beautiful study of the H_d in the case of a curve C with nodes and cusps. His primary technique is to construct the adjoint surfaces to H_d explicitly (see the appendix to chapter III of [25] for a sheaf-theoretic interpretation of this technique). His results are remarkable for their delicacy and precision. The question attacked is the following: What is the *irregularity*, $q = h^{1,0}$, of the surface H_d? The topological relevance of this question is clear since we are over $\mathbf{C}$, and consequently the irregularity is one half of the first Betti number.*

Zariski obtains necessary and sufficient conditions for q to be nonzero and rather precise information about q when it *is* nonzero. It is zero unless both d and the degree of the curve C are divisible by 6 (the number 6 is related to the nature of the cuspidal singularity: its associated knot is the trefoil, whose Alexander polynomial has the primitive 6th roots of unity as zeros). Suppose that the degree of C and d are both divisible by 6. Then the irregularity q of H_d is entirely determined by the degree of C and the position of the cusps of C in $\mathbf{P}^2$ (see p. 508 of [22]).

As Zariski proves at the end of [20], if C is irreducible and in general position with respect to the line at infinity, and if some H_d is irregular and hence has nontrivial first Betti number, there must be noncyclic coverings of $\mathbf{P}^2$ branched only over C, that is, G must be *noncyclic*. It follows that for the type of curve that he considers, he obtains a criterion for noncyclicity of G in terms of the (degree of the curve and the) actual placement of its cuspidal singularities in $\mathbf{P}^2$.

---

* Previous to Zariski's paper one may cite the following works concerning this problem: de Franchis,[17] who treated H_2 (double planes) for a general curve C, Comessati,[16] who treated H_3 (cyclic triple planes), and Zariski [17], who proved by topological means that if C is any irreducible curve, the first Betti number of H_d is zero when d is a power of a prime.

To emphasize the subtlety of this result, one need only cite the first nontrivial case where Zariski's result applies and which was studied extensively by Zariski. Namely, consider the case where C is a *sextic curve with six cusps*. Then if d is divisible by 6, the irregularity q of H_d is 1 or 0, depending on whether or not the six cusps lie on a conic. See also the discussion about this in paragraph 3, chapter VIII of [25].

In the course of establishing the above results, Zariski shows that certain systems of curves having base points at the cusps of an irreducible curve are *regular*. This keeps the set of cusps of such a curve from attaining certain positions in $\mathbf{P}^2$, and it also sets certain upper limits to the number of cusps an irreducible curve of a given degree can have. For example, there is no plane curve of degree 8 with 16 cusps [19], although the possible existence of such a curve can not be ruled out by standard considerations such as the Plücker relations or "postulational formulas." In Zariski's language the triple (degree, genus, number of cusps) = (8,5,16) is a *nongeometric* set of Plücker characters. The fact that there are such nongeometric sets of Plücker characters excited much interest at the time of its discovery. It is therefore curious that beyond Zariski's work this deep issue remains largely unstudied. Also, as far as the editors are aware, there has been no further progress in the delicate study of cyclic multiple planes for general d. There are many tantalizing questions here — there are even a number of less delicate topological issues to sort out. For example, for an irreducible plane curve C with arbitrary singularities, can one give some reasonable sufficient conditions for regularity of H_d in terms of the zeros of its "local Alexander polynomials"—that is, the Alexander polynomials of the knots associated with the singularities of C?

Topological Techniques

Along with the plane section theorem, a standard technique used by Zariski consists of calculating precise group presentations for G by relating G to the fundamental group of the intersection of $\mathbf{P}^2 - C$ with a general line. This technique goes back to Van Kampen;[59] see also Zariski's account in chapter VIII of [25], or Brieskorn.[12]

Zariski also studies how these group presentations change under deformation of the curve C, using the *continuity principle*:

The Poincaré group of a curve C maps surjectively to the Poincaré group of a generalization C' of C.

This principle shows that if a specialization of C has an abelian Poincaré group, then C itself does. A more delicate aspect of Zariski's method, however, consists in an explicit description of the change in group presentation that occurs when C generalizes to a curve possessing precisely one less cusp, or one less node [28]. This is applied, in particular, to the study of the generic plane section of the discriminant hypersurface in $\mathbf{P}^n$ (our example 2 above). The curves C_n obtained are rational, and they possess the maximal number of cusps that a rational curve of their degree may possess. Zariski shows that if one generalizes C_n to a curve C'_n possessing fewer cusps, then the Poincaré group of C'_n is cyclic.

The Problem of Irreducibility of the Family of Plane Curves with Nodes, and Commutativity of the Poincaré Group

Severi[58] published a proof that the family of such plane curves is irreducible, which was subsequently found to have an error in it. This result was only recently established by Harris[61], after many attempts including one by Zariski himself [98].

Zariski made use of this result to prove in [16] that an irreducible plane curve possessing only nodal singularities has an abelian (and hence cyclic) Poincaré group. Zariski's proof goes as follows: One first proves that the Poincaré group of a curve composed of m lines possessing only double points is abelian; this one does by an explicit analysis of the presentation of G. Then one uses the continuity property and Severi-Harris's result to conclude the proof.

Abhyankar[1] has proved the following theorem by algebraic methods:

Let C be a plane curve over any algebraically closed field such that the irreducible components C_α of C are smooth and intersect transversally. Then the tame (prime-to-p) algebraic Poincaré group $\pi_2(\mathbf{P}^2 - C)$ is abelian. More recently Oka[43] has proved that the commutativity for a union of curves C_α intersecting transversally follows from the same property for each component C_α.

There are two main points in the proof of Abhyankar's theorem (for a more detailed discussion, see Abhyankar[1] or Serre[56]). Let C_α be the irreducible components of C. First, one shows that the inverse image of C_α in any finite cover of $\mathbf{P}^2$ unramified outside C is irreducible. This is proved by noting that the inverse image of C_α is smooth, a local computation, and then applying Bertini's theorem. It follows that the decomposition group of C_α is the whole group $G = \pi_{1_{\text{tame}}}$. Next, one notes that the inertial subgroup I_α of C_α is abelian (Abhyankar's lemma). A local analysis at an intersection of C_α and C_β shows that I_α commutes with I_β. Thus the subgroup $I \subset G$ generated by the I_α is abelian and normal.

To complete the proof, it suffices to show that $I = G$. The reason for this is that if $Y \to \mathbf{P}^2$ is a finite covering classified by some subgroup of finite index $H \subset \hat{G}$ that contains I, then the branch locus Z of $Y \to \mathbf{P}^2$ must be in C and not contain any of the C_α; thus Z is of codimension ≥ 2. By the theorem of purity of the branch locus (Zariski [73]), Z must be empty; this forces $Y \to \mathbf{P}^2$ to be the trivial covering.

References

1. S. Abhyankar, *Tame coverings and fundamental groups of algebraic varieties, I-VI*, Amer. J. Math., vol. 81 (1959); vol. 82 (1960).

2. S. Abhyankar, *Ramification theoretic methods in algebraic geometry*, Annals of Math. Studies No. 43, Princeton, 1959.

3. J. W. Alexander, *Topological invariants of knots and links*, Trans. A.M.S., vol. 30 (1928) pp. 273-306.

4. K. Alibert and G. Maltsiniotis, *Groupe fondamentale du complémentaire d'une courbe à points doubles ordinaires*, Bull. Soc. Math. France, vol. 102 (1974) pp. 335-351.

5. D. Altman and S. L. Kleiman, *On the purity of the branch locus*, Compositio Math., vol. 23 (1971) pp. 461-465; and vol. 26 (1973) pp. 175-180.

6. E. Artin, *Theorie der Zöpfe*, Abh. Math. Sem. Hamburg, vol. 4 (1925) pp. 47-72.

7. M. Artin, A. Grothendieck, and J.-L. Verdier, *Théorie des topos et cohomologie étale*, exposé 16, Lecture Notes in Math. 305, Springer, Berlin, 1973.

8. M. Auslander, *On the purity of the branch locus*, Amer. J. Math., vol. 84 (1962) pp. 116-125.

9. M. Auslander and D. Buchsbaum, *On ramification theory in Noetherian rings*, Amer. J. Math., vol. 81 (1959) pp. 749–765.

10. Brauner K., *Zur Geometrie der Funktionen zweier Verändlichen: III. Klassifikation der Singularitäten algebroïder Kurven; IV. Die Verzweigungsgruppen*, Abh. Math. Sem. Hamburg, vol. 6 (1928) pp. 8–54.

11. E. Brieskorn, *Beispiele zur Differential topologie von singularitäten*, Invent. Math., vol. 2 (1966) pp. 1–14.

12. E. Brieskorn, *Special singularities — Resolution, Deformation and Monodromy*, mimeographed notes of the A.M.S. Summer Research Institute on algebraic geometry, 1974.

13. W. Burau, *Kennzeichnung der Schlauchknoten*, Abh. Math. Sem. Hamburg, vol. 9 (1932).

14. D. Cheniot, *Une démonstration du théorème de Zariski sur les sections hyperplanes d'une hypersurface projective* (to appear).

15. O. Chisini, *Sulla risolubilità per radicali delle equazioni contenenti linearmente un parametro*, Rend. Reale Instituto Lombardo di Sci. e Let., vol. 68 (1915) pp. 382–402.

16. A. Comessatti, *Sui piani tripli ciclici irregolari*, Rend. Circ. Mat. Palermo, vol. 31 (1911).

17. M. de Franchis, *Sulla varietà ∞^2 delle coppie di punti di due curve o di una curva algebrica*, Rend. Circ. Mat. Palermo, vol. 17 (1904).

18. P. Deligne, *Séminaire de géométrie algébrique, SGA4, Théorie des Topos*, exposé 17, Lecture Notes in Math. 305, Springer, Berlin, 1973.

19. I. V. Dolgačev, *On the purity of the degeneration loci of families of curves*, Invent. Math., vol. 8 (1969) pp. 34–54.

20. F. Enriques, *Sulla construzione delle funzioni algebriche di due variabile possedenti una data curva di diramazione*, Ann. Nat. Pura Appl., vol. 1 (1923).

21. L. Goeritz, *Die Betti schen Zahlen der zyklischen Überlage ungsräume der Knotenaussenräume*, Amer. J. Math., vol. 56 (1934) pp. 194–198.

22. H. Grauert and R. Remmert, *Espaces analytiquement complets*, Comptes Rendus Acad. Sci. Paris, vol. 245 (1957) pp. 882–885; also *Komplexe Räume*, Math. Annalen, vol. 136 (1958) pp. 245–318.

23. A. Grothendieck, *Séminaire de géométrie algébrique SGA1, Revêtements étales et groupe fondamental*, Lecture Notes in Math. 224, Springer, Berlin, 1971.

24. A. Grothendieck, *Cohomologie locale des faisceaux cohérents et théorèmes de Lefschetz*, exposé 10, North Holland, Amsterdam, 1968.

25. A. Grothendieck, *Un théorème sur les homomorphismes des schémas abéliens*, Invent. Math., vol. 2 (1966) pp. 59–78.

26. A. Grothendieck and J.-P. Murre, *The tame fundamental group of a formal neighborhood of a divisor with normal crossings on a scheme*, Lecture Notes in Math. 208, Springer, Berlin, 1971.

27. R. C. Gunning, *Jacobi varieties*, Princeton Univ., 1972.

28. H. Hamm and Lê Dũng Tráng, *Un théorème de Zariski du type Lefschetz*, to appear in Topology. Also Comptes Rendus Acad. Sci. Paris, vol. 272 (1971) pp. 946–949.

29. A. Hurwitz, *Über algebraische Korrespondenzen und das verallgemeinerte Korrespondenzprinzip*, Math. Ann. vol. 28 (1887) pp. 561–585.

30. N. Katz, *Séminaire de géométrie algébrique SGA 7, Groupes de monodromie en géométrie algébrique*, exposés 17, 18, Lecture Notes in Math. 340, Springer, Berlin, 1973.

31. G. Kempf, *On the geometry of a theorem of Riemann*, Ann. of Math., vol. 98 (1973) pp. 178–185.

32. S. Kleiman and D. Laksov, *Another proof of the existence of special divisors*, Acta Math., vol. 132 (1974) pp. 163–176.

33. S. Lefschetz, *L'analyse situs et la géométrie algébrique*, Gauthier-Villars, Paris, 1927.

34. I. G. Macdonald, *Symmetric products of an algebraic curve*, Topology, vol. 1 (1962) pp. 319–343.

35. A. Mattuck, *Symmetric products and jacobians*, Amer. J. Math., vol. 83 (1961) pp. 189–206.

36. A. Mattuck, *On symmetric products of curves*, Proc. A. M. S., vol. 13 (1962) pp. 82–87.

37. A. Mattuck, *Secant bundles on symmetric products*, Amer. J. Math., vol. 87 (1965) pp. 779–797.

38. A. Mattuck and A. Mayer, *The Riemann-Roch theorem for algebraic curves*, Ann. Scuola Norm. Sup. Pisa, 17 (1963) pp. 223–237.

39. S. Mori, *The endomorphism rings of some Abelian varieties* (to appear).

40. D. Mumford, *The topology of normal singularities and a criterion for simplicity*, Pub. Math. Inst. Hautes Études Sci., No. 9 (1961) pp. 229–246.

41. M. Nagata, *Remarks on a paper of Zariski*, Proc. Nat. Acad. Sci., 44 (1958) pp. 796–799.

42. M. Nagata, *Purity of branch loci in regular local rings*, Illinois J. Math., 3 (1959) pp. 328–333.

43. M. Oka, *The monodromy of a curve with ordinary double points*, Invent. Math., 27 (1974) pp. 157–164.

44. M. Oka, *On the fundamental group of a reducible curve in* $\mathbf{P}^2$ (to appear).

45. H. Pinkham, *Deformations of cones with negative grading*, J. Algebra, 30 (1974) pp. 92–102.

46. H. Popp, *Zur Reduktionstheorie algebraischer Funktionenkörper vom Tranzendenzgrad 1*, Archiv der Math., 17 (1966) pp. 510–522.

47. H. Popp, *Fundamentalgruppen algebraischer Mannigfaltigkeiten*, Lecture Notes in Math. 176, Springer, Berlin, 1970.

48. C. P. Ramanujam, *On a certain purity theorem*, J. Indian Math. Soc., 34 (1970) pp. 1–10.

49. M. Raynaud, *Profondeur et théorèmes de Lefschetz en cohomologie étale, cohomologie locale des faisceaux cohérents et théorèmes de Lefschetz locaux et globaux SGA2*, exposé XIV, North Holland, Amsterdam, 1968.

50. M. Raynaud, *Théorèmes de Lefschetz en cohomologie des faisceaux cohérents et en cohomologie étale*, Ann. Scient. École Norm. Sup., 7 (1974) pp. 29–52.

51. K. Reidemeister, *Knoten und Gruppen*, Abh. Math. Sem. Hamburg, 6 (1926) pp. 7–23.

52. J. F. Ritt, *On algebraic functions which can be expressed in terms of radicals*, Trans. A.M.S., 24 (1922) pp. 21–30.

53. R. L. E. Schwartzenberger, *Jacobians and symmetric products*, Illinois J. Math., 7 (1963) pp. 257–268.

54. H. Seifert, *Die Verschlingungs-invarianten der zyklischen Knotenüberlagerungen*, Abh. Math. Sem. Hamburg, 11 (1935) pp. 84–101.

55. J.-P. Serre, *Faisceaux algébriques cohérents*, Ann. of Math., 61 (1955) pp. 197–278.

56. J.-P. Serre, *Revêtements ramifiés du plan projectif*, Séminaire Bourbaki, exposé 204, 1960; Benjamin, New York, 1965.

57. F. Severi, *Le corrispondenze singolari fra i punti di una curva variabile in un sistema lineare sopra una superficie regolare*, Math. Annalen, 74 (1913) pp. 515–544.

58. F. Severi, *Vorlesungen über algebraische Geometrie, Anhang F,.* Teubnen, Leipzig, 1921.

59. E. R. Van Kampen, *On the fundamental group of an algebraic curve*, Amer. J. Math., 55 (1933).

60. A. N. Varchenko, теорема об эквисингулярности семейств алгебраических многообразий Uspekhi Matematicheskikh Nauk., 26 (1971) pp. 217–218.

61. J. Harris, *On the Severi problem*, Invent. Math., 84 (1986), pp. 445–461.

Zariski's Papers on the Foundations of

Algebraic Geometry and on Linear Systems

⊠ David Mumford

In the period 1937–1947, Oscar Zariski completely reoriented his research and began to introduce ideas from abstract algebra into algebraic geometry. Along with B. L. van der Waerden and André Weil, he undertook to completely rewrite the foundations of algebraic geometry without making any use of topological or analytical methods. There were two motivations for this: first, it became clear to Zariski, particularly after writing his Ergebnissebericht *Algebraic Surfaces* [25]† that many of the classical Italian "proofs" were not merely controversial but were really incomplete and imprecise at certain points. Second, it had become clear that it was both logical and useful to develop an "abstract" theory of algebraic geometry valid over an arbitrary ground field.

Two of the three main algebraic concepts that Zariski introduced into geometry and exploited most successfully were that of the integral closure of a ring and that of a valuation ring.‡ He introduces integral closure in [37], announced in [34], and applied it immediately to the resolution of singularities of curves and surfaces: [38], [39]. He introduces valuation rings in [35] to give an ideal-theoretic treatment of the Italian concept of the base conditions imposed by

---

† Bracketed numbers refer to references in the Bibliography following this Appendix. This list includes all of Zariski's published work.

‡ A third is that of the completion of a local ring which he exploited successfully in papers on formal holomorphic functions. (See discussion by M. Artin on p. 215.)

infinitely near points. The results of [35] were applied by Zariski and Schilling in [36] to give an algebraic proof of the theorem that an irrational pencil on an algebraic surface X can have base points only at the singularities of X. Zariski returned to the problem of base conditions and gave a new simpler treatment in Appendixes 3-5 to Volume II of *Commutative Algebra* [75]. Moreover, his results were extended to arbitrary rational singular points by Lipman.[2]

In [43] and [45], Zariski studied the effect of birational maps on normal singularities. In particular the theorem on p. 522 of [45] is the one which has been known ever since as "Zariski's Main Theorem." It states that if $f: X \to Y$ is a birational, regular map of varieties and if the local ring $o_{y,Y}$ of some point $y \in Y$ is integrally closed, then either $f^{-1}(y)$ is one point and f^{-1} is regular at y, or all components of $f^{-1}(y)$ is one point and f^{-1} is regular at y, or all components of $f^{-1}(y)$ have dimension ≥ 1. This theorem has been generalized a great deal in recent years. Grothendieck[1] partly with Deligne, Chapter 4, Sections 8.12 and 18.12, prove the following theorem which they call Zariski's Main Theorem:

If $f: X \to Y$ is a quasi-finite morphism of schemes (that is, $fg^{-1}(y_h)$ is finite for all $y \in Y$) and Y is quasi-compact, then f can be factored: $X \to Z \to Y$, where g is an open immersion and h is finite; that is, $\forall$ open affines $\mathrm{Spec}(A)$ in Y, $h^{-1}(\mathrm{Spec}(A))$ is an open affine $\mathrm{Spec}(B)$ in Y, and B is finite and integral over A. If one applies this to the case where Y is normal (that is, $o_{y,Y}$ integrally closed) and f is birational, it follows that in that case f itself must be an open immersion, which is essentially the original form of Zariski's Main Theorem.

Following the methods of Zariski's original proof, Peskine[6] has proved a local version of this generalization:

If $A \subset B$ are 2 rings, with B finitely generated over A, and $P \subset B$ is a prime ideal which is "isolated" (that is, P is maximal and minimal among prime ideals P' such that $P \cap A = P' \cap A$) then $\exists\, s \in B - P$ which is integral over A, such that $B_s = (A')_s$, where $A' = $ integral closure of A in B.

Finally, in papers [40] and [50], Zariski explored the algebraic significance of the geometric idea of a nonsingular, or simple point of a variety. In particular, in [50], the concept of a regular local ring is used. He discovered the basic fact that over an imperfect ground field k of characteristic p, there are really two different concepts of simple point: *regular* in the sense of having a regular local ring, and *smooth* in the sense that the usual Jacobian criterion is satisfied. (See definitions A and B in the Introduction to [50]; we are following Grothendieck's terminology.) Zariski shows that:

x is a smooth point $\Longleftrightarrow$ corresponding points x' over algebraically closed $k' \supset k$ are smooth

$\Longleftrightarrow$ corresponding points x' over algebraically closed $k' \supset k$ are regular

$\Longrightarrow x$ is a regular point

but that the last arrow cannot be reversed in general when k is imperfect. The main result of the paper is that the set of regular points is open (the corresponding question for smooth is trivial). For more general schemes, Nagata[5] discovered that sadly this was not necessarily true. Samuel[7] and Nagata[4] gave other criteria for the set of regular points to be open, and Grothendieck[1] with his concept of an "excellent ring" has extended Nagata's work and formalized it, Chapter 0, Sections 22, 23; Chapter 4, Section 7. See also Tate[8] for the effect of regular but nonsmooth points on the genus of a curve. One of the motivations for Zariski's work on simple points is his study of the two Bertini theorems in [42] and [48], which provide an excellent illustration of the distinction between the concepts of regular and smooth. Bertini's theorems state that if $\{D(\lambda)\}_{\lambda \in P}$ is a linear system of divisors on a variety X in characteristic zero, then (a) almost all of the $D(\lambda)$ have singularities only at the singularities of X and the base points of the linear system, and (b) either almost all the $D(\lambda)$ are irreducible, or else the linear system is composite with a pencil. Zariski proves (b) in [42], but in the middle of his proof (Lemma 5) uses characteristic zero. He returned to the question later in his *Introduction to the problem of minimal models in the theory of algebraic surfaces* [69, Section I.6], where he proves that if characteristic $= p$, either almost all $D(\lambda) = p^n \cdot E(\lambda)$, where $E(\lambda)$ is irreducible, or else the linear system is composite with a pencil.†
Another proof can be found in Matsusaka.[3] It is Theorem (a) however that is most interesting because it is definitely *false* in charac-

teristic p. Zariski shows in [48] that, in fact, the generic member of the pencil D^*, as a variety over the ground field $k(P)$, is regular except at the base points of the system and the singularities of X; but only if D^* is also smooth over $k(P)$ will almost all the $D(\lambda)$ have the same property.

Zariski's papers on the general topic of linear systems form a rather coherent whole in which one can observe at least two major themes which he developed repeatedly. One is the Riemann-Roch problem: to compute the dimension of a general linear system $|D|$ on a complete normal variety X and especially to consider the behavior of $\dim|nD|$ as n grows. The other is to apply the theory of linear systems in the 2-dimensional case to obtain results on the birational geometry of surfaces and on the classification of surfaces. In relation to his previous work, this research was, I believe, something like a dessert. He had worked long setting up many new algebraic techniques and laying rigorous foundations for doing geometry — and linear systems, which are the heart of Italian geometry, could now be attacked. In particular, the Italian theory could be recast from an algebraic point of view, freeing it of all dependence on the complex ground field and extending it to characteristic p; and many of its results could be extended from surfaces and curves to higher dimensional varieties.

In [56] he announces results on the dependence of the arithmetic genus on birational transformations. These results are proved in detail in a joint paper [57] with H. T. Muhly. Here, If $X \subset P^n$ is a projective variety, the arithmetic genus $p_a(X)$ is defined by

$$p_a(X) = (-1)^{\dim X}(P(0) - 1),$$

where

$$P(n) = \text{Hilbert polynomial of } X.$$

---

† If I may be allowed to interject a personal note, as a student of Zariski's I once attended a seminar on this book where each week Zariski would select, just before the hour, one of us to give that week's lecture. I happened to be the one called upon the week that we proved Bertini's theorem and, being a novice who was struggling to see any geometry at all behind the algebra, I started by saying that "for simplicity" we might as well restrict ourselves to characteristic zero. The response was a laugh but a firm request to keep the characteristic p case in mind.

Using the concept of a "proper" birational map $f\colon X_1 \to X_2$ (which means: for generic linear sections $X_1 \cdot H_1 \cdot \cdots \cdot H_k = Z^{(k)}$ of every dimension, $f[Z^{(k)}]$ is normal — no connection with the presently used concept of "proper" as in Grothendieck's elements), they prove that $p_a(X_1) = p_a(X_2)$ if (1) f is biregular and X_1 and X_2 are normal or if (2) f is birational and X_1 and X_2 are non-singular and of dimension 2 (their extension of (2) to dimension 3 misquotes Zariski's earlier paper [47] on resolution in dimension 3 and is therefore incomplete). Subsequently the problem has been clarified by two main developments: Serre's introduction[37] of coherent sheaf cohomology gave a new expression for the arithmetic genus. He showed that

$$P(n) = \sum_{i=0}^{\dim X} (-1)^i \dim H^i(X, \mathcal{O}_X(n)), \qquad \forall\, n \in \mathbf{Z};$$

hence if $n_0 = \dim X$,

$$p_a(X) = \dim H^{n_0}(\mathcal{O}_X) - \dim H^{n_0-1}(\mathcal{O}_X) + \cdots + (-1)^{n_0-1} \cdot \dim H^1(\mathcal{O}_X).$$

This shows immediately that $p_a(X)$ depends only on X as a scheme and not on the particular projective embedding. Moreover it suggests the conjecture: if X_1, X_2 are non-singular and birational, then

$$(1)\ \dim H^i(\mathcal{O}_{X_1}) = \dim H^i(\mathcal{O}_{X_2}), \qquad 1 \le i \le \dim X_1.$$

The second development is due to Matsumura[27] who showed that if $f\colon X_1 \to X_2$ is a birational map of non-singular varieties which can be factored,

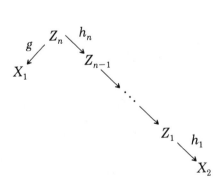

where g is a morphism and each h_i is a monoidal transformation with nonsingular center, then

$$\dim H^i(\mathcal{O}_{X_1}) \leq \dim H^i(\mathcal{O}_{Z_n}) = \dim H^i(\mathcal{O}_{X_2}), \qquad 1 \leq i \leq \dim X_1.$$

It follows from the results of Hironaka[19] that in char. 0 this factorization is always possible, hence (1) is true in char. 0.

In [61], Zariski takes up the central point in the Italian Riemann-Roch theorem for surfaces, which he calls the lemma of Enriques-Severi and in a very thorough analysis, extends it to normal varieties of any dimension and characteristic and deduces from it a Riemann-Roch inequality for general normal surfaces. In Zariski's form, the lemma states that if X is a normal variety, D is any divisor on X, and C_m is a generic hypersurface section of degree m of X, then if m is large enough, $\mathrm{tr}_{C_m}|D|$ is a complete linear system on C_m. In the language of sheaves, this means that the map

$$H^0(\mathcal{O}_X(D)) \to H^0(\mathcal{O}_{C_m}(D.C_m))$$

is surjective if $m \gg 0$. Zariski's proof is notable in giving a very good bound on the m needed for this to be the case. He returned to this lemma in the notes [87] (taken from lectures delivered in 1957–1958) where he gave a second proof much closer in spirit to Severi's original proof. As in the case of the invariance of the arithmetic genus, the problem was greatly simplified by the introduction of higher cohomology groups. Using these, the problem is to show that

$$H^1(\mathcal{O}_X(D)(-m)) = (0) \quad \text{if} \quad m \gg 0.$$

This is proven by methods of homological algebra in Serre;[37] yet another proof is described in Zariski's report [67]. The problem is also closely related to Kodaira's Vanishing Theorem: if X is nonsingular over k of char. 0 and L is an ample line bundle, then

$$H^i(L^{-1}) = (0), \qquad 0 \leq i < \dim X.$$

(Cf. Kodaira;[23] also Akizuki-Nakano,[9] Mumford,[28] Ramanujam,[34] Grauert.[17])

The use of higher cohomology groups also shows why the Riemann-Roch theorem in its classical form has no simple generalization to dimensions $n \geq 3$: what one can readily compute is $\chi(\mathcal{O}_X(D))$ and this differs from the sought-after $\dim H^0(\mathcal{O}_X(D))$ by too many terms. For the history of the Riemann-Roch theorem in higher

dimensions see Hirzebruch,[21] appendix by R. Schwarzenberger; and
Zariski [25], appendix to Ch. 4.

In [63], [77], and [79], Zariski looks in a new direction — at

(1) the function $n \to \dim |nD|$ and

(2) the rings $R_D = \bigcup_{n=0}^{\infty} \Gamma(\mathcal{O}_X(nD)) = \Gamma(X - \text{Support}(D), \mathcal{O}_X)$

and $R'_D = \bigoplus_{n=0}^{\infty} \Gamma(\mathcal{O}_X(nD))$

for arbitrary effective divisors D which need not be ample. He notes
in [63] that the finite generation of these rings is a natural generalization of Hilbert's 14th problem. He shows in [63] that when dim
$X = 2$, and D is irreducible then R_D is finitely generated. Subsequently, Rees[35] showed that R_D may not be finitely generated when
$\dim X = 3$; and Nagata[32] showed that Hilbert's 14th problem is false
too. In [77] and [79], Zariski analyzed the rings R'_D when dim $X = 2$
(these being isomorphic to particular rings of the type R_D when dim
$X = 3$) giving in particular a general structure theorem for the func-
tion $\dim |nD|$.

The remaining papers on linear systems concern the application
of linear systems to surfaces, especially to the study of exceptional
curves and to the characterization of rational and ruled surfaces.
Paper [26] (a joint paper with S. F. Barber) is an early work in which
classical language is still used. They study a birational morphism
$f: X_1 \to X_2$ between non-singular surfaces over a point $x \in X_2$ such
that $\dim f^{-1}(x) = 1$. Among other things, they prove that f factors
into a sequence of quadratic transformations, they study the intersection relations of the components E_i of $f^{-1}(x)$, and they character-
ize those configurations of curves $\{E_i\}$ on X_1 which arise from a
morphism f in this way. Many of the same results were proved
independently in a paper[15] by P. DuVal that appeared in the next
volume of the American Journal of Mathematics. Similar questions
are taken up by Zariski again in the monograph [69], but now in
more modern language and in all characteristics. Zariski begins with
a good deal of background including a new treatment of Bertini's
theorem valid in char. p. In the second part he deals again with the
factorization of birational morphism between non-singular surfaces
and gives a general theory of exceptional curves. One important
result is that a non-singular complete surface is always projective.

Subsequently Nagata[30] showed that this was false in dimension 3 (see also Hironaka[20] for a large class of such examples). The third part is a summary of the papers [70] and [74] which prove that if K/k is a function field of transcendence degree 2 and K is not isomorphic to $K_0(t)$, where tr. d.$_k K_0 = 1$, (i.e. the models of K are not ruled surfaces), then K has a unique minimal non-singular model X dominated by all other nonsingular models. Finally the results of these papers plus [71] together prove, as well, Castelnuovo's criterion: if X is a non-singular surface such that $p_a(X) = 0$ and $|2K_X| = \varnothing$ ($K_X =$ canonical divisor of X), then X is rational. Most of these papers can be described as belonging to "synthetic algebraic geometry," that is to say, they depend on the Riemann-Roch theorem to construct specific linear systems giving one quite explicit grasp on the surface in question. Zariski in fact revived this whole line of investigation which, in the hands of Enriques,[16] had led to a general classification of algebraic surfaces. To be specific, the situation which Zariski quickly finds if he assumes that his function field K has no minimal models is that K has a non-singular model F with an irreducible rational but possibly singular curve E on it such that after at least one quadratic transformation of F, the proper transform of E can be "blown down" to a simple point. In this case, he finds

$$p_a(E) = \sum_{i=1}^{m} \frac{s_i(s_i - 1)}{2},$$

$$(E^2) = -1 + n + \sum_{i=1}^{m} s_i^2,$$

$$(K \cdot E) = -1 - n - \sum_{i=1}^{m} S_i,$$

where

$s_i =$ multiplicities of singular points on E, infinitely near, possibly;
$K =$ canonical divisor class on F;

$$n + m > 0$$

Now if for instance, $(E^2) = 0$, then E is non-singular, $(E \cdot K) = -2$. So, by Riemann-Roch,

$$\dim |nE| \geq \frac{(nE \cdot nE - K)}{2} + p_a(F) - [\text{index of specialty } i(nE)].$$

So if $n \gg 0$, dim $|nE| > 0$ and nE moves in a pencil; then apply the classical theorem of Noether-Enriques that if F has a non-singular rational pencil on it, then F is ruled. In the cases $(E^2) > 0$, he examines instead one of the linear systems $|E + nK|$ or $|-K|$. The hardest case turns out to be $(K^2) = 2$, char. $= 2$ in which he has to look also at $|-2K|$, and via this he constructs a birational map to a certain specific singular quartic hypersurface whose rationality is then checked directly.

This line of research has been followed by many others since then: (1) Criteria for the contractibility of finite sets of curves were studied by Artin;[11] (2) The theory of rational and ruled surfaces was pursued by Andreotti,[10] Nagata,[31] and Hartshorne[18] among others; (3) Kodaira gave at the same time another rigorous treatment of Castelnuovo's criterion and went on first to establish all of Enriques' classification and later to carry it further, especially to non-algebraic compact complex analytic surfaces in a beautiful series of papers[24,25]; Šafarevitch[36] gave a seminar in which this theory was also worked out as well as more detailed investigations of $K3$-surfaces (surfaces X such that $K_X \equiv 0$ and $p_a(X) = 1$); Mumford[29] extended much of Enriques' theory to char. p; (4) Van der Ven,[38] Kodaira,[26] and Bombieri[13] studied the surfaces X where K_X is ample or "nearly so"; (5) Šafarevitch and Pjatetskij-Shapiro[33] recently have worked out a deep theory of $K3$-surfaces; (6) finally one of the most important corollaries of Castelnuovo's criterion is Lüroth's theorem in dimension 2: if $f: \mathbf{P}^2 \to X$ is a rational separable map of surfaces, then X is rational. This has recently been disproven in dimension 3.[12,14,2]

References

1. A. Grothendieck, *Eléments de la géometric algébrique*, Inst. Hautes Études Sci., Pub. Math., no. 4, 8, etc.

2. J. Lipman, *Rational singularities, with applications to algebraic surfaces and unique factorization*, Inst. Hautes Etudes Sci., Pub. Math., no. 36 (1970) p. 195.

3. T. Matsusaka, *The Theorem of Bertini on linear systems*, Mem. Coll. Sci. Kyoto, vol. 26 (1951) p. 51.

4. M. Nagata, *A jacobian criterion of simple points*, Ill. J. Math., vol. 1 (1957) p. 427.

5. M. Nagata, *On the closedness of singular loci*, Publ. Math. de l'I.H.E.S., no. 1 (1959) p. 29.

6. C. Peskine, *Une généralisation du "Main Theorem" de Zariski*, Bull. Sci. Mathématiques vol. 90 (1966) p. 119.

7. P. Samuel, *Simple subvarieties of analytic varieties*, Proc. Nat. Acad. Sci. U.S.A. vol. 41 (1955) p. 647.

8. J. Tate, *Genus change in inseparable extensions of function fields*, Proc. Amer. Math. Soc. vol. 3 (1952) p. 400.

9. Y. Akizuki and S. Nakano, *Note on Kodaira-Spencer's proof of Lefschetz's Theorem*, Proc. Japan Acad., vol. 30 (1954).

10. A. Andreotti, *On the complex structures of a class of simply connected manifolds*, in *Algebraic Geometry and Topology*, Princeton University Press, 1957.

11. M. Artin, *Some numerical criteria for contractibility of curves on an algebraic surface*, Amer. J. Math., vol. 84 (1962) pp. 485–496.

12. M. Artin and D. Mumford, *Some elementary examples of unirational varieties which are not rational*, Proc. London Math. Soc., vol. 25 (1972) pp. 75–95.

13. E. Bombieri, *Canonical models of surfaces of general type*, to appear.

14. H. Clemens and P. Griffiths, *The intermediate Jacobian of the cubic threefold*, Ann. of Math., vol. 95 (1972) pp. 281–356.

15. P. DuVal, *Reducible exceptional curves*, Amer. J. Math., vol. 58 (1936) p. 285.

16. F. Enriques, *Le Superficie Algebriche*, Zanichelli, Bologna, 1949.

17. H. Grauert and O. Riemenschneider, *Verschwindungssätze für analytische Kohomologiegruppen*, Invent. Math., vol. 11 (1970) pp. 263–292.

18. R. Hartshorne, *Curves with high self-intersection on algebraic surfaces*, Inst. Hautes Études Sci., Publ. Math., vol. 36 (1969), pp. 111–126.

19. H. Hironaka, *On resolution of singularities*, Proc. Internat. Congress in Stockholm, 1962, pp. 507–521.

20. H. Hironaka, *An example of a non-Kählerian deformation*, Ann. of Math., vol. 75 (1962) pp. 190–208.

21. F. Hirzebruch, *Topological methods in algebraic geometry*, third ed., Springer-Verlag, Berlin, 1966.

22. V. Iskovskikh and Y. Manin, *Three-dimensional quartics and counterexamples to the Lüroth problem*, Mat. Sbornik, vol. 86 (1971) pp. 140–166.

23. K. Kodaira, *On a differential-geometric method in the theory of analytic stacks*, Proc. Nat. Acad. Sci. U.S.A., vol. 39 (1953) pp. 1268–1273.

24. K. Kodaira, *On compact complex analytic surfaces*, I, II, and III, Ann. of Math., vol. 71 (1960) pp. 111–152; vol. 77 (1963) pp. 563–626; and vol. 78 (1963) pp. 1–40.

25. K. Kodaira, *On the structure of compact complex analytic surfaces*, I, II, III, IV, Amer. J. Math., vol. 86 (1964) pp. 751–798; vol. 88 (1966) pp. 682–721; vol. 89 (1967) pp. 55–83; vol. 90 (1968) pp. 1048–1065.

26. K. Kodaira, *Pluricanonical systems on algebraic surfaces of general type,* J. Math. Soc. Japan, vol. 20 (1968) pp. 170–192.

27. H. Matsumura, *Geometric structure of the cohomology rings in abstract algebraic geometry,* Mem. Coll. Sci. Kyoto, vol. 32 (1959) pp. 33–84.

28. D. Mumford, *Pathologies III,* Amer. J. Math., vol. 89 (1967) pp. 94–104.

29. D. Mumford, *Enriques' classification of surfaces I,* in *Global Analysis,* Princeton University Press, 1969, pp. 325–339.

30. M. Nagata, *Existence theorems for non-projective complete algebraic varieties,* Ill. J. Math., vol. 2 (1958) pp. 490–498.

31. M. Nagata, *On rational surfaces,* I and II, Mem. Coll. Sci. Kyoto, vol. 32 (1960) pp. 351–370; and vol. 33 (1960) pp. 271–293.

32. M. Nagata, *On the 14th problem of Hilbert,* Amer. J. Math., vol. 81 (1959) pp. 766–772.

33. I. Piatetskij-Sapiro and I. Šafarevich, *Torelli's theorem for algebraic surfaces of type K3,* Izvestia Akad. Nauk Ser. Mat., SSSR, vol. 35 (1971) pp. 530–572.

34. C. P. Ramanujam, *Remarks on the Kodaira Vanishing Theorem,* J. Indian Math. Soc., vol. 36 (1972) pp. 41–50.

35. D. Rees, *On a problem of Zariski,* Ill. J. Math., vol. 2 (1958) pp. 145–149.

36. I. Šafarevich (and others), *Algebraic surfaces,* Proc. Steklov Inst. Math., vol. 75 (1965).

37. J.-P. Serre, *Faisceaux algébriques cohérents,* Ann. of Math., vol. 61 (1955) pp. 197–278.

38. Van der Ven, *On the Chern numbers of certain complex manifolds,* Proc. Nat. Acad. Sci. U.S.A., vol. 55 (1966) pp. 1624–1627.

Zariski's Papers on
Holomorphic Functions

Michael Artin

Zariski's work on holomorphic functions occupied him almost exclusively from the mid-forties through 1950, culminating in his famous Memoir [58].† It was published in 1951, but Zariski had the main results several years earlier, and in fact he alluded to them already in 1946, in the Summa Brasiliensis paper [49]. The use of holomorphic functions in algebraic geometry was slowly emerging at this time, largely through the work of Weil[27] and Chevalley[5,6] on local rings, and of Zariski himself. Because of his interest in geometry in the large, Zariski quickly saw the importance of holomorphic functions along subvarieties, which he thought of as analogues of classical analytic functions. (This point of view was suppressed later in favor of viewing them as inverse limits, but we hope it may be re-emerging.)

Let W be a subvariety of a variety V, defined by a sheaf of ideals I on V. In the terminology of the Memoir, a *strongly holomorphic function* f along W is an equivalence class of sequences $\{f_i\}$ of functions regular along W, which are Cauchy sequences with respect to the I-adic metric. Zariski identifies such a function by means of its

---

† Bracketed numbers refer to references in the Bibliography following this Appendix. This list includes all of Zariski's published work.

"branches" f_w (its images) in the completions of the local rings of the points $w \in W$. A *holomorphic function* f along W is given by a collection of branches $f_w \in \mathcal{O}^*_{V,w}$, one for each $w \in W$, having the following property: for some affine open covering $\{V_i\}$ of V, there are strongly holomorphic functions on each V_i whose branches are the given ones f_w if $w \in W \cap V_i$.

Thus a strongly holomorphic function may be viewed as an element of the I-adic completion of the ring of functions on V, regular along W. This led Zariski to introduce from the start the notion of the completion R^* of an essentially *arbitrary* noetherian ring R with respect to an ideal m.[18] The exposition in [49] is very readable and makes an excellent introduction to completions in general, as well as to his Memoir. A nice feature of both of these papers is that the analytical nature of his theory is brought out clearly. In more recent treatments of completions, such as one by Bourbaki,[4] the major novelty is their emphasis on the flatness of R^* over R, a concept which was introduced in 1956 by Serre.[26]

It may be worthwhile to review the terminology of [49], for it differs from present usage. Mainly, the term *semi-local ring,* as used by Zariski, does not mean a ring with finitely many maximal ideals; this is Chevalley's terminology and is the common one at present. Instead, Zariski uses the adjective "semi-local" more generally, to refer to an m-adic ring R having the following property:

If $S \equiv 1$ (modulo m), then s is a unit in R.

He shows that this is equivalent with the condition

$$\mathrm{m} \subset \mathrm{rad}\, R,$$

where rad R is the Jacobson radical, called the *kernal* by Zariski. Such "semi-local" rings are now usually called *Zariski rings.* The localization of any noetherian affine scheme along a closed subscheme is a Zariski ring, and so the study of their completions leads to an essentially general theory.

In the Memoir, Zariski lays the foundations of a global theory of holomorphic functions and proves the following theorem on the invariance of the ring of holomorphic functions under rational transformations:

Let $T: V' \rightarrow V$ be a projective morphism of varieties. Assume that V is normal, and that the function field $K(V)$ is algebraically closed in $K(V')$.

Let W be a closed subvariety of V, and let $W' = T^{-1}(W)$. Then the rings of holomorphic functions $\mathcal{O}^*_{V,W}$ and $\mathcal{O}^*_{V',W'}$ are isomorphic.

Zariski applied this theorem to a "principle of degeneration" which extended his Main Theorem [45] (see Mumford's introduction to Volume I) to a very general connectedness theorem. His formulation of this principle of degeneration is explained in the survey articles [55] and [60], as well as in the introduction of the Memoir. It has been translated into the language of schemes and generalized slightly by Grothendieck,[13] to give the following assertion:

Let $f: V' \to V$ be a proper morphism of noetherian schemes such that $f_*\mathcal{O}_{V'} = \mathcal{O}_V$. Then the geometric fibres of f are connected.

The method of holomorphic functions was immediately recognized as having great potential. (It was called "bahnbrechend" by Krull in his review[19] of the Memoir.) But the principle of degeneration continued to be its main application for several years, and it was not until Grothendieck's work that its full power was realized. Important as the connectedness results are, they are now only one aspect of a method which has become a main tool of modern algebraic geometry.

Basically, Grothendieck has enriched the theory in two ways:

(1) He generalized the principal theorem, replacing the structure sheaf $\mathcal{O}$ by a coherent sheaf of modules, and f_* by the higher direct images $R^q f_*$. This extension was quite natural. It was at least partly foreseen by Zariski [67, p. 120] when he learned of Serre's work[25] on coherent sheaves, and was proved by Grothendieck a year or two later.

(2) More importantly, using techniques introduced by Serre,[26] Grothendieck has proved an *existence* theorem for coherent sheaves given formally,[13] and has applied it to many problems, such as computing the tame fundamental group of a curve in characteristic p.[14]

As an aid to a casual reader wishing to browse in the Memoir, here are a few salient features. There is an interesting discussion of some open questions on page 24, on which considerable work has been done in the meantime. Problems B and C have been answered negatively in their strict interpretations, but many positive results have been obtained by Grauert,[11] Hartshorne,[16] Hironaka,[18] Matsumura,[17] and Artin.[2] Problem A, which is still open, has also been clarified by all of this work.

The first main result is Theorem 10 on page 40, which asserts that, on an affine variety, a function which is holomorphic is strongly holomorphic, i.e., is in the completion of the affine coordinate ring. This appears as the coherence property of holomorphic functions in Grothendieck's elements.[13]

Then comes Part II, with the proof of the principal theorem. In contrast with Grothendieck's more general proof for the higher direct images $R^q T_*$, which uses descending induction on q and gives little intuition as to why the theorem is true, Zariski's approach is quite constructive. It is based on the classical method of reduction to relative dimension 1, which he uses also in his first proof of the Main Theorem [45].

Let $T: V' \to V$ be the given map, which we assume to be birational. There exists a normal variety V'' dominating V' such that the composed transformation $T'': V'' \to V$ is a composition of regular maps $\phi_i: V_{i-1} \to V_i$, and each V_{i-1} is a closed subset of $\mathbf{P}^1 \times V_i$. It is clear that V' may be replaced by V''. Then since he assumes the range normal, Zariski has to consider the normalization of each V_i, and so he is left with two cases:

(1) V' is a closed subset of $\mathbf{P}^1 \times V$;
(2) V' is the normalization of a closed subset of $\mathbf{P}^1 \times V$.

Case 2 is reduced to case 1 by a conductor argument, and the crucial step 1, the "blowing-up," is done on pages 61–64.

Very briefly, the argument goes this way: Say that $V = \operatorname{Spec} R$, where R is an integrally closed domain. Then V' will be the union of the spectra of two rings $R[t]$ and $R[t^{-1}]$, for some t in the field of fractions K. A holomorphic function ϕ is given by convergent sequences

$$f_i(t) \in R[t] \quad \text{and} \quad g_i(t) \in R[t^{-1}], i = 1, 2, \ldots ,$$

the f_i and g_i being polynomials with coefficients in R. These sequences must have the same limit on $\operatorname{Spec} R[t,t^{-1}]$, i.e., $f_i(t) - g_i(t^{-1}) = 0$ (modulo $\mathfrak{m}^{\rho_i} R[t,t^{-1}]$), where $\rho_i \to \infty$. We may therefore write this difference in the form $h_i(t) + h_i'(t^{-1})$, where the polynomials h_i and h_i' have coefficients in $\mathfrak{m}^{\rho_i}$. Let ξ_i be the rational function

$$f_i(t) - h_i(t) = g_i(t^{-1}) + h_i'(t^{-1}).$$

Zariski notes that this function has no poles on V'! For, if D is a prime divisor and t has no pole on D, the left side of the equation shows that ξ_i has no pole on D. If t has a pole on D, the right side shows that ξ_i has no pole there. Thus, $\xi_i \in R$ since R is integrally closed, and it is immediately seen that the sequence ξ_i converges to the holomorphic function ϕ.

Zariski returned to the connectedness theorem two more times, to give proofs using valuation rings [53], [66]. Both papers involve the notion of *prime divisor* [1] in a d-dimensional local domain $(\mathfrak{o},\mathfrak{m})$. This is a discrete rank 1 valuation ring (R,P) centered at $\mathfrak{o}$, such that the transcendence degree of R/P over $\mathfrak{o}/\mathfrak{m}$ is $d - 1$. In [53] he proves the following analytic result:

Theorem 2: If the local domain $\mathfrak{o}$ is analytically irreducible, then it is a *subspace* of R, i.e., $\mathfrak{p}^i \cap \mathfrak{o} \subset \mathfrak{m}^{\nu(i)}$, where $\nu(i) \to \infty$.

He concludes that if $F: V' \to V$ is a birational morphism and V is normal, then the local ring $\mathcal{O}_{V,f(p)}$ is a subspace of $\mathcal{O}_{V',p'}$. Zariski's Main Theorem follows easily from this fact.

Assuming that the singularities of the local domain can be resolved by monoidal transformations, one can deduce Theorem 2 from another important fact:

Theorem: A prime divisor (R,P) becomes of the first kind after a finite succession of monoidal transformations.

In other words, the procedure of replacing the local ring $(\mathfrak{o},\mathfrak{m})$ by the center of the valuation (R,P) on the monoidal transform of $(\mathfrak{o},\mathfrak{m})$ results, after a finite number of steps, in $(R,P) = (\mathfrak{o},\mathfrak{m})$. This theorem was extended to arbitrary regular local rings by Abhyankar.[1] It was used by Zariski several times: first in his proof [39], [69] that a birational transformation of smooth surfaces can be factored into quadratic transformations, and again in his paper [47] on resolution of singularities for three-folds. In [66], Zariski shows that the connectedness theorem for smooth varieties can also be derived from it.

A quite different and interesting approach to the principle of degeneration has been used by Chow.[7,8] He proves a completely general version constructively, using Chow coordinates and a generalized form of Hensel's lemma. Other proofs of the Main Theorem are described in Mumford's discussion.

In terms of stimulus to further research, two of Zariski's most influential papers are the ones on analytic irreducibility [52] and analytic normality [59] of normal varieties. Together with the work of Chevalley[5,6] and Cohen,[9] they form the beginning of the finer structure theory of local rings. Chevalley[6] proved that the local ring o of an algebraic variety is analytically unramified, i.e., that its completion o* has no nilpotent elements. In [52], Zariski reproves Chevalley's theorem and uses it to show that if o is normal, o* is an integral domain. In [59] he proves the stronger assertion that o* is in fact normal, again basing the argument on Chevalley's theorem.

At the end of paper [52], Zariski considers the problem of extending his results to more general local rings and poses several questions, among them the following: Suppose o is a local integral domain whose normalization ō is a finite o-module. Is o analytically unramified? This property of finiteness of integral closure was taken up by Nagata[23] and has become the central point of his theory. Nagata gave an example answering Zariski's question negatively, but he proved that if the normalization of o' is a finite module for every o' finite over o, then o is analytically unramified. This allowed him to extend Zariski's result to a wide class of rings. He also delineated the theory with several other important examples. Further examples have been given recently by Ferrand and Raynaud.[10]

The most important development in this area since Nagata's book appeared is Grothendieck's use of the concept of *formal smoothness* of o* over o, and his definition of *excellent* rings.[15] A systematic exposition combining Nagata's and Grothendieck's ideas has been given recently by Matsumura.[21] In a related direction the notions of *henselian ring* and of *henselization* of a ring along an ideal have been introduced by Azumaya[3] and Nagata,[22] and studied by Lafon,[20] Greco,[12] Raynaud,[24] and others. The henselization is an intermediate ring between R and R^* and has many of the properties of the completion.

For non-local rings, the first result on analytic irreducibility was obtained by Zariski in 1946 ([49], Theorem 9). The theory of completions of general rings is still far from definitive, and this is an active research area at the present time.

References

1. S. Abhyankar, *On the valuations centered in a local domain*, Amer. J. Math., vol. 78 (1956) pp. 332–336.

2. M. Artin, *Algebraization of formal moduli II, existence of modifications*, Ann. of Math., vol. 91 (1970) pp.

3. G. Azumaya, *On maximally central algebras*, Nagoya Math. J., vol. 2 (1950) pp. 119–150.

4. N. Bourbaki, *Algèbre Commutative*, Ch. 3, Hermann, Paris, 1961.

5. C. Chevalley, *On the theory of local rings*, Ann. of Math., vol. 44 (1943) pp. 690–708.

6. C. Chevalley, *Intersections of algebraic and algebroid varieties*, Trans. Amer. Math. Soc., vol. 57 (1945) pp. 1–85.

7. W.-L. Chow, *On the principle of degeneration in algebraic geometry*, Ann. of Math., vol. 66 (1957) pp. 70–79.

8. W.-L. Chow, *On the connectedness theorem in algebraic geometry*, Amer. J. Math., vol. 81 (1959) pp. 1033–1074.

9. I. S. Cohen, *On the structure and ideal theory of complete local rings*, Trans. Amer. Math. Soc., vol. 59 (1946) pp. 54–106.

10. D. Ferrand and M. Raynaud, *Fibres formelles d'un anneau local noethérien*, Ann. Sci. École Norm. Sup. 4ᵉ série, vol. 3 (1970) pp. 295–311.

11. H. Grauert, *Über Modifikationen und exzeptionelle analytische Mengen*, Math. Ann., vol. 146 (1962) pp. 331–368.

12. S. Greco, *Algebras over non-local Hensel rings I, II*, J. Algebra, vol. 8 (1968) pp. 45–59; and vol. 13 (1969) pp. 48–56.

13. A. Grothendieck, *Éléments de géométric algébrique III₁*, Inst. Hautes Études Sci., Publ. Math., vol. 11 (1961) pp. 130, 122, 149.

14. A. Grothendieck, *Géométrie formelle et géométric algébrique*, Séminaire Bourbaki, vol. 11 (1958–1959) exp. 182, Benjamin, New York, 1966.

15. A. Grothendieck, *Éléments de géométrie algébrique IV₂*, Inst. Hautes Études Sci., Publ. Math., vol. 24 (1965) p. 182ff.

16. R. Hartshorne, *Cohomological dimension of algebraic varieties*, Ann. of Math., vol. 88 (1968) pp. 403–450.

17. H. Hironaka and H. Matsumura, *Formal functions and formal embeddings*, J. Math. Soc. Japan, vol. 20 (1968) pp. 52–82.

18. H. Hironaka, *Formal line bundles along exceptional loci*, Algebraic Geometry, Papers Presented at the Bombay Colloquium, Oxford, Bombay, 1969, pp. 201–218.

19. W. Krull, Review of Zariski's Memoir [58], Zentralblatt Math., vol. 45 (1953) pp. 240–241.

20. J.-P. Lafon, *Anneau henséliens*, Bull. Soc. Math. France, vol. 91 (1963) pp. 77–107.

21. H. Matsumura, *Commutative algebra*, Benjamin, New York, 1970.

22. M. Nagata, *On the theory of Henselian rings, I, II*, Nagoya Math. J., vol. 5 (1953) pp. 45–57, and vol. 7 (1954) pp. 1–19.

23. M. Nagata, *Local Rings*, Interscience, New York, 1962.

24. M. Raynaud, *Anneaux locaux henséliens,* Lecture Notes in Math No. 169, Springer, Berlin, 1970.

25. J.-P. Serre, *Faisceaux algébriques cohérents,* Ann. of Math., vol. 61 (1955) pp. 197–278.

26. J.-P. Serre, *Géométrie algébrique et géométrie analytique,* Ann. Inst. Fourier (Grenoble), vol. 6 (1956) pp. 1–42.

27. A. Weil, *Foundations of algebraic geometry,* American Mathematical Society, Providence, R.I., 1962.

Zariski's Papers on
Resolution of Singularities

🔲 Heisuke Hironaka

The most important originality in Zariski's approach toward the problem of resolution of singularities, and for that matter toward algebraic geometry as a whole, is to use as much available power of modern algebra as possible, not only as techniques in each step of solving a specific problem but also in reformulating the problem from its foundation. For instance, in his way of setting the resolution problem (in sharp contrast to earlier works on the problem by Italian geometers and by J. Walker,[19] who gave a first rigorous proof of resolution of singularities for surfaces), we see as a self-evident matter the similarity between the singularity phenomena at the generic point of a subvariety of codimension s in any variety, and those of an s-dimensional variety at a point. We also easily find exactly where his assumption of characteristic zero is used. By this type of fundamental approach (not to mention specific techniques he invented to overcome specific difficulties in the problem), he made it much easier for other mathematicians in later works to follow the track and make further progress, especially Abhyankar's works in the case of positive characteristics and Hironaka's work in the higher dimensions in characteristic zero.

Zariski writes, in the introduction of his first algebraic proof of resolution of singularities of an algebraic surface [39],

We should say that the requirement of rigor is to be regarded as trivially satisfied in the present proof. More significant, however, is the clarification of the problem brought about by the use of the methods of modern algebra. . . . What is gained concretely thereby is the center of gravity of the proof is shifted from minute details to underlying concepts.

Singularities of algebraic curves are eliminated by integral closure, a conceptually very simple one-step process, as is done in Zariski [38, with Muhly]. This also makes very clear why the singularities of an algebraic curve can be resolved by a *finite* succession of quadratic (or Cremona) transformations, which had been studied earlier in minute details by Italian geometers. There the key is the *finiteness* of integral closure as is made clear in [38]. The problem of resolution of singularities becomes radically more intricate for algebraic surfaces. In [39], Zariski proves that the singularities of an algebraic surface can be eliminated by repeating alternately and a finite number of times the integral closure and the quadratic transformations (applied to all isolated singular points). This is proven roughly in three steps: (a) To classify the valuations of the function field of the given surface by the isomorphism type of their value groups and prove the local uniformization at every valuation by giving an explicit process depending upon the type of the valuation; (b) Using the local uniformization, to prove that a finite repetition of *integral closure and quadratic transformations* transforms the given surface into a surface which locally everywhere birationally dominates at least one nonsingular surface (not necessarily complete); (c) To analyze the factorization properties of *complete* (or integrally closed in a certain sense) ideals in the local rings of a normal surface, locally birationally dominating a nonsingular surface, and to find an explicit recipe to eliminate singularities. In fact, after (b) is accomplished, Zariski proves that the surface continues to be normal after quadratic transformations, and the factorization analysis of the complete ideals involved tells us exactly how many times the quadratic transformations should be repeated. Zariski proves that, after (b), the quadratic transformations give in fact the *minimal* resolution in the sense of birational dominations among those dominating the given surface. The minimal resolution exists for any algebraic surface,[16] but it is often different from the one obtained by the above process of Zariski even if the surface has only rational singularities.[16] The point is that the singularities of a normal surface after (b) are special kinds of rational singularities. (For the classification and the ideal theory of rational singularities, see Du Val,[17] Artin,[9] and Lipman.[16]

The local uniformization was then generalized to all dimensions (for an arbitrary base field of characteristic zero) by Zariski [41]. Here again the proof is based upon the classification of valuations, and the algorithm of repeated Cremona transformations is prescribed by the type of the value group of a given valuation. The result is very local and far from giving a resolution of singularities even for any small neighborhood of a given singular point, but the process is much more canonical and explicit than one can expect in the case of global resolution of singularities. More significant is the fact that the local uniformization is obtained by repeating Cremona transformations of the ambient space. As a by-product of the method of this proof, it is proven that, for every *rational* variety X and every valuation v of the function field of X, there exists a birational transformation $\mathbf{P} \to X$ that is well-defined at the center of v in $\mathbf{P}$, where $\mathbf{P}$ denotes the projective space of the same dimension as X.

In [44], Zariski gives another proof of resolution of singularities of an algebraic surface (this time over an arbitrary field of characteristic zero). He shows that, for surfaces, the resolution is a very easy consequence of the local uniformization. First of all, he notes a simple fact that the space of all valuations of a function field K/k is in a natural way a *compact* topological space. (It is the inverse limit of all projective models of K/k with respect to the canonical birational dominations.) This is incidentally proven in all dimensions in [46]. Thus the reduction of global resolution to local uniformization is done if the following fact is proven: If X_1 and X_2 are birationally related nonsingular algebraic varieties (not necessarily complete), then there exists a third nonsingular variety $\tilde{X}$, birationally related to X_1 and hence to X_2, such that, for each i, there exists an open subset U_i of $\tilde{X}$ for which the birational transformations $U_i \to X_i$ are both *proper* morphisms. Zariski notes that, to find such $\tilde{X}$, the following is enough:

(*) There exists a finite succession of monoidal (or quadratic) transformations with nonsignature centers, say $f_i \colon X_i' \to X_i$, for each i, such that if U_i' is the set of those points of X_i' having some corresponding points in X_j', where $j \neq i$, then,

(i) The U_i' are open and the birational correspondence from U_1' to U_2' is a *proper* morphism, and

(ii) The fundamental locus (= the set of indeterminacy points) of its inverse: $U_2' \rightarrow U_1'$ in U_2' is *complete* (that is, does not extend to the boundary of U_2').

Note that (ii) is satisfied, for instance, if the fundamental locus of $U_2' \rightarrow U_1'$ consists of only a finite number of points. Hence, in the case of surfaces, (ii) follows from (i), and (i) is immediate from Zariski's lemma that the union of any infinite sequence of local rings obtained by quadratic transformations and integral closure is a valuation ring.

The deduction of global resolution from local uniformization becomes substantially harder in dimension 3, as is seen in [47]. It is done in the following steps:

(1) Prove the local uniformization of an algebraic surface (in a three-dimensional nonsingular variety) only by repeating quadratic and monoidal transformations with nonsingular centers contained in the singular locus. (The most important property of such a process is that it naturally extends to the ambient variety without creating singularities.) Once this type of local uniformization is proven, there follows a constructive global resolution of the surface in the following form, which Zariski called the *theorem of Beppo Levi*[15]: Look at the set S of those points at which the surface X has the maximal multiplicity. If S contains an irreducible curve with singular points, then apply the quadratic transformations to the surface, whose centers are these points. If all the curves in S are nonsingular, then apply the monoidal transformation with one of these curves as center. If S contains no curves, then apply the quadratic transformation with any one of the points in S as center. Zariski proves this process eliminates all the singularities of the surface X after a finite number of steps.

(2) To prove (*) for three-dimensional nonsingular varieties X_1 and X_2, birationally related. Zariski does this by taking a linear system on X_1 which gives the birational transformation from X_1 to X_2 and then by applying the global resolution of (1) to the generic member of the linear system. The point is that it is easy to eliminate

any base point of a linear system of surfaces if it is a smooth point of the generic member. (The intersection of two independent generic members of the linear system consists of curves, whose singularities can be easily eliminated.) What Zariski gets in this manner (which incidentally works in all dimensions and in all characteristics with little modifications) is the deduction of *the elimination of fundamental locus* for a birational transformation, that is, (*) with (i), without requiring (ii), from the global resolution of embedded subvarieties. To get (*) with both (i) and (ii), Zariski proves a more exact form of (*) for the case of surfaces. Namely, he solves the *factorization problem* for a birational transformation of surfaces, that is, when X_1 and X_2 are surfaces, f_1 and f_2 of (*) can be found in such a way that the birational correspondence from U_1' to U_2' of (i) is an *isomorphism*.

The proofs of resolution of algebraic surfaces in [39] and [44] are written in such a way that they extend to the case of arbitrary characteristics as soon as the local uniformization in dimension two is obtained. This essential difficulty in positive characteristic was later overcome by Abhyankar,[1] who first reduced the problem to the case of multiplicity p (p = characteristic), by the techniques of Galois theory and ramification theory, and then established an algorithm for polynomials of degree p whose coefficients are power series in two variables. This algorithm has been simplified and generalized (not to the case of more variables but to more abstract situations) by Abhyankar himself.[2-5,7] Abhyankar thus obtained the local uniformization, and hence the resolution in the form of Zariski's [39] and [44], for two-dimensional schemes of finite type over "good" Dedekind domains.[4] A portion of Abhyankar's algorithm[2] has been conceptualized in terms of the Newton polygon (or Newton polyhedron), so as to give a simpler proof of resolution for an arbitrary excellent surface.[12]

Zariski's work in dimension 3 [47] has been extended to almost all positive characteristic cases by Abhyankar.[6] (Characteristics 2, 3, and 5 are excluded in this work of Abhyankar.) Abhyankar's book[6] follows Zariski's [47] almost faithfully except for two essential points: *local uniformization in dimension 3* and *local uniformization of an embedded surface by means of quadratic and monoidal transformations*. (See (1) above.) By a comparatively simple global geometric method, due to Albanese[8] and recently brought up to attention by

Du Val[18] and, especially from the point of view of arbitrary characteristics, by M. Artin (unpublished note) one can transform an algebraic variety of dimension 3 so that the singularities of multiplicities > 3! are all eliminated. After this is done, if the characteristic $p > 3!$, then the algorithm with respect to at least one transversal parameter becomes completely similar to the case of characteristic zero. In such cases, the uniformization problem is reduced to the same of one less dimension, here to the case of surfaces for which one needs the full strength of Abhyankar's algorithms.[5,7] With this and Zariski's ideas in [47], the resolution of singularities for three-dimensional variety in characteristic > 5 is reduced to the resolution of an embedded algebraic surface by quadratic and monoidal transformations with nonsingular centers, due to Abhyankar.[5,7]

Zariski's resolution papers are written in such a way that, whenever possible, the proof in a particular step is done for all characteristics. A typical example of this is Lemma 7.1 of [47], that asserts: If X is a surface embedded in a three-dimensional nonsingular variety, and if $f: X' \rightarrow X$ is the quadratic transformation with center $x \in X$, then every point of $f^{-1}(x)$ at which the multiplicity of X' is equal to that of X at x, belongs to the *projective line* in $f^{-1}(x)$ corresponding to the directrix of the tangential cone $C_{X,x}$. Here the directrix means the vector space consisting of those translations that map the cone $C_{X,x}$ into itself. This idea and the result were generalized by Hironaka.[13,14]

In [62], Zariski proposes a possible inductive proof of resolution of singularities in all dimensions. The suggested idea is to look at a generic projection of a given variety to a projective space of the same dimension and then to apply the induction assumption to the branch locus of this finite projection. When the branch locus consists of a finite number of nonsingular hypersurfaces having *normal crossings* everywhere, the covering can be rather easily analyzed, as was done by Jung in the two-dimensional case, and therefore the resolution of singularities of the given variety finds its recipe. This paper is only a partial result as far as the inductive proof of resolution is concerned. Several years later Zariski [78] and [84] took up this approach once again and showed how it can be successfully applied to the case of a surface imbedded in a nonsingular three-dimensional variety. Where the branch locus is nonsingular, the surface is equisingular along the singular locus. This is the case in which the singularity of the surface can be resolved by a finite number of monoidal transformations having the singular loci as their centers, which are nonsingular by themselves. Moreover this process induces parallel resolution of singularities of all the transversal sections of the surface, and in fact it is completely prescribed by the resolution process of any one transversal section curve. In the general case, there are at most a finite number of *exceptional* singular points where the branch locus is singular. Then Zariski shows that after a finite number of quadratic transformations with exceptional singular points as centers, all the remaining exceptional singular points become *quasi-ordinary,* which means that the branch locus is a normal crossing (of two smooth analytic curves). At a quasi-ordinary singular point, the surface as a covering is given by a fractional power series of suitable two variables (similar to Puiseux series in one variable). From this, he extracts a fractional exponent (r_1, r_2) (analogous to the first characteristic exponent of a Puiseux series) describing the exact process which is a combination of monoidal and quadratic transformations and which reduces the multiplicity of the surface. Incidentally this last step is intrinsically contained as a special case in Lemma (D,1), Chapter IV, of Hironaka[11] (viewed as a step in deducing Theorem I from Theorem II in Hironaka's net of inductions).

Hironaka[11] proposed a different induction by means of the Weierstrass preparation theorem and of the language of general schemes (due to Grothendieck) and proved the resolution of singularities in all dimensions (but strictly in the characteristic zero case). The essentially new features of Hironaka's approach are the techniques developed to deal with the ideal bases of subvarieties of codimensions > 1, especially (a) the notion of *normal flatness* (which generalizes equimultiplicity in the case of hypersurfaces, exclusively considered by Zariski) and (b) the numerical characters v^* of singularities. In Hironaka,[11] the problems about the *total transform into normal crossings* and the *elimination of fundamental locus* are also solved simultaneously with the resolution by a single net of inductions. Bennett[10] studied the *Hilbert-Samuel function* of a scheme at a singular point and showed that this replaces v^* and has better properties than v^* in many instances with regard to the effects of monoidal transformations and specialization of singularities. Some of Bennett's theorems are given simpler proofs in Hironaka.[13]

References

1. S. Abhyankar, *Local uniformization on algebraic surfaces over ground fields of characteristic p ≠ 0*, Ann. of Math., vol. 63 (1956) pp. 491–526.

2. S. Abhyankar, *Reduction to multiplicity less than p in a p-cyclic extension of a two dimensional regular local ring*, Math. Ann., vol. 154 (1964) pp. 28–55.

3. S. Abhyankar, *Uniformization of Jungian local domains*, Math. Ann., vol. 159 (1965) pp. 1–43.

4. S. Abhyankar, *Uniformization in a p-cyclic extension of a two dimensional regular local domain of residue field of characteristic p*, Wissenschaftliche Abh. des Landes Nordrhein-Westfalen, vol. 33 (1966) pp. 243–317.

5. S. Abhyankar, *An algorithm on polynomials in one indeterminate with coefficients in a two dimensional regular local domain*, Ann. Mat. Pura Appl., vol. 71 (1966) pp. 25–60.

6. S. Abhyankar, *Resolution of Singularities of Embedded Algebraic Surfaces*, Academic Press, New York and London, 1966.

7. S. Abhyankar, *Nonsplitting of valuations in extensions of two dimensional regular local domains*, Math. Ann., vol. 170 (1967) pp. 87–144.

8. G. Albanese, *Transformazione birazionale di una superficie algebrica qualunque in un'altra priva di punti multipli*, Rend. Circolo Matem. Palermo, vol. 48 (1924) pp. 321–332.

9. M. Artin, *On isolated rational singularities of surfaces*, Amer. J. Math., vol. 88 (1966) pp. 129–136.

10. B. Bennett, *On the characteristic functions of a local ring*, Ann. Math. vol. 91 (1970) pp. 25–87.

11. H. Hironaka, *Resolution of singularities of an algebraic variety over a field of characteristic zero*, Ann. Math. vol. 79 (1964) pp. 109–326.

12. H. Hironaka, *Characteristic polyhedra of singularities*, J. Math. Kyoto Univ., vol. 7 (1968) pp. 251–293.

13. H. Hironaka, *Certain numerical characters of singularities*, J. Math. Kyoto Univ., vol. 10 (1970) pp. 151–187.

14. H. Hironaka, *Additive groups associated with points of a projective space*, Ann. Math., vol. 92 (1970) pp. 327–334.

15. B. Levi, *Resoluzione delle singolarita puntuali delle superficie algebriche*, Atti. Accad. Sci. Torino, vol. 33 (1897) pp. 66–86.

16. J. Lipman, *Rational singularities, with applications to algebraic surfaces and unique factorization*, Inst. Des Hautes Études Sci., Pub. Math., no. 36 (1969) pp. 195–279.

17. P. Du Val, *On isolated singularities of surfaces which do not affect conditions of adjunction*, I., Proc. Camb. Phil. Soc., vol. 30 (1933–1934) pp. 483–491.

18. P. Du Val, *Removal of singular points from an algebraic surface,* Universite d'Istanbul, Fac. des Sci., Memoires (1948) pp. 21--25.

19. R. J. Walker, *Reduction of singularities of an algebraic surface,* Ann. of Math., vol. 36 (1935) pp. 336–365.

Zariski's Papers on Equisingularity

⬔ Joseph Lipman and Bernard Teissier

The vision toward which these papers point is this: to seek a natural way of stratifying any algebraic or complex analytic variety X so that X is *equisingular along the strata*, i.e., the singularities which X has at the various points of each stratum are *equivalent* in some convincing sense.

An excellent introduction to the theories of equisingularity and saturation created in [81,82,85,89,90,93,97], is provided by Zariski himself in the expository papers [80,86,88,91,95]. In addition to reviewing salient features, we will indicate here some of the developments that have grown out of those theories. For more along these lines, see the report of Teissier.[31]

One of Zariski's basic ideas is that the equisingularity of a *hypersurface* $X \subset \mathbf{C}^N$ along a nonsingular subspace $Y \subset X$ around a point $0 \in Y$ should be defined (inductively, on the codimension of Y in X) by the equisingularity of the branch locus (i.e., reduced discriminant variety) $B_\pi \subset \mathbf{C}^{N-1}$ along $Y_\pi = \pi(Y)$ around $\pi(0)$, $\pi{:}X \to \mathbf{C}^{N-1}$ being a suitably general finite projection. The underlying feeling of a strong link between singularities and their "generic branch loci" can be traced back to Zariski's papers on fundamental groups [16–20,28,29]. (It is interesting to compare Zariski's ideas in these papers with recent proofs of the local and global versions of the Zariski-Lefschetz theorem given by Cheniot,[6] Hamm-Lê,[8] and Var-

chenko.[36]) The theory of saturation received some of its initial moti-
vation from Whitney's work on topological triviality of analytic
varieties along smooth subvarieties (cf. [85,§6]). Altogether, topology plays an important backstage role in Zariski's theory; and the
conjunction of discriminant and topology provides the basis for
many connections between his work on algebro-geometric equisingularity and recent work of others on monodromy, singularities of
differentiable mappings, and analysis on singular varieties (cf.
Teissier,[34] Varchenko,[40] and the end of section 3 below).

   A really satisfactory theory of equisingularity exists only for the
case when Y has codimension one in X. Here equisingularity of X
along Y at 0 means that for some π, B_π is nonsingular. (It should be
understood that we are thinking always of reduced *algebroid* varieties, or of *germs* of reduced complex analytic spaces). This case,
studied in detail in [82], serves as a model for all further work in the
area. There are many different criteria for equisingularity in codimension one, of algebro-geometric, differential-geometric, or topological nature. Each of these provides a theme for further development in higher codimension. But there some of the beautiful
interconnections between the criteria vanish, and of others only a
shadow is visible; the search for more substance remains a major
challenge.

   More specifically (cf. [82]), when B_π is nonsingular, Zariski
showed that the singular locus $S = \mathrm{Sing}(X)$ is mapped isomorphi-
cally to B_π by π and that $\pi^{-1}(B_\pi) = S$ (this is the "non-splitting
principle", cf. Teissier, p. 616[31]) and in particular S is nonsingular
and of codimension one. Taking $Y = S$, we see that there exist
retractions $X \to Y$ and that each of them displays X as a family of
reduced plane curve germs parametrized by Y. The nonsingularity
of B_π means that the irreducible components of any two curves in
this family can be matched up in such a way that corresponding
components have the same characteristic Puiseux exponents, and
corresponding pairs of components have the same intersection multiplicity. (This germinal fact is implicit in Jung's work on local
uniformization.[11]) This in turn means that the curves are *equivalent*
from the viewpoint of resolution of singularities or, topologically, as
embedded germs in $\mathbf{C}^2$. Conversely, any family of plane curve germs
that has all its fibers reduced and equivalent in one of the above
senses has singular locus (say Y) isomorphic to the parameter space

(which is assumed nonsingular), and all projections $X \rightarrow Y \times \mathbf{C}$ "transversal" to X(i.e., in a direction not tangent to X at the origin) have nonsingular branch locus. Finally, given a hypersurface X whose singular locus Y is nonsingular and of codimension one, X is equisingular along Y if and only if the famous conditions (a) and (b) of Whitney[45] hold for the pair $(X - Y, Y)$. It can be shown in numerous ways that for any nonsingular Y of codimension one in X, the points of Y where X is equisingular form a dense Zariski-open subset of Y.

Complete as the theory is in codimension one, it does not exhaust all plausible notions of "non-variation of singularity type." For instance there are examples of Pham (cf. also Berthelot[4]) showing that the topology of a plane curve does not determine the topology of the versal unfolding of an equation of this curve and that very simple geometric features of the discriminant of this unfolding can change as the curve is deformed in an equisingular way.[21]

The codimension-one theory does not work as it stands for varieties over fields of characteristic >0, cf. Abhyankar.[1a,b] Perhaps in positive characteristic the concept of equivalence of plane curve singularities given in [81] (and further developed by Lejeune-Jalabert,[46] Moh,[47] and Fischer[48]) is not the definitive one.

We will now describe briefly some attempts to adapt the various equivalent ways of looking at codimension-one equisingularity to the case where the smooth subvariety Y has arbitrary codimension in the hypersurface X and also to the case where X is not a hypersurface. (Schickhoff even looks at some of these matters in the context of Banach spaces.[24])

1. Branch Loci

The significance of the existence of equisingular projections π (those for which B_π is equisingular along Y_π) is not entirely clear. The theorem in [94] (cf. also Speder, p. 574[26]) is encouraging. Stronger positive evidence is provided first of all by the theorem of Varchenko, which states that if a family of hypersurface germs admits an equisingular projection (Y being the family of origins), then the family itself is topologically isomorphic to $X_0 \times Y$ for a suitable embedded germ X_0.[36,37,38] Secondly, Speder has shown that if X is "generically equisingular" along Y, then the pair $(X$-Sing X, $Y)$ satisfies the Whitney conditions (i.e., X is "differentially equi-singular" along Y [88], definition 2).[26] ("Generic" equisingularity is defined inductively by the condition that for "almost all" π, B_π is generically equisingular along Y_π).

For families X of isolated singularities of surfaces in $\mathbf{C}^3$, with smooth singular locus Y (of codimension two), Briançon[3] and Speder[27] show that the existence of one transversal equisingular projection already implies differential equisingularity. This also follows from a result of Lipman (unpublished) to the effect that the existence of such a projection implies the existence of a strong simultaneous resolution of the singularities of the family X, and Teissier's result:[33] "strong simultaneous resolution implies that the Whitney conditions hold" (the first result is proved only for families of surfaces, while the second holds quite generally). On the other hand, there are the following two examples of Briançon and Speder:

(1)   Let $X \subseteq \mathbf{C}^4$ be given by

$$z^5 + ty^6z + y^7x + x^{15} = 0,$$

and let Y be the singular locus $x = y = z = 0$. For the projection $\pi(x,y,z,t) = (z,y,t)$, B_π is equisingular along Y_π. But X is not differentially equisingular along Y. Hence no transversal projection is equisingular; this answers negatively problem 1 on the second last page of [88].

(2) X: $z^3 + tx^4z + x^6 + y^6 = 0$

Y: $x = y = z = 0$.

Here X is differentially equisingular along Y; but again it can be shown that no transversal projection is equisingular.

The idea of using discriminants also appears from a completely different direction in the study of singularities, namely when it is realized that the number of vanishing cycles $\mu^{(N+1)}(X,0)$ — or Milnor number[17] — of a hypersurface germ $(X,0) \subset (\mathbf{C}^{N+1},0)$ with isolated singularity is the order of vanishing of the discriminant of some map $(\mathbf{C}^{N+1},0) \to (\mathbf{C},0)$ having $(X,0)$ as fiber and that the discriminant of a general projection $f: (X,0) \to (\mathbf{C},0)$ vanishes to order $\mu^{(N+1)}(X,0) + \mu^{(N)}(f^{-1}(0),0)$ (cf. Teissier, section 5.5[34]). Actually $\mu^{(N)}(f^{-1}(0),0)$ does not depend on f, so we write $\mu^{(N)}(X,0)$ instead.

Now it is easy to prove that $\mu^{(N+1)}(X,0)$ depends only on the topological type of the hypersurface $(X,0)$, but this is *not* so for $\mu^{(N)}(X,0)$.
In fact, in the above example (1) of Briançon and Speder, considered
as a family X_t of surfaces (with parameter t), the topological type of
X_t does not depend on t (for t small), whereas $\mu^{(2)}(X_t,0)$ is different
for $t \neq 0$ than for $t = 0$. In particular this shows that the topological
type of a hypersurface germ does *not* determine the topological type
of its general hyperplane section. To come back to $\mu^{(N+1)}$, Lê and
Ramanujam proved that if it is constant in a family of hypersurfaces
$(X_t,0)$ with isolated singularities and $N \neq 2$, then the fibers $(X_t,0)$
all have the same topological type.[12] Timourian showed that this
implies that the family is locally topologically trivial.[35] However,
as we have just seen, topological triviality does not imply that
the family of discriminants of general projections $(X_t,0) \to (\mathbf{C},0)$ is
trivial.

Apropos, there is a remarkable equivalence between *differential
equisingularity* of a family of hypersurfaces with isolated singularities and *constancy of the sequence of Milnor numbers* of the members of the family together with their general linear sections of
various dimensions. This area of investigation was opened up by
Teissier[30] and further developed by Briançon and Speder. In fact,
one of the ideas introduced in Teissier is the relationship between
Zariski's discriminant conditions and the feeling that a "good" notion of equisingularity should have the following property:[31] if a
hypersurface $X \subset \mathbf{C}^N$ is equisingular along Y, then for a sufficiently
general nonsingular hypersurface $H \subset \mathbf{C}^N$ with $H \supset Y$, the intersection $X \cap H$ is equisingular along Y.

2. Saturation

There is nevertheless a fascinating theory when B_π is equisingular
along Y_π in the most trivial sense, viz. B_π is *analytically a product*
along Y_π. This is the theory of *equisaturation*. In order to capture
algebraically the topological type in situations more general than
that of plane curves, Zariski invented the notion of the *saturation* $\tilde{\mathfrak{o}}$
of a local ring $\mathfrak{o}$. For brevity, we deal here with "absolute saturation,"
in which case $\tilde{\mathfrak{o}}$ is defined by Zariski only when $\mathfrak{o}$ is either the local

ring of a point on a hypersurface ([85, theorem 8.2],* [93, theorem 3.4]), or o is one-dimensional ([93, appendix A]; cf. also Lipman[15] and Böger, Satz 5[5]). This $\tilde{o}$ is a local ring between o and its normalization, and $\tilde{o}$ is radicial over o [85,§4] (also Lipman[16]), so that in the analytic case the germs X and $\tilde{X}$ corresponding to o and $\tilde{o}$ are locally homeomorphic, [85,§5] (also Seidenberg[25]). If o_1 and o_2 are the local rings of two hypersurface germs X_1 and X_2, and if the saturations $\tilde{o}_1$ and $\tilde{o}_2$ are isomorphic, then X_1 and X_2 are topologically equivalent as embedded germs [85,§6]; and the converse is true if X_1 and X_2 are plane curves [90,§7]. Given $X \supset Y$ as before, and a retraction $\rho{:}X \to Y$, (X,ρ) is *equisaturated* along Y if the fibers $\rho^{-1}(y)$ ($y \in Y$) have isomorphic saturations at their origins (this is a loose translation of [85, definition 7.3]). A basic fact is that X is equisaturated along Y if and only if for some sufficiently general π, B_π is analytically a product along Y_π [85,§7]. In particular, when Y has codimension one in X then equisaturation of X along Y is equivalent with equisingularity of X along Y.

Equisaturation of X (with local ring o) along Y also means that the germ $\tilde{X}$ corresponding to the local ring $\tilde{o}$ is analytically a product along Y. Since X and $\tilde{X}$ are homeomorphic, this implies that X is topologically a product along Y. Zariski proves more, namely that the *pair* $X \subset \mathbf{C}^N$ is topologically trivial along Y [85,§7].

Here a rather curious thing happened. Pham and Teissier tried to interpret Zariski's work, starting from the idea that topological triviality should be proved by integrating Lipschitz vector fields on X since they have the property of being integrable, of course, but also of extending locally to the ambient $\mathbf{C}^N$, by a pretty result of Banach. They were encouraged by the fact that Zariski's computations in [85] looked like the use of Lipschitz conditions. Therefore Pham and Teissier introduced a purely algebraic description, using the concept of integral dependence on ideals, of the sheaf of *locally Lipschitz meromorphic functions* $\tilde{\mathcal{O}}_X$ on a reduced space $(X,\mathcal{O}_X)$ and defined the absolute Lipschitz saturation of $\mathcal{O}_{X,x}$ as $\tilde{\mathcal{O}}_{X,x}$.[23] They indicated that in the case of *hypersurfaces,* Zariski saturation and Lipschitz saturation *coincide* (a counter-example in the non-hyper-

---

* Theorem 8.3 of [85] does not hold as stated, but it does hold for hypersurfaces (cf. first paragraph in introduction to [85], and Böger, p. 247[5]).

surface case was given by Zariski [93, introduction]). The relation between analytic triviality of B_π along Y_π and topological triviality of X along Y had then the following simple analytical explanation: any vector field on Y_π extends to a vector field on $\mathbf{C}^{N-1}$ tangent to B_π, and this can be lifted to a vector field on X with coefficients which are *meromorphic* but satisfy (locally) a Lipschitz inequality and therefore are bounded; this lifted vector field extends to the ambient space, and if we take a basis of constant vector fields on Y to start with, the integration of corresponding vector fields in $\mathbf{C}^N$ provides a topological (even Lipschitz) trivialization of $X \subset \mathbf{C}^N$ along Y.

Lipschitz and Zariski saturation also coincide in the one-dimensional case (Lipman, p. 808, remark ii[16]). In [89] and [90] Zariski investigates thoroughly the structure and automorphisms of one-dimensional saturated local rings. The simplest version of the "structure theorem" [85, theorem 1.12] may be interpreted as saying that complete equicharacteristic one-dimensional saturated (i.e., equal to their saturation) local domains over, say, $\mathbf{C}$, are of the form $\mathbf{C}[[t^{a_1}, t^{a_2}, \ldots, t^{a_n}]]$ for suitable integers $a_1, \ldots, a_n$ (cf. *Math Reviews*, vol. 38, no. 5775). A class of one-dimensional rings which includes the saturated ones is studied by Lipman.[14] Notable among the algebraic features of one-dimensional saturated rings is the existence of "many automorphisms" ([93, appendix A]; also Böger, Satz 5[5]). This reflects the fact that saturation kills the *moduli* [92] of plane curve germs, in the previously mentioned sense that such germs have equivalent singularities at their origins if and only if they have isomorphic saturations. It is particularly enlightening, compared to the "Lipschitz" definition of saturation, to look at this result geometrically. Consider a nonplanar curve germ Γ. "Almost all" plane projections of Γ will have the same saturation as Γ. (This is the geometric meaning of the *existence of saturators* [85, proposition 1.6], a fact which also underlies the equality of one-dimensional Lipschitz and Zariski saturation.) Hence these plane projections have equivalent singularities at their origins. But conversely, *all* plane branches belonging to the same equivalence class can be obtained — up to isomorphism — as sufficiently general projections of a *single* Γ, namely the germ whose local ring is the saturation of the local ring of any one of the equivalent plane curves.

The algebraic theory of Lipschitz-saturation was taken up and improved on by Lipman[15,16] and Böger.[5,5a] Stutz provided new insight into the meaning of Lipschitz equisaturation when X is no longer a hypersurface, but Y is still of codimension one.[28,29] The joint theory of Zariski and Lipschitz saturation has been used by Nobile to prove an interesting theorem that implies in particular that any germ of reduced complex analytic surface is Lipschitz equivalent to an algebraic surface germ;[18] and by Treissier to give an algebraic proof of the fact that the constancy of Milnor's number in a family of plane curve germs implies that the family is equisingular (a result proved topologically by Lê-Ramanujam, see above).[32] To conclude on this topic, let us note that for a reduced complex analytic space X, the existence of a partition of X into nonsingular constructible strata X_α such that X is locally Lipschitz-trivial (and not just topologically trivial) along each stratum, seems to be completely open when X has dimension ≥ 3. However, Verdier has proved the existence of a stratification with "rugose" triviality, and rugosity is a Lipschitz-like condition, but relative to the stratification.[41]

3. Simultaneous Resolution of Singularities

Zariski proposes to geometers the following program for resolving singularities. Find for each complex analytic variety $X \subset \mathbf{C}^N$ a natural stratification with the following property: if $H \subset \mathbf{C}^N$ is a smooth hypersurface which avoids the "exceptional points" (i.e., the zero-dimensional strata), and cuts all the positive-dimensional strata transversally, then some suitable process of resolving the singularities of $X \cap H$ should propagate along the strata to resolve all the singularities of X outside the exceptional points. Thus, by induction on dimension, one would resolve almost all singularities of X. The remaining step would be to transform exceptional points into non-exceptional ones. For surfaces in $\mathbf{C}^3$, this idea is realized in [78] (cf. also [84, introduction]); the underlying fact is that the singularities of an equisingular family of plane curves can be simultaneously resolved by monoidal transformations [82, theorem 7.4]. A big problem in higher dimensions is that no *canonical* process for resolving singularities is known. Nevertheless, one would hope at least to be able to find natural stratifications which are "monoidally stable" in the sense that a certain class of permissible blow-ups $f: X' \to X$ would be *stratified* relative to the canonical stratifications on X' and X (i.e., f maps any stratum of X' smoothly onto some stratum of X).

There are several possible definitions of simultaneous resolution (cf. Teissier[33]), the strongest of which, as mentioned above, implies differential equisingularity. (Note: the family given in the above example (1) of Briançon-Speder admits a "weak" simultaneous resolution, though it is not differentially equisingular.) Several authors have approached equisingularity from the point of view of simultaneous resolution, and in some cases have succeeded in showing the nonsingularity of the local moduli space, a result which is not obvious even for plane curves (cf. Wahl,[42,43] Nobile,[19,20] and Teissier [92, appendix]).

The problem of finding criteria for simultaneous resolution in more general situations has its interest enhanced by the discovery by Arnol'd(§11)[2], Kushnirenko,[13] and Varchenko,[39,40] of very interesting "equiresolvable" families of functions having isolated critical points where the resolution can be explicitly constructed by a toroidal map $Z \to \mathbf{C}^{N+1}$ from the datum of the Newton polyhedron of the function, the families in question being made of "almost all" (in a precise sense) functions having a given Newton polyhedron. They also computed from the Newton polyhedron many invariants of the singularities, which are in fact invariants of the resolution, e.g., the zeta function of the monodromy, the "initial exponent" of the Fuchsian equation corresponding to the Gauss-Manin connection associated to the singularity, etc.

4. Differential Equisingularity (X Not Necessarily a Hypersurface)

For non-plane-curve germs, there is no satisfactory theory of equivalence of singularities. For example, any two irreducible curve germs in $\mathbf{C}^N$ ($N > 2$) are topologically equivalent. Nevertheless Stutz was able to generalize large portions of Zariski's equisingularity theory to the case where X is no longer a hypersurface, but $Y = \mathrm{Sing}(X)$ is still nonsingular and of codimension one;[28] and he brought out connections between equisingularity and the tangent cones C_4, C_5 of

Whitney (§3).[44] We mentioned above the equivalence of equisingularity and differential equisingularity for families of plane curves. The following generalization is a distillation of results in Stutz[28] and Abhyankar.[1]

Theorem: Let X be a reduced d-dimensional complex analytic variety, let $Y = \mathrm{Sing}(X)$ be smooth and of dimension $d - 1$, and let $0 \in Y$. The following are equivalent:

(1) The *Whitney conditions* (a), (b) hold for the pair $(X - Y, Y)$ at every point in a neighborhood of 0 in Y.

(2) Every irreducible component X' of X at 0 contains Y (at least near 0), and the Zariski tangent cone T' ($\equiv$ Whitney's C_3) of X' at 0 is a d-plane; furthermore, if a sequence of points $x_i \in X' - Y$ approaches 0 and the tangent planes $T_{x_i} X'$ have a limit, then that limit is T'. (In other words $C_3 = C_4$ at 0; this is essentially a generalization of the *Jacobian criterion* [82,§5].)

(3) (*Simultaneous resolution*) If $v{:}\bar{X} \to X$ the normalization of X, then (after replacing X by a suitable neighborhood of 0) we have:
(a) X is equimultiple along Y;
(b) $\bar{X}$ is nonsingular; and
(c) v induces an etale covering $(v^{-1}(Y))_{\text{reduced}} \to Y$.
Moreover, when these equivalent conditions hold, then for every projection $\pi{:}X \to \mathbf{C}^d$ transversal to X, the branch locus B_π is nonsingular, and $\pi^{-1}(B_\pi) = Y$ (near 0). Conversely, if there exists a projection π with B_π nonsingular of dimension $d - 1$, and if every component of X contains and is equimultiple along $\pi^{-1}(B_\pi)$ near 0 (which is automatically so if X is a hypersurface), then the above conditions hold.

Teissier studies a refinement of differential equisingularity, called "c-cosecance,"[34] that grew out of ideas of Hironaka.[9] This equisingularity condition *is* stable for generic hypersurface sections (cf. end of section 1 above).

We mention also, in closing, a still open question of Zariski [88]: if two hypersurface germs have the same (embedded) topological type, do they have the same multiplicity? A step toward an affirmative answer is taken by Ephraim.[7] In this vein there is an intriguing result of Hironaka's that in a Whitney stratification of an arbitrary X, the closure of any stratum has the same multiplicity (possibly zero) at all points of any other fixed stratum.[10]

5. Paper [97] (A General Theory of Equisingularity): Branch Loci Revisited

In this fundamental paper, Zariski introduces the concept of the dimensionality type d.t.$_k(V,Q)$ of an algebroid hypersurface V at a point Q of V, with respect to a fixed coefficient field k of the local ring $\mathfrak{o}$ of V at its closed point P. The definition is by induction on the dimension, as follows: Set $\mathfrak{o} = k[[x_1, \ldots, x_{r+1}]] = k[[X_1, \ldots, X_{r+1}]]/(f)$, where $f(X_1, \ldots, X_{r+1}) = 0$, $f \in k[[X_1, \ldots, X_{r+1}]]$ is the equation of an algebroid hypersurface. Zariski introduces a new algebraic concept of a "generic projection" by adding infinitely many new independent variables $u_{i,A} = (u)$ where $A \in \mathbf{Z}_0^{r+1}$, $1 \le i \le r$, and considering formal power series

$$x_i^* = \sum_{A \in \mathbf{Z}_0^{r+1}, |A| \ge 1} u_{i,A} x^A \qquad (1 \le i \le r)$$

which in a precise sense define a generic projection into the affine space $A_{k^*}^r$ over the field k^* generated over k by the $u_{i,A}$. Zariski then defines the discriminant Δ_u^* of V with respect to this generic projection π_u; Δ_u^* is an algebroid hypersurface defined over k^*, and he defines the "image" Q^* of Q by π_u: He then defines inductively

$$\text{d.t.}_k(V,Q) = 1 + \text{d.t.}_{k^*}(\Delta_u^*, Q^*)$$

and d.t.$_k(V,Q) = 0$ if Q is a simple point of V. Intuitively d.t.$_k(V,P)$ is the codimension in V of the equisingularity stratum of P in V. The main theorem in [97] is that indeed the subsets $V(\sigma)$ of V consisting of the points of V where the dimensionality type of V is equal to a given integer σ form a stratification of V (by nonsingular subvarieties). Given now an algebraic hypersurface V over a field k, and defining the dimensionality type via the completions of the local rings, Zariski can then define an equisingular stratification for any algebraic hypersurface (an important fact, the semicontinuity of the dimensionality type for the Zariski topology along any algebraic subvariety W/k of V, is proved by Hironaka[49]). One of the beauties of Zariski's stratification is that, being defined by the constancy of a numerical invariant, it is uniquely defined (once k is fixed). Indeed the question of the independence of d.t.$_k(V,P)$ on the field of representatives k is still open in general, although Zariski himself has important (unpublished) partial results. Another outstanding question is whether the dimensionality type can be computed by using only generic *linear* projections. In the complex-analytic framework this has been proved in the case where dim $V = 3$ and V has a singular locus of dimension 1 by Briançon and Henry.[50]

References

1. S. S. Abhyankar, *A criterion of equisingularity*, Amer. J. Math., vol. 90 (1968) pp. 342–345.

1a. S. S. Abhyankar, *Remarks on equisingularity*, Amer. J. Math., vol. 90 (1968) pp. 108–144.

1b. S. S. Abhyankar, *Note on coefficient fields*, Amer. J. Math., vol. 90 (1968) pp. 346–355.

2. V. I. Arnol'd, *Critical points of smooth functions*, Proc. Internat. Congress of Mathematicians, Vancouver 1974, vol. 1, pp. 19–40, Canadian Math. Congress, 1976.

3. J. Briançon, *Contribution à l'étude des déformations de germes de sous-espaces analytiques de* C^n, Thèse, Université de Nice, 1976.

4. P. Berthelot, *Classification topologique universelle des singularités d'après F. Pham*, Astérisque, vol. 16 (1974) pp. 174–213.

5. E. Böger, *Zur Theorie der Saturation bei analytischen Algebren*, Math. Ann., vol. 211 (1974) pp. 119–143.

5a. E. Böger, *Über die Gleichheit von absoluter und relativer Lipschitz-Saturation bei analytischen Algebren*, Manuscripta Math., vol. 16 (1975) pp. 229–249.

6. D. Cheniot, *Une démonstration du théorème de Zariski sur les sections hyper-planes d'une hypersurface projective* . . . , Compositio Math., vol. 27 (1973) pp. 141–158.

7. R. Ephraim, C^1 *preservation of multiplicity*, Duke Math. J., vol. 43 (1976), pp. 797–803.

8. H. Hamm, Lê D. T., *Un théorème de Zariski du type de Lefschetz*, Ann. Sci. École Norm. Sup. 4e série, vol. 6 (1973) pp. 317–366.

9. H. Hironaka, *Equivalences and deformations of isolated singularities*, Woods Hole conference on Algebraic Geometry, Amer. Math. Soc., 1964.

10. H. Hironaka, *Normal cones in analytic Whitney stratifications* Inst. Hautes Études Sci. Publ. Math., vol. 36 (1969) pp. 127–138.

11. H. W. E. Jung, *Darstellung der Funktionen eines algebraischen Körpers zweier unabhängigen Veränderlichen* . . . , J. Reine Angew, Math., vol. 133 (1908) pp. 289–314.

12. Lê D. T., C. P. Ramanujam, *The invariance of Milnor's number implies the invariance of the topological type*, Amer. J. Math., vol. 98 (1976) pp. 67–78.

13. A. G. Kushnirenko, *Polyèdres de Newton et nombres de Milnor*, Inventiones Math., vol. 32 (1976), pp. 1–32.

14. J. Lipman, *Stable ideals and Arf rings*, Amer. J. Math., vol. 93 (1971) pp. 649–685.

15. J. Lipman, *Absolute saturation of one-dimensional local rings*, Amer. J. Math., vol. 97 (1975) pp. 771–790.

16. J. Lipman, *Relative Lipschitz-saturation*, Amer. J. Math., vol. 97 (1975) pp. 791–813.

17. J. Milnor, *Singular points of complex hypersurfaces*, Annals of Math. Studies, vol. 61, Princeton University Press, 1968.

18. A. Nobile, *On saturations of embedded analytic rings*, Thesis, Massachusetts Institute of Technology, 1971 (to appear).

19. A. Nobile, *Equisingular deformations of Puiseux expansions*, Trans. Amer. Math. Soc., vol. 214 (1975) pp. 113–135.

20. A. Nobile, *On equisingular deformations of plane curve singularities*, preprint.

21. F. Pham, *Remarques sur l'équisingularité universelle*, preprint, Université de Nice, 1971.

22. F. Pham, *Fractions Lipschitziennes et saturation de Zariski des algèbres analytiques complexes*, Actes du Congrès International des Mathématiciens, Nice 1970, vol. 2, pp. 649–654, Gauthier-Villars, Paris, 1971.

23. F. Pham, B. Teissier, *Fractions Lipschitziennes d'une algèbre analytique complexe et saturation de Zariski*, preprint, Centre de Math., École Polytechnique, 1969.

24. W. Schickhoff, *Whitneysche Tangentenkegel, Multiplizitätsverhalten, Normal-pseudoflächheit und Aquisingularitätstheorie für Ramissche Räume*, Schriftenreihe Math. Instit. Universität Münster, 2. Serie, Heft 12, 1977.

25. A. Seidenberg, *Saturation of an analytic ring*, Amer. J. Math. vol. 94 (1972) pp. 424–430.

26. J.-P. Speder, *Équisingularité et conditions de Whitney*, Amer. J. Math. vol. 97 (1975) pp. 571–588.

27. J.-P. Speder, *Équisingularité et conditions de Whitney*, Thèse, Université de Nice, 1976.

28. J. Stutz, *Equisingularity and equisaturation in codimension 1*, Amer. J. Math. vol. 94 (1972) pp. 1245–1268.

29. J. Stutz, *Equisingularity and local analytic geometry*, Proc. Symposia in Pure Math. vol. 30, pp. 77–84, Amer. Math. Soc. 1977.

30. B. Teissier, *Cycles évanescents, sections planes, et conditions de Whitney*, Astérisque, vols. 7, 8 (1973) pp. 285–362.

31. B. Teissier, *Introduction to equisingularity problems*, Proc. Symposia in Pure Math. vol. 29, pp. 581–632, Amer. Math. Soc. 1975.

32. B. Teissier, *Sur diverses conditions numériques d'équisingularité des familles de courbes* . . . , preprint, Centre de Math., École Polytechnique, 1975.

33. B. Teissier, *Sur la résolution simultanée comme condition d'équisingularité*, preprint, Centre de Math., École Polytechnique, 1975.

34. B. Teissier, *The hunting of invariants in the geometry of discriminants*, Proc. Nordic Summer School on Singularities (Oslo, 1976), Sijthoff and Noordhoff, Groningen, 1977.

35. J. G. Timourian, *The invariance of Milnor's number implies topological triviality*, Amer. J. Math. vol. 99 (1977) pp. 437–446.

36. A. N. Varchenko, *Theorems on the topological equisingularity of families of algebraic varieties and families of polynomial mappings*, Math. USSR Izvestija, vol. 6 (1972) pp. 949–1008.

37. A. N. Varchenko, *The relation between topological and algebro-geometric equisingularities according to Zariski*, Functional Anal. Appl., vol. 7 (1973) pp. 87–90.

38. A. N. Varchenko, *Algebro-geometrical equisingularity and local topological classification of smooth mappings*, Proc. Internat. Congress of Mathematicians, Vancouver 1974, vol. 1, pp. 427–431, Canadian Math. Congress, 1976.

39. A. N. Varchenko, *Zeta-function of monodromy and Newton's diagram*, Inventiones Math., vol. 37 (1976) pp. 253–262.

40. A. N. Varchenko, *Newton polyhedra and estimation of oscillating integrals*, Functional Anal. Appl., vol. 10 (1976) pp. 175–196.

41. J.-L. Verdier, *Stratifications de Whitney et théorème de Bertini-Sard*, Inventiones Math., vol. 36 (1976) pp. 295–312.

42. J. Wahl, *Equisingular deformations of plane algebroid curves*, Trans. Amer. Math. Soc., vol. 193 (1974), 143–170.

43. J. Wahl, *Equisingular deformations of normal surface singularities*, I, Annals of Math., vol. 104 (1976), 325–356.

44. H. Whitney, *Local properties of analytic varieties*, in "Differential and Combinatorial Topology" (Marston Morse symposium, edited by S. S. Cairns) pp. 205–244, Princeton University Press, 1965.

45. H. Whitney, *Tangents to an analytic variety*, Annals of Math., vol. 81 (1965) pp. 496–549.

46. M. Lejeune-Jalabert, *Sur l'équivalence des singularités des courbes algébroides planes*, Thése, Université de Paris VII, 1973.

47. T. T. Moh, *On characteristic pairs of algebroid plane curves for characteristic p*, Bull. Inst. Math. Acad. Sinica, vol. 1 (1973) pp. 75–91.

48. K. G. Fischer, *The decomposition of the module of n-th order differentials in arbitrary characteristic*, Can. J. Math., vol. 30 (1978) pp. 512–517.

49. H. Hironaka, *On Zariski dimensionality type*, Amer. J. Math., vol. 101 (1979).

50. J. Briançon and J. P. G. Henry, *Equisingularité générique des familles de surfaces à singularités isolées*, Preprint, Centre de Math., École Polytechnique, No. M367.0778 (July 1978).

 APPENDIX B

BIBLIOGRAPHY OF

OSCAR ZARISKI

[1] *I fondamenti della teoria degli insiemi di Cantor*, Period. Mat., serie 4. vol. 4 (1924) pp. 408–437.

[2] *Sulle equazioni algebriche contenenti linearmente un parametro e risolubili per radicali*, Atti Accad. Naz. Lincei Rend., Cl. Sci. Fis. Mat. Natur., serie V, vol. 33 (1924) pp. 80–82.

[3] *Gli sviluppi più recenti della teoria degli insiemi e il principio di Zermelo*, Period. Mat., serie 4, vol. 5 (1925) pp. 57–80.

[4] *Sur le développement d'une fonction algébroide dans un domaine contenant pinsieurs points critiques*, C. R. Acad. Sci., Paris, vol. 180 (1925) pp. 1153–1156.

[5] *Il principio de Zermelo e la funzione transfinita di Hilbert*, Rend. Sem. Mat. Róma, serie 2, vol. 2 (1925) pp. 24–26.

[6] *R. Dedekind, Essenza e Significato dei Numeri. Continuità e Numeri Irrazionali, Traduzione dal tedesco e note storico-critiche di Oscar Zariski* ("Per la Storia e la Filosofia delle Matematiche" series), Stock, Rome, 1926, 306 pp. The notes fill pp. 157–300.

[7] *Sugli sviluppi in serie delle funzioni algebroidi in campi contenenti più punti critici*, Atti Accad. Naz. Lincei Mem., Cl. Sci. Fis. Mat. Natur., serie VI, vol. 1 (1926) pp. 481–495.

[8] *Sull'impossibilità di risolvere parametricamente per radicali un'equazione algebrica f(x,y) = 0 di genere p > 6 a moduli generali*, Atti Accad. Naz. Lincei Rend., Cl. Sci. Fis. Mat. Natur., serie VI, vol. 3 (1926) pp. 660–666.

[9] *Sulla rappresentazione conforme dell'area limitata da una lemniscata sopra un cerchio*, Atti Accad. Naz. Lincei Rend., Cl. Sci. Fis. Mat. Natur., serie VI, vol. 4 (1926) pp. 22–25.

[10] *Sullo sviluppo di una funzione algebrica in un cerchio contenente più punti critici*, Atti Accad. Naz. Lincei Rend., Cl. Sci. Fis. Mat. Natur., serie VI, vol. 4 (1926) pp. 109–112.

[11] *El principio de la continuidad en su desarrole historico*, Rev. Mat. Hisp. Amer., serie 2, vol. 1 (1926) pp. 161–166, 193–200, 233–240, 257–260.

[12] *Sopra una classe di equazioni algebriche contenenti linearmente un parametro e risolubili per radicali,* Rend. Circolo Mat. Palermo, vol. 50 (1926) pp. 196–218.

[13] *On a theorem of Severi,* Amer. J. Math., vol. 50 (1928) pp. 87–92.

[14] *On hyperelliptic θ-functions with rational characteristics,* Amer. J. Math., vol. 50 (1928) pp. 315–344.

[15] *Sopra il teorema d'esistenza per le funzioni algebriche di due variabili,* Atti Congr. Internaz. Mat. 2, Bologna, vol. 4 (1928) pp. 133–138.

[16] *On the problem of existence of algebraic functions of two variables possessing a given branch curve,* Amer. J. Math., vol. 51 (1929) pp. 305–328.

[17] *On the linear connection index of the algebraic surfaces $z'' = f(x,y)$,* Proc. Nat. Acad. Sci. U.S.A., vol. 15 (1929) pp. 494–501.

[18] *On the moduli of algebraic functions possessing a given monodromie group,* Amer. J. Math., vol. 52 (1930) pp. 150–170.

[19] *On the non-existence of curves of order 8 with 16 cusps,* Amer. J. Math., vol. 53 (1931) pp. 309–318.

[20] *On the irregularity of cyclic multiple planes,* Ann. of Math., vol. 32 (1931) pp. 485–511.

[21] *On quadrangular 3-webs of straight lines in space,* Abh. Math. Sem. Univ. Hamburg, vol. 9 (1932) pp. 79–83.

[22] *On the topology of algebroid singularities,* Amer. J. Math., vol. 54 (1932) pp. 453–465.

[23] *On a theorem of Eddington,* Amer. J. Math., vol. 54 (1932) pp. 466–470.

[24] *Parametric representation of an algebraic variety,* Symposium on Algebraic Geometry, Princeton University, 1934–1935, mimeographed lectures, Princeton, 1935, pp. 1–10.

[25] *Algebraic Surfaces*, Ergebnisse der Mathematik, vol. 3, no. 5., Springer-Verlag, Berlin, 1935, 198 pp.; second supplemented edition, with appendices by S. S. Abhyankar, J. Lipman, and D. Mumford, Ergebnisse der Mathematik, vol. 61, Springer-Verlag, Berlin-Heidelberg-New York, 1971, 270 pp.

[26] (with S. F. Barber) *Reducible exceptional curves of the first kind*, Amer. J. Math., vol. 57 (1935) pp. 119–141.

[27] *A topological proof of the Riemann-Roch theorem on an algebraic curve*, Amer. J. Math., vol. 58 (1936) pp. 1–14.

[28] *On the Poincaré group of rational plane curves*, Amer. J. Math., vol. 58 (1936) pp. 607–619.

[29] *A theorem on the Poincaré group of an algebraic hypersurface*, Ann. of Math., vol. 38 (1937) pp. 131–141.

[30] *Generalized weight properties of the resultant of $n + 1$ polynomials in n indeterminates*, Trans. Amer. Math. Soc., vol. 41 (1937) pp. 249–265.

[31] *The topological discriminant group of a Riemann surface of genus p*, Amer. J. Math., vol. 59 (1937) pp. 335–358.

[32] *A remark concerning the parametric representation of an algebraic variety*, Amer. J. Math., vol. 59 (1937) pp. 363–364.

[33] (In Russian) *Linear and continuous systems of curves on an algebraic surface*, Progress of Mathematical Sciences, Moscow, vol. 3 (1937).

[34] *Some results in the arithmetic theory of algebraic functions of several variables*, Proc. Nat. Acad. Sci. U.S.A., vol. 23 (1937) pp. 410–414.

[35] *Polynominal ideals defined by infinitely near base points*, Amer. J. Math., vol. 60 (1938) pp. 151–204.

[36] (with O. F. G. Schilling) *On the linearity of pencils of curves on algebraic surfaces*, Amer. J. Math., vol. 60 (1938) pp. 320–324.

[37] *Some results in the arithmetic theory of algebraic varieties*, Amer. J. Math., vol. 61 (1939) pp. 249–294.

[38] (with H. T. Muhly) *The resolution of singularities of an algebraic curve,* Amer. J. Math., vol. 61 (1939) pp. 107–114.

[39] *The reduction of the singularities of an algebraic surface,* Ann. of Math., vol. 40 (1939) pp. 639–689.

[40] *Algebraic varieties over ground fields of characteristic zero,* Amer. J. Math., vol. 62 (1940) pp. 187–221.

[41] *Local uniformization on algebraic varieties,* Ann. of Math., vol. 41 (1940) pp. 852–896.

[42] *Pencils on an algebraic variety and a new proof of a theorem of Bertini,* Trans. Amer. Math. Soc., vol. 50 (1941) pp. 48–70.

[43] *Normal varieties and birational correspondences,* Bull. Amer. Math. Soc., vol. 48 (1942) pp. 402–413.

[44] *A simplified proof for the resolution of singularities of an algebraic surface,* Ann. of Math., vol. 43 (1942) pp. 583–593.

[45] *Foundations of a general theory of birational correspondences,* Trans. Amer. Math. Soc., vol. 53 (1943) pp. 490–542.

[46] *The compactness of the Riemann manifold of an abstract field of algebraic functions,* Bull. Amer. Math. Soc., vol. 45 (1944) pp. 683–691.

[47] *Reduction of the singularities of algebraic three dimensional varieties.* Ann. of Math., vol. 45 (1944) pp. 472–542.

[48] *The theorem of Bertini on the variable singular points of a linear system of varieties,* Trans. Amer. Math. Soc., vol. 56 (1944) pp. 130–140.

[49] *Generalized semi-local rings,* Summa Brasiliensis Mathematicae, vol. 1, fasc. 8 (1946) pp. 169–195.

[50] *The concept of a simple point of an abstract algebraic variety,* Trans. Amer. Math. Soc., vol. 62 (1947) pp. 1–52.

[51] *A new proof of Hilbert's Nullstellensatz,* Bull. Amer. Math. Soc., vol. 53 (1947) pp. 362–368.

[52] *Analytical irreducibility of normal varieties,* Ann. of Math., vol. 49 (1948) pp. 352–361.

[53] *A simple analytical proof of a fundamental property of birational transformations,* Proc. Nat. Acad. Sci. U.S.A., vol. 35 (1949) pp. 62–66.

[54] *A fundamental lemma from the theory of holomorphic functions on an algebraic variety,* Ann. Mat. Pura Appl., series 4, vol. 29 (1949) pp. 187–198.

[55] *Quelques questions concernant la théorie des functions holomorphes sur une variété algébrique,* Colloque d'Algèbre et Théorie des Nombres, Paris, 1949, pp. 129–134.

[56] *Postulation et genre arithmétique,* Colloque d'Algèbre et Théorie des Nombres, Paris, 1949, pp. 115–116.

[57] (with H. T. Muhly) *Hilbert's characteristic function and the arithmetic genus of an algebraic variety,* Trans. Amer. Math. Soc., vol. 69 (1950) pp. 78–88.

[58] *Theory and applications of holomorphic functions on algebraic varieties over arbitrary ground fields,* Mem. Amer. Math. Soc., no. 5 (1951) pp. 1–90.

[59] *Sur la normalité analytique des variétés normales,* Ann. Inst. Fourier (Grenoble), vol. 2 (1950) pp. 161–164.

[60] *The fundamental ideas of abstract algebraic geometry,* Proc. Internat. Cong. Math., Cambridge, Massachusetts, 1950, pp. 77–89.

[61] *Complete linear systems on normal varieties and a generalization of a lemma of Enriques-Severi,* Ann. of Math., vol. 55 (1952) pp. 552–592.

[62] *Le problème de la réduction des singularités d'une variété algébrique,* Bull. Sci. Mathématiques, vol. 78 (January–February 1954) pp. 1–10.

[63] *Interprétations algébrico-géométriques du quatorzième prob-*

lème de Hilbert, Bull. Sci. Math., vol. 78 (July–August 1954) pp. 1–14.

[64] Applicazioni geometriche della teoria delle valutazioni, Rend. Mat. e Appl., vol. 13, fasc. 1–2, Roma (1954) pp. 1–38.

[65] (with S. Abhyankar) Splitting of valuations in extensions of local domains, Proc. Nat. Acad. Sci. U.S.A., vol. 41 (1955) pp. 84–90.

[66] The connectedness theorem for birational transformations, Algebraic Geometry and Topology (Symposium in honor of S. Lefschetz), edited by R. H. Fox, D. C. Spencer, and A. W. Tucker, Princeton University Press, 1955, pp. 182–188.

[67] Algebraic sheaf theory (Scientific report on the second Summer Institute), Bull. Amer. Math. Soc., vol. 62 (1956) pp. 117–141.

[68] (with I. S. Cohen) A fundamental inequality in the theory of extensions of valuations, Illinois J. Math., vol. 1 (1957) pp. 1–8.

[69] Introduction to the problem of minimal models in the theory of algebraic surfaces, Publ. Math. Soc. Japan, no. 4 (1958) pp. 1–89.

[70] The problem of minimal models in the theory of algebraic surfaces, Amer. J. Math., vol. 80 (1958) pp. 146–184.

[71] On Castelnuovo's criterion of rationality $p_a = P_2 = 0$ of an algebraic surface, Illinois J. Math., vol. 2 (1958) pp. 303–315.

[72] (with Pierre Samuel and cooperation of I. S. Cohen) Commutative Algebra, vol. I, D. Van Nostrand Company, Princeton, N.J., 1958.

[73] On the purity of the branch locus of algebraic functions, Proc. Nat. Acad. Sci. U.S.A., vol. 44 (1958) pp. 791–796.

[74] Proof that any birational class of non-singular surfaces satisfies the descending chain condition, Mem. Coll. Sci., Kyoto Univ., series A, vol. 32. Mathematics no. 1 (1959) pp. 21–31.

[75] (with Pierre Samuel) Commutative Algebra, vol. II, D. Van Nostrand Company, Princeton, N.J., 1960.

[76] (with Peter Falb) *On differentials in function fields*, Amer. J. Math., vol. 83 (1961) pp. 542–556.

[77] *On the superabundance of the complete linear systems |nD| (n-large) for an arbitrary divisor D on an algebraic surface*, Atti del Convegno Internazionale di Geometria Algebrica tenuto a Torino, Maggio 1961, pp. 105–120.

[78] *La risoluzione delle singolarità delle superficie algebriche immerse*, Nota I e II, Atti Accad. Naz. Lincei Rend., Cl. Sci. Fis. Mat. Natur., serie VIII, vol. 31, fasc. 3–4 (Settembre-Ottobre 1961) pp. 97–102; e fasc. 5 (Novembre 1961) pp. 177–180.

[79] *The theorem of Riemann-Roch for high multiples of an effective divisor on an algebraic surface*, Ann. Math., vol. 76 (1962) pp. 560–615.

[80] *Equisingular points on algebraic varieties*, Seminari dell'Istituto Nazionale di Alta Matematica, 1962–1963, Edizioni Cremonese, Roma, 1964, pp. 164–177.

[81] *Studies in equisingularity I. Equivalent singularities of plane algebroid curves*, Amer. J. Math., vol. 87 (1965) pp. 507–536.

[82] *Studies in equisingularity II. Equisingularity in co-dimension 1 (and characteristic zero)*, Amer. J. Math., vol. 87 (1965) pp. 972–1006.

[83] *Characterization of plane algebroid curves whose module of differentials has maximum torsion.* Proc. Nat. Acad. Sci. U.S.A., vol. 56 (1966) pp. 781–786.

[84] *Exceptional singularities of an algebroid surface and their reduction*, Atti Accad. Naz. Lincei Rend., Cl. Sci. Fis. Mat. Natur., serie VIII, vol. 43, fasc. 3–4 (Settembre-Ottobre 1967) pp. 135–146.

[85] *Studies in equisingularity III. Saturation of local rings and equisingularity*, Amer. J. Math., vol. 90 (1968) pp. 961–1023.

[86] *Contributions to the problem of equisingularity*, Centro Internazionale Matematico Estivo (C.I.M.E.), Questions on Alge-

braic varieties. III ciclo. Varenna, 7–17 Settembre 1969, Edizioni Cremonese, Roma, 1970, pp. 261–343.

[87] *An Introduction to the Theory of Algebraic Surfaces,* Lecture Notes in Mathematics, No. 83, Springer-Verlag, Berlin, 1969.

[88] *Some open questions in the theory of singularities,* Bull. Amer. Math. Soc., vol. 77 (1971) pp. 481–491.

[89] *General theory of saturation and of saturated local rings, I. Saturation of complete local domains of dimension one having arbitrary coefficient fields (of characteristic zero),* Amer. J. Math., vol. 93 (1971) pp. 573–648.

[90] *General theory of saturation and of saturated local rings, II. Saturated local rings of dimension 1,* Amer. J. Math., vol. 93 (1971) pp. 872–964.

[91] *Quatre exposés sur la saturation,* Notes prises par J. J. Risler, Astérisque, 7 et 8 (1973) pp. 21–29.

[92] *i.e problème des modules pour les branches planes,* Cours donné au Centre de Mathématiques de l'Ecole Polytechnique, octobre-novembre (1973). Rédigé par François Kmety et Michele Merle, pp. 1–144. Avec un Appendice de Bernard Teissier.

[93] *General theory of saturation and of saturated local rings, III. Saturation in arbitrary dimension and, in particular, saturation of algebroid hypersurfaces,* Amer. J. Math., vol. 97 (1975) pp. 415–502.

[94] *On equimultiple subvarieties of algebroid hypersurfaces,* Proc. Nat. Acad. Sci. U.S.A., vol. 72 (1975) pp. 1425–1426.

[95] *The elusive concept of equisingularity and related questions.* Algebraic geometry: The Johns Hopkins Centennial Lectures (supplement to the American Journal of Mathematics) (1977) pp. 9–22.

[96] *A new proof of the total embedded resolution theorem for algebraic surfaces (based on the theory of quasi-ordinary singularities),* Amer. J. Math., vol. 100 (1978) pp. 411–442.

[97] *Foundations of a general theory of equisingularity on r-dimensional algebroid and algebraic varieties, of embedding dimension r + 1*, Amer. J. Math., vol. 101 (1979) pp. 453–514.

[97a] *Abstract of the paper* "Foundations of a general theory of equisingularity on r-dimensional algebroid and algebraic varieties, of embedding dimension r + 1," *Symposia Matematica*, vol. XXIV (Instituto Nazionale di Alta Matematica Francesco Severi, Rome, 1979).

[98] *Dimension-theoretic characterization of maximal irreducible algebraic systems of plane nodal curves of a given order n and with a given number d of nodes*, Amer. J. Math., vol. 104 (1982) pp. 209–226.

◩ INDEX OF NAMES ◪

Numbers in italic indicate pages on which footnotes are referenced.